Ownership and Performance
in Electric Utilities

Ownership and Performance in Electric Utilities:
The International Evidence on Privatization and Efficiency

MICHAEL G. POLLITT

Published by the Oxford University Press
for the Oxford Institute for Energy Studies
1995

Oxford University Press, Walton Street, Oxford OX2 6DP
Oxford   New York
Athens   Auckland   Bangkok   Bombay
Calcutta   Cape Town   Dar es Salaam   Delhi
Florence   Hong Kong   Istanbul   Karachi
Kuala Lumpur   Madras   Madrid   Melbourne
Mexico City   Nairobi   Paris   Singapore
Taipei   Tokyo   Toronto
and associated companies in Berlin Ibadan

Oxford is a trade mark of Oxford University Press

British Library Cataloguing in Publication Data
available

ISBN 0-19-730015-4

Cover design by Peter Tucker, PGT Design, Oxford
Typeset by Philip Armstrong
Printed by Bookcraft, Avon

"Even youths grow tired and weary
and young men stumble and fall;
but those who hope in the Lord
will renew their strength."
Isaiah 40: 30-31a

To Him who gave me strength

ABSTRACT

Ownership and Efficiency in Electric Utilities:
The International Evidence on Privatization and Efficiency

The electricity supply industry (ESI) is one of the most important sectors in a modern industrial economy. The importance of the industry in economic development has resulted in the state having a substantial ownership interest in the ESI in many countries. However in recent years there have been widespread moves to liberalize, restructure and privatize ESIs across the world. This book seeks to review the previous theoretical and empirical literature on ownership and productive efficiency and then to present new empirical evidence investigating the claim that privatization of the electricity supply industry can be expected to reduce production costs. Our empirical evidence compares the relative productive efficiency of international samples of publicly owned utilities (MUNIs) and privately owned utilities (IOUs) using the latest measurement techniques. The empirical analysis allows competing measurement techniques to be compared and evaluated.

ACKNOWLEDGEMENTS

It gives me great pleasure to write these acknowledgements and to thank some of the many people who have helped me in the preparation of my D.Phil thesis and hence this book.

I would like to start by thanking all the organizations who have contributed financially to the writing of my thesis. I acknowledge the support of a studentship from the Department of Education (N.I.) for my first three years on the M.Phil and D.Phil in Oxford. I also received support from the George Webb Medley Fund and Brasenose College for the financial costs of collecting the data for my book. Brasenose gave me a Hulme Continuation Grant towards my fourth year of graduate study. Balliol, Worcester, Trinity and Brasenose Colleges have provided me with much appreciated college lectureships at various times over the past three years. Commonwealth House has provided me a Deputy Wardenship and highly conducive surroundings to live in while I was writing up. Finally, I must thank the Oxford Institute for Energy Studies for publishing the final product.

The collection of the data for this book was a huge undertaking, spread over more than 18 months. I have incurred many professional debts in data collection and can only acknowledge a few of them here. The Electricity Association library opened up their collection of international sources to my examination. Many companies replied to my requests for data and a few commented on my work and made helpful suggestions. Without these replies this would not be an analysis of the 'international' electricity supply industry. John Kelly of the American Public Power Association generously offered to conduct a survey of US public utilities to collect missing data for the transmission and distribution study in Chapter 8. Above all, the book was helped by London Economics who gave me the chance to work for them on their project on comparative international performance of electric utilities during 1992–3. This project gave me access to most of the data for Chapters 6 and 7; without their help these chapters would not have been possible. In particular I wish to thank Michael Webb and Clive Harris at London Economics for their advice and help throughout the project. The presentation and interpretation of the results benefited greatly from having the critical comments of industry professionals.

Within the Oxford Sub-Faculty of Economics my debts are large and numerous. I especially thank Piotr Jasinski for his continuing interest in my work and his many helpful suggestions. Piotr kindly proof-read Chapters 2 and 3 and made many incisive comments. Peter Sinclair at Brasenose suggested the idea of a book on the international electricity industry and has always been supportive. Continuing thanks are due to my M.Phil. supervisor, Professor Christopher Bliss, for his support and constructive criticism. Technical assistance was given to me by Bill Macmillan at the School of Geography, who helped me to master data envelopment analysis, and by Guiseppe Mazzarino, who helped me with the econometrics. Professor John Vickers provided good ideas for taking the analysis forward at the halfway stage and was responsible for getting me the job with London Economics. Robert Mabro, at the Oxford Institute for Energy Studies, has been an extremely patient and understanding publisher. Above all however my thanks go to my book supervisor, George Yarrow, for his openness, encouragement and criticism over the years. His concern for tackling real world problems using rigorous analytical techniques has inspired me professionally. All remaining errors are, of course, my own.

Special thanks are also due to my D.Phil. examiners, Martin Slater (from Oxford) and Tom Weyman-Jones (from Loughborough), for their encouragement and constructive comments.

Finally, I want to thank my family and friends for all their love and support over the last few years. Writing a book is a lonely business and I cannot say how many times people close to me picked me up when things were not going as well or as quickly as I might have hoped. Special thanks go to all my friends in the Christian Union at Brasenose, my fellow residents at Commonwealth House and my friends at St.Aldates Church who continually encouraged me with words, actions and prayers. Others will forgive me if I single out Ian deVilliers and Andrew Dulley from Brasenose, Michael and Celia Mowat at Commonwealth House and Simon and Kathryn Gee, from St.Aldates, for their constant love and encouragement. Thanks are also due to Debbie Hockedy for finding me a publisher. Of my fellow students in the faculty, I must thank Bill Russell, that old Aussie 'dog', for all his support and encouragement through four years (plus interest) of graduate study. Bill believed in my ability to do economics when I thought no one else did, I will never forget that. Above all however my love and thanks go to my dear mother, finishing this work was as much for her as for myself.

CONTENTS

TABLES

FIGURES

ABBREVIATIONS

A+H	Atkinson and Halvorsen reference
APPA	American Public Power Association
AV	Average
BTU	British Thermal Unit
C	Listing code for cooperatively owned utility
CEGB	Central Electricity Generating Board
COLS	Corrected Ordinary Least Squares
COOP	Cooperatively owned utility
CRS	Constant returns to scale
DEA	Data Envelopment Analysis
DMU	Decision Making Unit
DRS	Decreasing returns to scale
DSA	Deterministic Statistical Approach
EdF	Electricité de France
ESI	Electricity supply industry
FGD	Flue-Gas Desulphurization Unit
FGL	Fare et al. (1985a, b) references
FSTAT	US EIA Financial Statistics of Selected Electric Utilities
HPC	US EIA Historic Plant Cost and Annual Production Expenses for Selected Electric Plants
I	Listing code for privately owned utility
IOU	Privately owned utility
IRS	Increasing returns to scale
JEPIC	Japan Electric Power Information Centre
km	kilometres
kW	kilowatt (measure of generating capacity)
kWh	kilowatt hour (measure of electric energy = 3412.1 Btu)
M	Listing code for publicly owned utility
MAX	Maximum
MED	Median
MES	minimum efficient scale
MIN	Minimum
MUNI	Publicly owned utility
MVA	Megavolt Amp (measure of transformer capacity)
MW	Megawatt (1000 kW)
O+M	Operation and maintenance
OLS	Ordinary Least Squares

PPA	Parametric Programming Approach
psf	proximity scale factor
RTS	Returns to scale
RWE	Rheinisch-Westfalisches Elecktritätswerk
SD	Standard deviation
SFM	Stochastic Frontier Method
TBTU	Btu$*10^{12}$
TWh	Terawatt hour (kWh$*10^{9}$)
US EIA	US Energy Information Agency

CHAPTER 1

INTRODUCTION

[P]rivatisation increases productive efficiency whether or not a monopoly is involved. Pressures from shareholders looking for return on their investment – considerably enhanced when these shareholders are also managers and employees – give a clear incentive to privatised firms to organise their internal affairs as efficiently as possible and seek the maximum competitive terms from their suppliers.

J. Moore MP (1986), p. 95.

The electricity supply industry is one of the largest and most important industries in a modern industrial economy. In many countries the state has traditionally owned and controlled a large proportion of the assets of electric utility companies. However in recent years there have been moves to restructure state-owned electricity assets, introduce formal regulatory regimes and privatize state-owned electricity companies. A central argument for privatization programmes across the world is that private ownership of a firm leads to lower costs than would be achieved under public ownership.

This book seeks to investigate the claim that privately-owned electric utilities have lower production costs than publicly-owned electric utilities using data on electricity generation, transmission and distribution from 14 countries. The analysis is conducted using the latest techniques for measuring cost efficiency and this allows the techniques to be compared and evaluated. The 14 countries included in this study are the USA, the UK, France, Germany, Australia, New Zealand, Greece, Ireland, Thailand, Taiwan, South Africa, Canada, Denmark and Italy.

The decision to privatize should be based on a detailed cost-benefit analysis (Jones et al., 1990). This analysis must include calculations of the net benefits of each of the various feasible alternative forms of privatization as well as the net benefits of alternative forms of government ownership. A key element of this analysis will be the extent to which privatization lowers production costs. The book quantitatively examines the cost reductions likely to result from privatization within the ESI.

This short introductory chapter is in four sections. In Section 1.1 we sketch some of the moves towards restructuring and privatization being made in the international ESI. We examine the theoretical background to ownership and efficiency questions in the ESI and the need for an empirical study in Section 1.2. In Section 1.3 we discuss the contributions the book makes to the existing literature and introduce the methodology of the book. Section 1.4 briefly outlines the contents of the later chapters.

1.1 The Current State of Restructuring in the International ESI

The Electricity Supply Industry can be thought of as being divided into four functions: generation, transmission, distribution and supply. James Capel (1990) defines these functions as follows:

Generation – the production of electricity.
Transmission – the transfer of electricity in bulk across the country.
Distribution – the delivery of electricity in bulk over local networks.
Supply – the acquisition of electricity and its sale to customers.

Privatization in the ESI is a process which begins with the vertical separation (financial and then often real) of the generation, transmission and distribution functions; proceeds with opening up of the transmission grid to independent generators; and goes on to the corporatization and eventual whole or partial privatization of state-owned electricity companies. This is not the only model for the development of the ESI but it is certainly a model which is attracting a lot of attention in both the developed and developing world.[1] Across the world, state-owned electricity industries are in the process of restructuring through vertical separation, and the required legislation is being passed to enable private competitors to enter the market and/or to enable full or partial transfer of state-owned ESI assets to the private sector.

In the UK the process of transferring an almost wholly state-owned ESI into a collection of privately-owned generation, transmission and distribution utilities is almost complete. The government only retains ownership of the two nuclear power production companies. The UK is in the vanguard of privatization in Europe and the UK experience in restructuring and privatization is being closely watched by other governments with large public sector ESIs.[2] Portugal has recently completed a radical unbundling of its formerly vertically integrated industry. Finland is close to the initial partial privatization of the state-owned electricity company, IVO. In Ireland the state-owned vertically integrated utility, the ESB, has proposed changes to its working practices and one-third of workers face redundancy. In Germany and Austria transfers of ownership in municipally owned utilities are proposed or have already taken place. In Italy the state-owned electric utility, ENEL, was turned into a joint stock company in July 1992 and a stock market listing is planned. In the meantime margins are being raised in order to increase the rate of return on the companies' assets ahead of privatization. In France EdF is under pressure from the European Commission to open up its domestic electricity market to foreign competition. Power workers have already taken strike action to protest at the possible ownership change, citing the UK experience with ESI privatization as a potentially undesirable British import. Unions, management and government have resisted radical change so far. In Greece the planned privatization of the state-owned PPC was delayed by a change of government.

In Eastern Europe restructuring of national ESIs is under way.[3] In Hungary the national electricity board, MVM, has separated production, transmission and distribution operations. It is expected that 49 per cent of MVM will be privatized once the restructuring is complete. Poland has transferred some generating stations to the control of the Ministry of Privatization with a view to possible asset sales. Belarus is privatizing auxiliary companies in the power sector such as construction companies. Latvia has converted the state-owned electricity company, Latvenergo to a joint stock company. The huge Russian electricity industry is being considered for privatization and the Russian government has engaged western advisors. Proposals exist for the vertical separation of the Ukrainian electricity industry and the introduction of access for private generators to the Romanian electricity grid.

Outside Europe similar trends in restructuring and ownership transfer in the ESI are observable.[4] In Canada publicly-owned provincial utilities are being exposed to increased competition from independent generators and one provincial utility, Nova Scotia Power Corporation, was privatized in 1992. In the USA there is a large privately-owned electricity sector but further competition is being encouraged in the wholesale generation sector through improved access to transmission systems. In Australia the vertical separation of generation, transmission and distribution is advancing and an interstate electricity grid is nearing completion. In New Zealand a process of corporatization and deregulation has occurred and eventual privatization of the state-owned generation and transmission utility, Electricorp, looks likely. The South African utility, Eskom, has been considered as a candidate for privatization but plans have been shelved for the foreseeable future. In Thailand the main generation and transmission utility, EGAT, was registered on the Bangkok stock exchange in May 1992 and sales of the government's shareholding are proceeding. The Philippines are considering privatization of the dominant state-owned utility, NAPOCOR. In Taiwan the state-owned utility, Taipower, is a possible privatization candidate.

The World Bank (1993) notes the widespread move towards restructuring and encouraging private sector investment and involvement in the ESI within developing countries. Corporatization is currently being implemented in Jordan, Malaysia and Nigeria, among others. Private sector involvement of varying degrees has been proposed or is being encouraged in Argentina, Chile, China, Côte d'Ivoire, Guinea, India, Korea, Malaysia, Mexico, Pakistan, Philippines and Turkey, among others. Independent power production for sale to the grid is now being encouraged in Costa Rica, Dominican Republic, Jamaica, Pakistan and Philippines. It is not hard to see how many of these changes could eventually result in the privatization of valuable state-owned ESI assets.

1.2   The Theoretical Background and the Need for an Empirical Study

A firm (or unit of production) which can produce the same amount of the same type of output as another at a lower cost is said to be more productively efficient than the other firm. The theoretical literature on the link between ownership and productive efficiency has at least three strands. The most prominent is the property rights literature, of which the opening quotation from a UK Treasury Minister is a popular expression. The argument goes back to Alchian (1965) where he argues that the inability to transfer ownership rights under public ownership prevents the capitalization of gains in efficiency and hence reduces the incentives of the owners to seek such gains. A taxpayer cannot sell his implicit share in the state-owned utility and hence will not monitor the performance of its managers. A second strand is the public choice literature, following Niskanen (1971), which emphasizes the inefficiency associated with the bureaucracy charged with running a public utility; bureaucrats and politicians maximize their own budgets and this rarely leads to minimum-cost production. The third strand is drawn from the literature on private monopolies. This recognizes that private utilities are often regulated monopolies and that as such they may be more inefficient than public monopolies. The seminal paper here is that of Averch and Johnson (1962) who suggest that profit maximizing private monopolies facing rate of return regulation will employ more capital than is socially efficient. All these general conclusions have been disputed[5] but it would be fair to say that on balance theory suggests privately-owned utilities should be more efficient than publicly-owned utilities.

Any debate about private vs. public ownership of an industry involves more than a simple ownership transfer of the existing firms and the cost-benefit analysis of privatization is highly industry specific. Usually it only concerns industries where there is a substantial degree of monopoly power accruing to existing firms. It is the allocative inefficiency which this monopoly creates which may require government intervention either in the form of some degree of public ownership or some type of regulation of the private firms in the industry. The degree of public ownership may take various forms, from full nationalization to the purchase of a percentage of the shares in one or more of the private firms (mixed ownership). Public ownership may not preclude franchising and thus the continuation of effective private control, albeit within the terms of the franchise. The regulation of private firms may also take several forms such as moral suasion, strict enforcement of anti-trust laws, price control or rate of return regulation. Arguably there is no such thing as an unregulated large firm in a modern capitalist economy as the threat of anti-trust action, government regulation, or even loss of government orders always exists.

The cost-benefit analysis of privatization thus has many elements and the calculation of the socially optimal ownership-regulation mix involves knowledge of the direct costs of regulation and the shape of the demand and cost curves in the industry. This is a formidable information requirement. Focusing on just the question of productive efficiency reduces the information requirement and improves the tractability of the empirical problem. It might be speculated that the differences in net social welfare under regulated private and public ownership in the presence of identical productive efficiency are likely to be small for a large industry producing a small number of homogeneous products. Thus productive efficiency is likely to be the central determinant of any recommendation on the advisability of ownership change in an industry such as the ESI.

In any industry capital, labour and raw materials are transformed using a technology into an output which can be consumed. The ESI is a vertically integrated industry which may be divided into three distinct processes (or functions): generation, transmission and distribution. In 1986 the ESI in the UK accounted for 5% of the gross capital stock, ½% of total employment and 30% of primary energy consumption.[6] The nature of the output of the industry purchased by final consumers differs by location of the consumer, the quantity consumed per consumer, the time of day at which consumption occurs and other factors. For example the electricity used by a household in London is not the same 'good' as that used by a factory in Arizona. The nature of the consumed product fundamentally affects the distribution and transmission costs making any cross firm comparison more complex. In electricity generation the product, electric energy, as it appears at the power station is reasonably homogeneous across countries and firms. This is not to say that distribution and transmission systems do not influence the factors employed in generation or that the output from power stations does not exhibit different characteristics; it is to make a reasonable simplifying assumption to allow analysis to proceed.

However in electricity transmission and distribution the problems of identifying inputs and outputs and environmental variables are more acute. There are many different outputs and inputs that could be characterized. Are not all transmission and distribution systems uniquely a product of geography and the topology of supply and demand? Despite such difficulties it is possible to make some adjustments for environmental factors and to undertake efficiency comparisons. Electricity companies have access to a similar range of technologies worldwide, with most power stations and other capitals being built by one of a small number of transnational corporations. In theory every electricity company is free to choose the least cost technique available, given the input prices it faces.

The dominant ownership forms in the ESI are privately franchised oligopolists, regulated by rate of return criteria, and 100% state- or municipally-owned monopolists. Following the US literature we will label private – investor owned – utilities IOUs and public – or municipally owned – utilities MUNIs. In Chapter 6 we also identify co-operatively owned utilities as COOPs but these are only used to increase the sample size. In the appendices the code I is always used to denote IOUs, the code M to denote MUNIs and the code C to denote COOPs. Firms involved in generation may or may not be involved in transmission and distribution, or indeed other activities e.g. gas supply.

1.3   The Contribution and Methods of this Book

The book seeks to address four major gaps in the previous literature. Firstly, most previous studies use data which come from the early 1970s or earlier. This is a problem because of the changing technology and structure of the ESI and because the early studies are written in the period before privatization became a major political issue. We introduce new data from 1986, 1989 and 1990. Secondly, there are very few studies which compare performance across countries. Most studies use

US data while a few recent studies examine efficiency in one non-US country only. Given the international nature of the current interest in privatization, an international study would seem to be appropriate. Thirdly, many earlier studies use unsophisticated techniques, while the sophisticated studies tend to use only one of the several methodologies available for calculating the comparative economic efficiency of production units. We use the four methodologies for calculating efficiency scores (Data Envelopment Analysis [*DEA*], Parametric Programming Approach [*PPA*], Deterministic Statistical Approach [*DSA*] and Stochastic Frontier Method [*SFM*]), outlined in the review of Lovell and Schmidt (1988), and this allows for extensive 'methodology cross-checking' (Charnes et al., 1988) of results. As a by-product of the analysis we can then offer suggestions as to the relative merits of the various methods for measuring productive efficiency. Fourthly, we seek to add to the very small literature on comparative efficiency in the electricity transmission and distribution functions. The book includes the first *DEA* study of efficiency in electricity transmission only and one of the few *DEA* studies of distribution.

The original contributions of the book are in the four empirical chapters (5–8). The two review chapters (2–3) are necessarily short and selective given the large and growing literature in this area. The methodology chapter (4) appears in order to report the details of the methodologies used in the later empirical chapters. The aim is to employ the latest methods for measuring productive efficiency on new data in order to produce robust conclusions on the question of the comparative efficiency of IOUs and MUNIs in the international ESI. We use the latest techniques to estimate production unit level efficiency scores which can then form the basis for comparing classes of firms/production units.

The efficiency scores are calculated by measuring the distance of an actual production unit from a derived production or cost frontier – the frontier being constructed from the units in the sample being analysed. These efficiency scores take values between 0 and 1, with 1 implying 100% efficiency. A value of less than 1 indicates the proportionate amount by which the inputs could be reduced (or inversely the proportionate amount by which the output could be increased) if the unit became 100% efficient. We also perform regression analyses of these efficiency scores (for generation only) and of costs in the electricity transmission and distribution functions.

Throughout this book we distinguish two main types of productive efficiency: allocative and technical. Technical efficiency scores measure the distance of an individual unit from the production frontier and allocative efficiency measures the amount by which costs could be reduced if the actual factor mix was adjusted to the efficient factor mix. Whenever we refer to allocative efficiency, unless otherwise stated, we mean it in this sense of productive efficiency. Allocative and technical efficiency scores can be multiplied to give a composite efficiency measure which we call the overall (productive) efficiency score. Once the various efficiency scores have been calculated rank order tests are then used to test for significant differences in efficiency between ownership types.

1.4   An Outline of the Book

Chapters 2 to 8 contain the substantive material of the book. In Chapter 2 we briefly examine the theoretical evidence on the links between ownership and productive efficiency. In Chapter 3 we review previous studies on the links between ownership and productive efficiency in the ESI. Chapter 4 outlines the four methodologies in Lovell and Schmidt (1988) for measuring productive efficiency in individual production units which we employ in the following empirical chapters. In Chapter 5 we compare allocative and technical efficiency in IOUs and MUNIs in a sample of 95 electricity generating firms operating in eight countries in 1986, using both the parametric technique of Atkinson and Halvorsen (1986) and the *DEA* technique of Fare et al. (1985a). In Chapter 6 we examine the technical efficiency of IOUs and MUNIs in a sample of 768 electric power plants operating in 14 countries in 1989, using the *DEA*, *PPA*, *DSA* and *SFM* techniques. Further regression/Tobit analysis of the efficiency scores is performed for 213 base load plants in the larger sample. Chapter 7 analyses overall and allocative productive efficiency using the *DEA*, *PPA*, *DSA* and *SFM* methodologies on a sample of 164 base load plants from the sample in Chapter 6. Regression analysis of the overall efficiency scores is also conducted. Chapter 8 extends the analysis to the electricity transmission and distribution functions. *DEA* and OLS techniques are used to analyse comparative efficiency in samples of 129 US utility transmission systems and 145 US and UK utility distribution systems operating in 1990. Chapter 9 briefly summarizes the results of Chapters 2 to 8 and offers a final conclusion.

Notes
1. IEA (1994b) suggests that the ESIs of OECD countries can be classified into one of three structural forms. Firstly, systems operated by vertically integrated utilities protected from competition eg. France and the USA. Secondly, systems characterized by vertical separation and limited

competition e.g. Germany, Spain and the Netherlands. And finally, systems which have both vertical separation and horizontal competition e.g. UK and Norway.

2. See IEA (1993a), IEA (1994b) and *Power in Europe* (Various).
3. See IEA (1994a) for a review.
4. See IEA (1993a) for information on Canada, USA and New Zealand; annual reports for information on Eskom and Australia; and *Power in Asia* (1994) for information on Thailand, Philippines and Taiwan.
5. See Chapter 2 for a more detailed discussion of these three sets of theories.
6. Sources: Electricity Council (1986), CSO (1987a,b), IEA (1985).

CHAPTER 2

THEORIES OF OWNERSHIP AND PRODUCTIVE EFFICIENCY

2.1 Introduction

An owner of property rights possesses the consent of his fellow men to allow him to act in particular ways.

Demsetz (1967), p.347.

Does the fact that a firm is publicly or privately owned matter from the point of view of the cost efficiency of the firms? In this chapter we seek to address this question by reviewing the theoretical writings on the likely effects of ownership on productive efficiency. We do this in order to establish the need for an empirical investigation of the impact of ownership on costs within the electricity supply industry.

The allocation of property rights with respect to a firm defines the ownership type of that firm. Public ownership, in a democracy, allocates the right to make decisions about the conduct of a firm's business to the representatives of the people. The public, i.e. the taxpayers,[1] own the firm but of necessity vest control in the hands of their representatives. These representatives (or at least the subset of representatives who form the government) are entrusted to run the firm in such a way as to maximize social welfare (however it is defined). Public representatives in turn devolve control to a bureau or commission which oversees the management of the firm. In privately owned plcs, the shareholders appoint directors who oversee managers to take decisions on their behalf with the objective of profit maximization. Both ownership types involve a principal–agent problem. The major difference between these two ownership types is the control structure faced by managers. Although the primal maximands are different we might expect the cost-minimization duals of the two ownership types to be very similar. This is especially true with respect to large public companies supplying output to a large representative cross section of voters i.e. when the social costs of production are approximately equal to private costs of production. In such a case as the ESI, the wishes of those on whose behalf the property rights are exercised should involve the minimization of the costs of production of a given output.

In this chapter we identify three classes of literature – property rights, public choice and private monopoly – which seek to formulate what effect, if any, ownership has on productive efficiency. The literatures are not logically distinct but natural extensions of one another[2] and simply provide a convenient way of organizing our review. In the following three sections we examine each literature in turn and suggest how they could apply to the ESI. Section 2.5 offers a conclusion.

2.2 Property Rights Theories

This literature is by far the most important strand and pre-empts the other two. It has its roots in the work of Pigou (1932) and Coase (1960) on pollution externalities.

> Property rights convey the right to benefit or harm oneself or others. The recognition of this leads easily to the close relationship between property rights and externalities.
>
> Demsetz (1967), p.347.

Just as suboptimal levels of pollution arise due to a lack of property rights or to the initial distribution of property rights, differences in the productive efficiency of firms according to ownership type arise because of the definition and allocation of rights with respect to the firms.

Pigou (1932) explained the existence of suboptimal levels of pollution as resulting from a lack of property rights. If no one is endowed with the right to exploit a resource (e.g. the water in a river) there is little possibility that an optimal final allocation of rights will occur. Utilitarian social welfare could be improved if property rights were defined and trading permitted. Coase (1960) refined the analysis by noting that reallocations of rights, even in cases where initial property rights are fully defined, are costly. Thus initial allocations of rights should be such as to minimize the transaction costs involved in moving towards the optimal final allocation. In his famous example, borrowed from Pigou, of the railway running through the cornfield creating sparks which might set light to the corn, Coase questions the lack of basis in Pigou's conclusion to make the railway liable for the cost of any fires. The basis to be used in allocating previously non-existent rights should be the minimization of transaction costs which in this case might well involve making the farmers liable for any fire damage, presumably because this saves on litigation costs and contract expenses. The history of property rights illustrates that ownership tends to evolve towards a cost-minimizing allocation of ownership rights as the nature of scale economies, negotiating costs and externalities change.[3]

Coase and Pigou were concerned that ad hoc allocations of rights based on established legal practice were not necessarily economically efficient. The subsequent literature on the economics of law has sought to build on their pioneering work and to ensure that all the costs and benefits of alternative legal decisions are calculated in the process of reaching a legal judgement.[4] It was Alchian (1965) who identified the crucial difference between MUNIs and IOUs as the high cost which public ownership imposes on the transfer of property rights pertaining to the firm. A taxpayer cannot sell his share in the public utility except, imperfectly, by moving out of the tax area. By contrast the private shareholder can, by selling his shares, capitalize his profits and losses. In Pigou's terms the market for public shares is missing or at best highly imperfect, while for Coase transaction costs are much higher than under an alternative (private) initial allocation of property rights.

How does the restricted transferability of rights affect the control structures of the two types of firm? Firstly, the inability of the taxpayer to capitalize his gains and losses in a public utility reduces his incentive to minimize costs. For example, say that a large investment now in new plant has a high positive net present value. If the taxpayer has a shorter tax horizon than the project due to the prospect of retirement or migration then he will not wish to pay higher taxes now. A private shareholder would make the investment even though he was going to sell his shares (provided capital markets were efficient enough) – because the value of his investment will be capitalized in the valuation of his shares. Secondly, under a private initial allocation of rights ownership gravitates to those who know the business or are more interested in monitoring it. In the presence of an efficient stock market takeover threats exist to firms that do not minimize costs. Shareholders whose propensities to take risks are more nearly in line with a firm's fundamental riskiness will be attracted to it. Finally, public ownership may involve higher monitoring costs. The setting up of a bureaucracy to oversee public companies, by introducing an opaqueness into the firm's decision-making process, might make it more difficult for individual taxpayers to directly influence managerial decisions.[5] The opposite may be true: the public may be endowed with rights of access to managers by the state through such bodies as consumer councils.[6] The costs of monitoring an investment are an important determinant of any decision to examine how well managers are representing the objectives of their principal(s). Higher monitoring costs will lower incentives to seek cost reducing opportunities.

The continued public ownership in the 1990s of some firms is rarely justified on the grounds of productive efficiency. Other social objectives are cited[7] and these may well be detrimental to cost minimization.

They are not socially efficient in terms of the simple sum of consumer and producer surplus. Electricity nationalization has allowed for cross-subsidization of the coal industry in the UK[8] (this also happens in Germany), employment of surplus labour,[9] the support of R+D and technology in the UK, the cross-subsidization of high-cost users (non-marginal cost pricing to peak users) and as the instrument of macroeconomic policy eg. via investment planning in the 1960s.[10] All of these sources of productive inefficiency have been discredited as inefficient means of achieving stated social objectives. This is interesting, as no rational shareholder would have contemplated any of these decisions.

The relatively bleak picture the property rights literature draws of the incentives facing taxpayers to seek out cost-minimization is not wholly justified. While it may be true that shareholders have more incentive to minimize costs it is the link between owners and managers (the principal–agent problem) that needs to be examined carefully. Private electricity companies tend to be large firms employing hundreds of millions of dollars of capital and having thousands of shareholders. Ownership is diffuse and free-riding is surely a pervasive problem when it comes to the monitoring of managerial decisions. There is a board of directors who should represent shareholders' interests in much the same way as the ministry of energy might represent taxpayers' interests. Directors however are usually trained managers themselves, rather than large shareholders, who from anecdotal evidence abuse their position of trust (at least to a minor extent) for business contacts and the extraction of ever higher directors' remunerations. At least the civil servants monitoring public utilities cannot usually gain financial rents from their positions (though some do, especially in developing countries). Managerial incentives within large private companies are also imperfect. Rees (1984b) models managers of MUNIs as maximizing output in the face of unions trying to maximize wage rates and numbers employed and subject to a break-even constraint. The influence of the government is reduced to a constraint which comes in the form of a profit target or an external financing limit. The result is overcapacity, lower than optimal prices and a labour bias. However, managerial theories of the firm[11] indicate that large IOUs exhibit similar tendencies to deviate from cost-minimization.

The ESI consists of a set of highly technical businesses within which managers have high firm-specific knowledge unobtainable or useless to non-specialist shareholders. If managerial theories of the firm are correct we might expect a high degree of managerial rent-seeking in the industry. If working for a publicly-owned firm carries a high degree of social responsibility or even selects managers with preferences for public service rather than personal rent-seeking this might leave unexploited some personal utility gains which privileged insider managers could exploit. A crucial assumption of all the theoretical investigations of the welfare effects of privatizing a firm and switching from a public sector to a private sector incentive scheme is that the managers have the same preferences (Bös, 1991). While this assumption is mathematically convenient, few academic economists would accept the parallel belief that there is no difference in preferences between public and private sector economists! It is possible that working for privately-owned firms carries higher prestige in some countries or states and thus allows firms to attract better managers. Better 'team spirit' in IOUs may improve productivity in the absence of effective monitoring by encouraging increased effort.[12] Pay structures within IOUs might be more incentive-based than in MUNIs due to restrictions on salary levels and structures (perhaps as a result of linkage to civil servants' pay) and this might be expected to raise IOU managerial performance. Indeed Bös (1991) suggests that managerial incentive schemes in the public sector will always be less successful in bringing forth optimal effort than in the private sector.[13] Longer tenure in public firms (as an offset to lower pay and as a result of powerful public sector unions) may make it more difficult to sack underperforming staff. The knowledge that loss-making is possible (i.e. bankruptcy does not threaten managerial rewards) in a context of poor monitoring of MUNIs might lead to reduced managerial performance. Vickers and Yarrow (1991a) point out that bankruptcy is not an issue in the ESI (at least in the UK) as the regulator has as one of his objectives the financial viability of the existing firms in the industry. Casual observation of the reorganization of the ESI in the UK over the last few years suggests that the privatized industry does exhibit higher managerial rent-seeking and higher managerial effort. It is not clear whether this change in managerial behaviour represents a move towards or a move away from the social optimum.

The overall effect on productive efficiency is a matter for empirical research. The transfer of ownership requires managerial co-operation to be effectively undertaken; this provides an opportunity for at least part of any gains from privatization to be extracted as increased managerial rent, as in previous privatizations.[14] The 'paradox of privatization' (Kay and Thompson, 1986) is that the greater the competitive pressure that it exerts on managers in an industry, the more difficult it is to secure the support of public sector managers for ownership transfer and attendant restructuring. Thus support for privatization can only be bought at the price of higher salaries (or expensive payoffs of existing managers) or reduced competitive pressure in the post-privatization market (i.e. leaving the industry structure unchanged).[15]

Some increase in salaries can however be justified on the grounds of 'catching up' with private sector pay rates.

The Alchian view also is rather optimistic about the role of the capital market as an efficient arbiter of risk and control. The earlier history of the private ESI in the UK was not a happy one. Kennedy (1976) in his economic survey of the UK before 1914 cites the ESI as an example of the 'failure thesis' suggested by the UK's apparent inability to grasp the technological opportunities of the second industrial revolution. The ESI in the UK, in contrast to that in Germany and the USA, spread only slowly up to 1914 and by that date half of the private capital in the industry had come from overseas. A surprising figure, at a time when the UK was the world's largest exporter of capital.[16] The UK capital market of the time apparently viewed the industry as too risky – several relatively small capital issues from well established companies failed.[17] No student of British economic history can have much time for untested claims that capital markets are inherently good judges of risk in capital intensive industries which comprise the basic infrastructure of a capitalist economy. Alchian's point about the gravitation of control to those with knowledge of the business similarly requires statistical evidence. There seems little reason to suppose that the marginal British Telecom shareholder[18] is any better informed than the average taxpayer supplied with the same information from the managers. There is also the associated idea that efficient takeovers of poorly managed firms will discipline managers and improve control.[19] The UK evidence on takeovers is mixed especially with respect to large firms with market power in the financial markets (Cowling et al.,1980). Roe (1990) notes in the USA the effects of Federal financial acts (such as the Glass-Steagall Act and the Investment Company Act of 1940) in reducing the efficiency of the capital market.[20] Nearly all non-US MUNIs would be components of their national index of leading shares if they were privatized without being broken up. All four of the recently privatized UK electricity generating companies are members of the FTSE 100[21] suggesting some scope for the exercise of monopoly power.

2.3 Public Choice Theories

The property rights literature focuses on the incentives facing owners to seek cost reductions. Public choice theories focus on the incentives facing politicians and the bureau charged with running a public enterprise to minimize costs. The key question is how well does the political process represent the interests of taxpayers. Within the property rights framework taxpayers have only very limited rights with respect to property owned by them and managed in their name. They can only exercise a preference at infrequent intervals, once every 3–7 years[22] in the case of non-US public utilities, and even then the preference is expressed over a bundle of issues within which the conduct of the managers and bureaux concerned with electricity is likely to be a very minor issue. The cost efficiency of public investments is readily swamped by other political issues. It is safe to assume that all taxpayers want cheaper electricity but in deciding how to cast their vote it is hard to see this as a burning electoral issue. There are exceptions to this: the productive efficiency of public companies in the UK has become an electoral issue, while in the USA municipal ownership of electric power plants, by allowing local voting on a smaller number of issues may lead to closer monitoring.[23] Stigler (1973) notes the similarity between economic and political competition and this suggests that the better the political system is at representing voters' preferences the more efficient will be the management of MUNIs.

If taxpayers do not effectively control the enterprise then who does? Olson (1965) suggests that consumers and taxpayers are large and unorganized groups in a democratic system while successful lobby groups tend to be small and oligopolistic. Small but powerful groups, particularly business associations, find it easy to organize and pursue their collective self interest. In the context of the ESI the industry forms a powerful lobby against changes which might improve efficiency. This is especially true for a large monopolistic public sector industry when compared with a fragmented private sector where lobbying is more difficult to organize.[24] Related to this is the idea that public firms are more vulnerable to union control. Olson argues that the latent power of unions to negotiate closed shop deals forces workers to join unions and hence gives unions lobbying power as a 'by-product' (similar arguments apply to professional associations). Unions can then lobby against cost reducing policies in the ESI (see Kotowitz and Mathewson (1982) for a theoretical treatment). Although unions can be powerful in public enterprises (Rees, 1984b) there is little theoretical reason why a strong union cannot reduce efficiency equally effectively in a privatized enterprise (Bös, 1986).

Niskanen (1971, 1975) also examines the sources of effective control in a public enterprise. Public companies are not run by taxpayers but by bureaucrats and politicians. Politicians are assumed to buy the output of bureaucrats. These individuals have their own objective functions which via the political process must recognize the presence of voter preferences. Bureaucrats maximize utility functions which include the size of the bureau and the size of their discretionary budgets as arguments, while politicians are assumed to vote maximize.[25] Thus these individuals take decisions given the very weak influence of voter preferences for cost efficiency. It is easy to see how bureaucrats and politicians can maximize their own objectives to the detriment of social welfare. For bureaucrats charged with delivering a fixed amount of output within a budget the incentive is to overbudget and to attempt to produce more bureaucratic output than is socially optimal. For politicians the incentive is to shift the costs and the benefits so that the net benefits to their constituency are positive[26] or to redistribute gains and losses within their constituency to their advantage.[27] This leads to political optimization which can conflict with cost efficiency. In particular the public firm produces only those outputs which are considered to be important and are measured by the politicians or bureaucrats who monitor the firm's performance (Lindsay, 1976).[28]

Relevant examples of political optimization include the nuclear waste in the UK which does not get stored in disused coal mines in marginal constituencies in the Midlands but has to be stored at existing nuclear landfill sites leading to extra expense and risk. In Italy the nuclear programme has ground to a halt as no constituency has agreed to have a new station in its area.[29] Since the oil shocks of the 1970s Italy has made no significant moves to reduce its dependence on imported fossil fuels and now imports 10%[30] of its distributed electricity from France. There are also the direct resource costs of bureaucracy and politicians' time which public ownership imposes. Senior managerial time has to be spent answering ministers' and senior civil servants' questions and in complying with the complicated and often conflicting guidelines which the bureaucracy and the legislature lay down for the management of public utilities. Political short-termism frequently means that projects with positive net present values are often not undertaken in order to meet current year financial targets.[31]

The political process introduces distortions to the control structure in MUNIs. We are however comparing the control structure in public firms with that in large regulated IOUs. In the firm level dataset we shall be using in Chapter 5 the smallest private company by output, Metro Edison (I46), has over $80m of historic cost capital. Bureaucracy and political influence have not been eliminated, only limited in scope. In the USA and in all other countries the political process still arbitrates the construction of new power stations and decides where they may be built and of what type they should be. Regulatory commissions demand large quantities of information and lay down large numbers of guidelines over prices, security of supply, rights of connection, safety of production etc.[32] The 1990 Electricity Act in the UK gave the Secretary of State for Energy virtually unlimited powers to take decisions over the industry if he views them as in the national interest.[33] Demsetz (1968) points out that the existence of rights of interference means that the market valuation of the firm and hence its incentives to cost-minimize are distorted. In the USA it seems that the regulation of IOUs allows higher standards (e.g. of safety) to be imposed than in public utilities elsewhere because the costs are not borne by the taxpayer but by customers and shareholders.[34] The reluctance of the UK government to retro-fit CEGB power stations with FGDs (Flue-Gas Desulphurization Units) and the increase in statutory environmental expenditures by the privatized water companies after years of underinvestment provide notable examples of how other social objectives may be easier to achieve (due to unbundling) under private ownership and regulation to the detriment of cost-minimization.[35]

Stigler (1971) in his critique of regulation goes much further. His argument is that regulation imposes costs but does not yield benefits. Regulatory agencies are subject to capture and may be used by the industry to defend the status quo, preventing new entry and maintaining profitability in spite of inefficiency. For Demsetz (1968) competition for the field takes care of the monopoly problem and of the incentive to minimize costs by allocating the franchise to the lowest bidder (who only wins the franchise by making a minimum cost bid). This conclusion is controversial not least for its neglect of issues of incumbent power and for its neglect of social issues such as environmental pollution which may be considered to be more important than issues of monopoly pricing. Stigler and Demsetz suggest that the keenness of electric utilities to accept regulation is convincing evidence[36] that it is preferable to competition.[37] If regulation cannot be effective and large deadweight social losses are occurring then an obvious solution to consider is public ownership.

2.4   Private Monopoly Theories

Our criticism of the negative conclusions for public ownership from public choice theory centred on the counterbalancing bureaucratic costs imposed by regulation on large IOUs. These were essentially composed of the direct costs of regulatory agencies and compliance and of the costs of the reduction in competition which entry restrictions to regulated industries impose. The final strand of the literature is one which has had a significant influence on regulatory policy in the USA and looks precisely at the effects of the different regulatory regimes on privately-owned firms' incentives. This literature begins with the Averch-Johnson (A-J) thesis (1962). Although this literature predates the public choice literature it is logically later as Stigler (1971) points out. A-J focus on the type of regulation rather than questioning the underlying rationale for regulation. A-J recommend better regulation while Stigler advocates the elimination of regulation in favour of competition for the field.

The A-J thesis examines the effects of rate of return regulation on the first-order conditions for profit maximization that a firm faces. The rationale for regulation is that the firm has market power and can raise prices significantly above marginal cost and earn excess returns on its assets. Rate of return regulation limits these returns to no more than x% of capital employed where: $r \leq x < m$; r = market rate of return; m = unconstrained rate of return. The firm now has an incentive to overinvest in capital to increase the size of its rate base. Refinements to the original A-J theory throw the strength of the conclusion into doubt. The introduction of lags (Bailey and Coleman, 1971) in changing the rate base provides strong short-term incentives to minimize costs though strategic action becomes more worthwhile the closer the review. For example a firm might inflate costs in the final period to secure a favourable review depending on its discount rate and the risk of having the rise in capital disallowed in its rate base. Similarly, the introduction of uncertainty in the review date itself may reduce incentives for strategic action (Bawa and Sibley, 1980) though Pint (1992) disputes this. If investment involves sunk costs, there is an incentive for the regulator to set price equal to marginal cost, the firm produces but makes a loss on its investments, thus dynamic inconsistency in the regulatory process may lead to incentives to underinvest (Greenwald, 1984).[38] Crain and Zardkoohi (1980) point out that the continued existence of a probability of the arrival of new competitors or favourable rate reviews means that the firm still has an incentive to minimize costs, so that it can seek to exploit the rents so created. In the UK a recognition of the shortcomings of rate of return regulation in theory and practice in the USA led to an alternative proposal: *RPI-X* price control (Littlechild, 1983). This may look different in theory[39] to rate of return regulation but the calculation of X is usually made with some reference to the rates of return so that in fact the original case for such a formula was overstated (Vickers and Yarrow, 1988b).[40]

The nature of the regulator's problem is essentially one of asymmetric information: the firm knows how to manipulate capital costs in order to maximize profits in the presence of a regulatory constraint, but the regulator can only imperfectly observe costs (and other variables that may be relevant) by incurring a regulatory resource cost. If the regulatory body knew exactly the minimum cost of capital required to produce a given output this problem would not arise. This problem was first formalized by Baron and Myerson (1982) in a principal–agent framework and has since spawned a large literature.[41] A major criticism of these models is their reliance on transfers from the regulators to achieve the optimal solution; in practice such transfers are not permitted and should be ruled out by assumption. The essential result is that the firm's information monopoly allows it to extract a rent which involves departure from the social optimum (Leibenstein, 1966);[42] this rent can be reduced – by the introduction of such features as ex post auditing (Baron and Besanko, 1984) or learning (Baron and Besanko, 1987) about the firm in a dynamic setting – but not eliminated. A further criticism of these models is the portrayal of the regulator as an aggressor. Nowell and Shogren (1991) point out that in US utility regulation the firm is the aggressor; the firm must choose when to request a rate rise in the face of future price uncertainty.

All the theories confirm that better information is the key to more effective regulation. The US regulators now no longer rely on just company-provided aggregate capital cost data to calculate maximum permitted prices, but on allowable rate bases from which certain capital expenditures may be excluded if deemed unnecessary. Such hindsight review reduces the risk premium firms pay to avoid construction cost uncertainty to the optimal (lower) level (Lyon, 1991). Improvements in regulatory technology since the early 1970s are judged to have reduced the incentives to deviate from cost-minimization (Stelzer, 1988).[43] 'Yard-stick' regulation (Shleifer, 1985) may provide further advances in the effectiveness of regulation in some industries, e.g. electricity distribution. In an industry with several monopolists operating in separate markets, using the same technology, the value of X for each firm is set equal to the average of the cost reductions achieved by the other firms in the industry. This gives optimal incentive for the firm to seek cost reductions while allowing control of monopoly prices.[44] A key problem is that actual firms do not have the same technology and operating environment.[45]

Once again it is a matter of evidence as to whether regulation does lead to incentives to deviate from cost-minimization. A-J 's paper did lead to better regulation and under stricter regimes there seems a likelihood of underinvestment relative to the optimum. However the general conclusions on the balance of theoretical evidence would seem to be that there is probably little difference in the incentives created by different regulatory regimes, designed to reduce the exploitation of monopoly power,[46] and that the magnitude of the distortion which they introduce with respect to the incentive to minimize costs is likely to be small and declining over time, as regulation improves. Even if the general theoretical conclusion seems to be that private regulated monopolies tend to overinvest relative to the optimum, while publicly-owned firms tend to have too much labour relative to the optimum[47] this still leaves it to empirical testing to determine the relative efficiency of IOUs and MUNIs.

2.5   Conclusion

Nationalization or public direction of production is a way of reallocating property rights in order to reduce the costs of private sector transactions which would improve social welfare. For example, the utilitarian welfare losses which occur as a result of the existence of private sector monopoly only occur because price discrimination is expensive to administer (transaction costs) and to police (enforcement costs). In the absence of these costs of property rights a private monopolist could realize the maximum value of the social surplus. Public ownership of a monopoly allows social welfare to be maximized as a result of the availability of marginal cost pricing as a policy option and the elimination of the incentive to maximize monopoly profits. The move towards the social optimum involves much lower transaction and enforcement costs. Of course the very act of government-decreed ownership change is costly because of transfer costs and these transfer costs (where they involve welfare losses[48]) must enter into any cost-benefit calculation of ownership change.[49] Our concern is whether ownership transfer will improve social welfare via improvements in both allocative (output price) and productive efficiency. This implies that the simple observation that costs are lower in private firms (an increase in productive efficiency) is not sufficient to recommend privatization. The expected cost reduction should compensate for the allocative losses arising from supernormal pricing and profits, the transfer costs and welfare losses arising from redistribution and the substitution of privatization revenue for tax revenue.

We have compared two forms of ownership and have argued that although there may be different types of regulation and bureaucracy these differences are likely to introduce only small differences in the incentives facing the managers within the broad classes of MUNIs and IOUs in the ESI. There are other forms of ownership in the ESI such as the mixed enterprise[50] and the co-operative. In Chapters 6 and 7 we include co-operatives when calculating measures of productive efficiency, however given the small number of (US) co-operatives we disregard them for the purposes of comparing the relative performance of ownership forms. Parker and Hartley (1991) identify four different public ownership forms[51] which correspond to different public sector

regulatory schemes. They argue that there has been differential performance between these forms in the UK.[52] We abstract from additional
disaggregation of our two main ownership forms and compare publicly-
owned firms with privately-owned firms which we assume are subject
to regulation. The necessity of bundling private ownership and regulation has been widely recognized in the literature.[53]

> In the end, what matters is how the combination of ownership and regu-
> lation under private ownership compares with ownership and (implicit or
> explicit) regulation in the public sector.
>
> Vickers and Yarrow (1991a), p. 116.

In this chapter we have shown that there is little theoretical reason
to suppose that for an industry such as the ESI one or other ownership
form will be superior. Thus we have established a need for empirical
analysis to test the relative performance of the two ownership forms.
The suggestion is that the principal–agent problem between the 'owners'
and the managers is likely to be just as great in large regulated IOUs
as in MUNIs. However we observe that the theoretical evidence does
suggest that public ownership might be relatively poorer at making
efficient investment decisions. Both the property rights literature and
the public choice literature highlight the scope for relatively poor
decision making and political interference in large investment decisions
within publicly-owned firms.

Notes

1. There is a distinction to draw here between voters and taxpayers. Our
   general premise is that the two groups are identical, this is clearly a gross
   generalization. While the public consists of all those entitled to vote, only
   taxpayers have a direct incentive to seek cost efficiency and indeed it is
   taxpayers who will be most affected by ownership transfers e.g. by lower
   taxes as a result of privatization proceeds. It could therefore be argued
   that many of the shareholders in a public firm, the non-taxpaying voters,
   have little or no incentive to seek cost efficiency. Further, distributional
   considerations suggest that if cost inefficiency benefits some taxpayers
   more than it costs them in higher taxes they will not seek efficiency gains.
2. We take this division from Brynes (1985) and Brynes et al. (1986). Bartel
   and Schneider (1991) suggest five strands in the literature, in the context
   of the performance of the Austrian public enterprise sector. They add
   interest group theories and X-inefficiency theories to our list – we discuss
   interest group theories under 'public choice' theories and regard X-
   inefficiency as a definition of inefficiency rather than a theory of how
   differences in inefficiency arise.
3. It has long been recognized that property rights are fundamentally linked
   to productive efficiency. Demsetz has a fascinating account of how land

rights evolved among American Indians and were well established by 1750 in response to the efficiency gains which their definition and reallocation could capture as a result of the coming of the fur trade, thus preventing overhunting (Demsetz (1967), p.359).

4. See Veljanovski (1990) for a review of this literature.

5. i.e. 'Red Tape'.

6. See Melling (1965) on the role of statutory consumer bodies in ensuring the accountability of the UK ESI in the 1960s.

7. Rees (1984a) cites four possible objectives for MUNIs: economic efficiency, profitability, effects on income distribution and relationship with macroeconomic policy.

8. Robinson (1988) estimates the magnitude of the overcharging of the CEGB by British Coal (BC) at £300m in the financial year 1986–87. Taylor (1990) analyses the current coal contract between the ESI and BC and argues that while the marginal tonne of coal is exchanged at close to the world market price, the average price is still a long way above the price of imported coal. The relatively high sulphur content and hence the greater environmental costs of British coal mean that the true social costs of the cross-subsidization are even higher than these two studies would suggest.

9. See Tieber (1985) on the use of public enterprises in macroeconomic stabilization policy in Austria.

10. See Pryke (1982).

11. See Tirole (1988), pp.36–55, for a review of these theories.

12. Alchian and Demsetz (1972).

13. Bös considers possible several incentive schemes for public sector managers – profit based, output based, cost based and social welfare based. He concludes that a profit based scheme is not feasible given the social objectives of the firm and that output and cost based schemes cannot approximate to the private sector optimum; social welfare based schemes can work in theory but are unlikely to be justifiable to the voter.

14. See Helm (1988) and Yarrow (1989b).

15. Of the recent UK privatizations, British Telecom and British Gas provide particularly good examples of this phenomenon.

16. 1865–1912 the UK exported £4bn of capital while by 1914 there was only £4m of private capital employed in the ESI (Kennedy, 1976).

17. Two issues by Crompton's, totalling £125,000, failed to be fully subscribed in the early 1890s (Kennedy, 1976).

18. Whether individual or institutional.

19. See Hay and Morris (1979), pp.474–82, for a review of the theoretical arguments.

20. In particular Roe notes the laws prohibiting interstate banking and bank shareholdings in industrial companies. He argues that banks represent powerful potential monitors of firm performance, a role which they perform with some success in Japan and Germany.

21. On 16 November, 1993, the two generating-only companies – National Power and Power Gen – were capitalized at £5.099bn and £3.637bn

respectively, while the integrated utilities – Scottish Power and Scottish Hydro-Electric – were capitalized at £3.211bn and £1.488bn respectively (*Financial Times* 16 November, 1993).

22. Three years for general elections in Australia and seven years for president-ial elections in France.

23. The debate surrounding the Community Charge or Poll Tax in the UK focused on the incentives which the tax gives local voters to monitor the cost efficiency of their elected representatives.

24. Note that the relative power of lobby groups in a democracy to lobby for socially inefficient policies stems from the relative ease of free riding among taxpayers (or voters) as a group.

25. Wyckoff (1990) shows that slack maximizing (effort minimizing) bureaucrats have similar incentives with regard to cost-minimization to those who budget maximize.

26. We note two papers on the existence of shifting costs to outside the constituency. Maloney et al. (1984) finds that electricity prices are signific-antly higher for companies with higher extra state exports of electricity. Couch et al. (1992) finds a correlation between the level of state funding for a school and the presence of state representatives on the school board for a sample of schools and representatives in Alabama.

27. For example by the cross-subsidization of large business users of electricity by small residential consumers in order to elicit large political campaign donations in the USA (Peltzman, 1971).

28. Lindsay studied the performance of a sample of publicly owned VA hospitals in the USA. Official figures indicate that these hospitals were low cost and operated at high utilization. Unpublished data revealed that the good measured performance was a function of much longer average stays in the VA hospitals than for comparable procedures in the private sector. This implied lower numbers of expensive operations and less than socially optimal performance in the public hospitals.

29. Lucas (1985).

30. ENEL Accounts (1986).

31. See comments in House of Commons Select Committee on the Environ-ment (1989b) on possible energy savings in the National Health Service.

32. See Joskow and Rose (1989), p.1486, who suggest that the environmental standards required of the US ESI might be excessive.

33. See *Power in Europe* (1988) No. 38 "UK Electricity Privatization 1 'And this is called freedom ?'"

34. This is a question of incidence, see Joskow and Rose (1989), pp.1486–95, for a discussion of the redistributive effects of regulation.

35. It is not clear that unbundling is socially optimal – bundling may effectively internalize more of the relevant social externalities associated with indi-vidual social issues.

36. If the only purpose of regulation is to reduce monopoly pricing then shareholders must be worse off (have lower profits) under effective regu-lation than when unregulated. This would seem to imply that regulated private firms should seek to have regulation reduced or eliminated.

37. See Demsetz (1968).
38. Besanko and Spulber (1991) suggest that a non-linear rate of return mechanism can correct this.
39. Observationally they are very similar; the regulatory authorities lay down permissible maximum price rises in both cases.
40. Pint (1992) suggests that under stochastic reviews price cap and rate of return regulation may not be equivalent.
41. See Caillaud et al. (1988) for a survey of these theories.
42. Leibenstein (1966) suggested that X-inefficiency, i.e. observed production inside the possibility frontier, was the result of (a) incomplete labour contracts (b) an unknown production function (c) inputs not being marketed per se or not being marketed on equal terms.
43. The regulatory technology is still far from perfect, excessive disallowals have left some power companies with high debt burdens which they are unable to reduce by raising prices.
44. The principal–agent problem is solved because each firm is given a price formula which allows it to retain residual profits: it faces an optimal incentive scheme.
45. Thus, for a given level of effort, firms may not be capable of achieving the same X.
46. Regulation designed for the achievement of other social objectives, such as the reduction of pollution, may have significantly different effects by type.
47. See Pint (1991) for a recent theoretical comparison with these conclusions.
48. E.g. the direct transaction and negotiation costs involved in ownership transfer.
49. See Jones et al. (1990) and Shapiro and Willig (1990).
50. For example the German utility – RWE – might be considered a mixed enterprise. This form is not considered because our statistical sample includes so few firms that could be so classified. The theoretical arguments suggest that the mixed enterprise will be more productively efficient than the MUNI but less efficient than the IOU (see Eckel and Vining (1985) for such an argument).
51. Government department, quasi-government agency, public corporation and wholly owned PLC.
52. They investigate the performance of ten UK public enterprises which went through changes in regulatory states. They suggest that theoretically and empirically the order of efficiency is: private PLC > wholly owned PLC > public corporation > quasi-government agency > government department. Their evidence certainly suggests changes in public sector regulation can improve performance. However as only one of the corporations (British Airways) was actually privatized the evidence for privatization over better public sector organization is weak.
53. See for example Yarrow (1989b) and Stelzer (1989).

CHAPTER 3

PREVIOUS STUDIES

3.1 Introduction

Before presenting our own empirical evidence on the effect of ownership on efficiency it is helpful to review the previous empirical literature on the electricity supply industry of relevance to the ownership and efficiency question. This literature is large and varied due to the sustained interest in the subject and the availablity of a large amount of high quality data on the US industry. The literature contains many insights and methodological innovations.

There have been a large number of previous empirical studies of relevance to the general ownership and efficiency question. The literature covers several industries but the largest number of papers seems to have been written on the ESI.[1] Some general comments can be made on this empirical literature. Firstly, it is mostly based on data relating to US power stations and there are only a relatively small number of published non-US studies. Of the five comparative international studies[2] we shall review, only one involves sophisticated economic or econometric techniques. Secondly, ESI studies are mainly for thermal power stations only, nuclear and other non-renewable types of generation are generally omitted.[3] The techniques used may well rule out the inclusion of nuclear but this leads to an incompleteness for which there seems to be little justification – the optimal choice of technology is an important determinant of efficiency. A few recent studies examine distribution but none looks solely at transmission: most examine generation. Finally, the studies on the ESI are usually cross-sectional in character and use data from the early 1970s or before and thus are clearly out of date; of the sophisticated studies we only look at four which use data after 1978.[4] It is a matter for empirical investigation as to whether the management of MUNIs has improved since the late 1970s – though it might be suggested that the threat of privatization and the renewed interest in ownership transfer has led to an improvement in the operation and management of public corporations. In the UK the major improvements in performance (even if only financial) of privatized companies have occurred in the run-up to privatization rather than in the aftermath (Yarrow, 1989b).

We shall draw on evidence from the ESI and from other industries where it may be relevant to the ESI; however we recognize that the links between ownership and efficiency are likely to be industry specific. Before considering the literature explicitly on ownership and efficiency we will examine the evidence on the related issues of competition, structure and regulation in Section 3.2. In Section 3.3 we discuss the US empirical work on ownership and efficiency. Section 3.4 examines the non-US and international studies of efficiency in the ESI. Section 3.5 offers a conclusion on the likely effects of privatization of the ESI in the light of recent developments in the UK.

3.2 Related Issues

Privatization, as Ramamurti (1989) points out,[5] is not so much about ownership as it is about competition and regulation. We have already argued that we are justified in defining two major types of firms in the ESI – the public company and the private regulated monopolist. This implies that we have already recognized the relevance of issues of the structure of the industry (and thus competition) and the importance of regulation. If differences in structure or regulation are determinants of differences of productive efficiency between firms then comparisons of efficiency between our chosen two ownership types may be influenced by these factors. There are basically three structural issues: the nature of competition, economies of scale and the degree of vertical integration in the ESI. After we have looked at these, we will turn to the issues relating to regulation.

3.2.1 Degree of Competition

In the simplest economic theories the degree of competition facing a firm does not affect its incentive to minimize the costs of producing its output. All firms maximize profits regardless of the strength of the competition and by duality this implies cost minimization. However for large (or even small) managerial firms the degree of competition does affect the incentive to cost minimize. Competition carries a risk of bankruptcy and a need to fight for market share and hence output – for managers with preferences for lower risk, higher output and less effort competition is likely to have a disciplining effect. Competition, by allowing the comparison of managerial performance, also improves monitoring. This improvement in monitoring and incentives is clearly independent of ownership type, thus it may be that any efficiency comparison based on ownership may be picking up the effects of differences in the competitive environments facing the firms.

Boardman and Vining (1989, 1992) criticize previous studies of the effects of ownership for failing to allow for the degree of competition as a determinant of observed differences. In the limit, under perfect competition, there could be no difference in efficiency between MUNIs and IOUs. This is true but under the conditions of perfect competition there would be no need to consider ownership transfers in the first place – as social welfare could not be improved by such a transfer. It is precisely because of imperfect competition that ownership is an issue. In the case of electricity the degree of competition is limited by statute in virtually every country, thus variations in this potentially important variable are likely to be small. Boardman and Vining's (1989) study of the largest 500 non-US manufacturing firms,[6] in the year 1983, comes to the conclusion that private firms are more efficient than public when they operate in competitive markets. Boardman and Vining (1992) conduct a similar study based on the largest 500 firms in Canada in 1985. They come to the same conclusion using a similar methodology.[7] Picot and Kaulman (1989) also investigate performance in an international setting. They use Fortune Foreign 500 data for the period 1975–84 on firms in 15 industries with unregulated markets in the UK, Canada, France, Germany, Italy and Sweden. Their results show that MUNIs have lower productivity, lower rates of return and lower increases in profits for given increases in size.

The above three studies are subject to the same criticisms: the samples of firms consisted of the world's most successful private companies vs. a sample of very large politically important public firms, several of whom were taken into public ownership to save them from bankruptcy as a result of bad management in the private sector.[8] Given the diversity of the data set it is not at all clear what, if any, conclusions for the best form of ownership for a particular state-owned enterprise can be drawn from their analysis. Together, however, these studies do suggest that where monopoly is not an issue, private ownership is to be preferred. This leads us to the question of whether the ESI exhibits the characteristics of a monopoly.

Several authors have suggested that the assumption that the ESI is a natural monopoly is wrong. Helm (1988) separates the UK ESI into seven idealized vertical levels[9] and suggests that only one, the national grid, is a strict natural monopoly. Generation is classified as competitive/oligopolistic. Distribution is classed as a local natural monopoly. Stigler and Friedland (1962) [S+F] argued that regulation of the US ESI was ineffective because there was an insufficient monopoly element to the prices which regulation sought to control. They further contended that regulation in the absence of monopoly, by controlling prices, reduced quality of service and that even if there was some monopoly pricing it was too costly to detect it. It could be argued that improved regulatory techniques make S+F look unduly pessimistic with respect to the effectiveness of regulation. The prospects for unregulated 'competition' in the ESI would seem to be limited; it is difficult to think of any capital-intensive industry which retains a competitive market structure in the absence of regulation. Capital markets are just too risk averse and imperfect.[10] The Helm classification system minimizes the importance of vertical economies within the ESI. Kaserman and Mayo (1991) suggest that even if generation capacity exhausts economies of scale, divestment to create competition in generation may not be optimal if distribution does not exhaust economies of scale.[11] We would therefore like to suggest that each of the three key businesses in the ESI – generation, transmission and distribution[12] – exhibit important monopoly elements and should face regulatory arrangements. There are two important issues lying behind the above authors' assertions – minimum efficient scale (MES) in the ESI and the optimal degree of vertical integration.

3.2.2 *Economies of Scale and Vertical Structure*

The question of scale is important because regulation so often defines the area of operation of an electric utility. It may be that the size of the company so defined is incompatible with cost minimization. Thus if observed differences in cost efficiency reflect the proximity of the scale of operation to the minimum, it may be wrong to attribute differences in cost efficiency to ownership type. However if the company can choose its scale then it is legitimate to attribute scale inefficiency to the owners. For example a finding that the CEGB could reduce costs by splitting into several operational units clearly represents poor decision making/monitoring by the 'owners' of the CEGB. For national MUNIs scale is a choice variable but for local MUNIs such as in the USA where there is a large number of single-plant public companies, scale inefficiency is outside the control of the firm's owners.[13] IOUs are limited in scale by regulation but this only matters if the firm is too small to exploit scale economies as larger firms can split into more efficient operational units. We have argued that we are seeking to compare MUNIs with regulated IOUs and therefore that inefficient regulation is a legitimate part of any comparison, if common to all regulated firms.[14] The nature of scale economies is potentially of great importance in deciding the structure of the industry which privatization and regulation should seek to establish.

The empirical evidence on the existence of scale economies suggests that the electricity generating industry exhibits a classic U-shaped average cost curve with falling average cost up to the 1500–4000MW range. This surprising evidence is very interesting especially when we observe that at privatization the two UK generating companies National Power and Power Gen had c.30,000MW and c.18,000MW respectively.[15] We shall review nine papers on the nature of scale economies in the US ESI: six at the firm level, three at the plant level.[16]

Wallace and Junk (1969), W+J, find that in 1964–5 operating costs in MUNIs were 74% higher per kWh than in IOUs, while there continued to be substantial surplus capacity at private plants. They attributed this fact to the federal tax-interest[17] subsidy to large numbers of small public power producers which resulted in 40% more capital per kWh at public plants and suggested that the subsidy should be removed and MUNIs purchase cheaper surplus power from IOUs. W+J's study covered 900 power systems, and the number of systems has been substantially reduced since 1964–5. However the results do suggest that MUNIs are significantly less scale efficient than IOUs.

Nerlove (1968) fits a generalized Cobb-Douglas cost function to 1955 data on 145 firms in the US ESI and detects the presence of increasing returns to scale. This result is not very robust, as Nerlove points out, because OLS tends to smooth the estimated cost function even if the true cost function indicates a U-shaped average cost function. On splitting the data into two output size categories this seems to be the case.[18]

Christensen and Greene (1976) using data on 124 firms in 1955 and on 114 firms in 1970 examined economies of scale by fitting a translog cost function to the data in the two years. They concluded that the use of the more general translog functional form resulted in a flattening of the U identified by Nerlove for the 1955 data. For the 1970 data they found an essentially L shaped average cost curve, with a large range over which average cost curves appear to be flat. In 1970 the bounds of the region in which no significant economies or diseconomies exist was 19,800mkWh to 67,100mkWh, however the upper bound is not very credible due to the small number of sample firms in this region.[19]

Huettner and Landon (1977), using data on 74 utilities in 1971, conduct a comprehensive study of returns to scale in the ESI, they confirm the non-robustness of the Nerlove study and find that of six expense categories[20] only sales expenses exhibits IRS (increasing returns to scale) over the whole of the observed output range. Generation has a U-shaped cost curve with a minimum occurring at 1600MW, however the U is very flat with only a 1% increase in average costs at 9000MW and 2.4% at 100MW. The key elements of the cost function yielding these results are the presence of squared terms on the output related variables, to pick up the U in the average cost curve, and the replacement of the output variable (Q) by K, peak capacity, and U, the rate of utilization of peak capacity, to deal with peak load costs.[21]

Roberts (1986) points out that the Huettner and Landon study and others like it fail to take adequate account of the way that service area characteristics effect scale economies. This leads to several important issues relating to the characteristics of demand and how they affect costs. For the sake of empirical tractability we cannot address these issues in the present analysis but we should be aware of them. Electric energy is defined not just by power ratings, eg kW, but also by time of day, time of year and voltage. Furthermore, power ratings apply to particular consumers and cables. The cost of supplying the aggregate output, measured in kWh, is thus a function of all the above variables. Importantly decisions made at one stage of a vertically integrated industry affect decisions in other stages. If demand profiles, voltages and distribution of consumers differ markedly between our firms this may lead to significant variations in costs independent of ownership type. The observation of small and inefficient generation companies in the USA may be a reflection of the prohibitive transmission costs which make it uneconomic to exploit economies of scale in generation. There is, however, little evidence to suggest that these variables do vary significantly or systematically across our sample of firms.

Roberts' own study attempts to model costs more fully by taking account of the characteristics of the demand facing the firm. The sample consists of 65 vertically integrated US IOUs in 1978. The multi-product translog cost function used includes variables for capital employed in transmission and distribution, labour employed, size of service area and number of customers. This specification allows the calculation of economies of size and consumer density. His main conclusions are that there are economies of output density, diseconomies in the number of consumers and that increasing consumer density has an insignificant effect on average cost. This has implications for our study – the size of the area served by each of our utilities varies widely but this has a negligible impact on costs. The suggestion is that while densely populated areas require shorter cables they become more expensive to lay.

The New Zealand Ministry of Energy (1989) investigates economies of scale in the New Zealand electricity distribution industry. This study uses data on 60 distribution companies operating in 1987 and specifies four translog functional forms with associated share equations for the firms in the industry.[22] In the four input single output case MES occurs at 2315mkWh while in the three input single input case the minimum occurs at 1748mkWh. These figures imply 8–11 firms in a restructured industry. However the cost savings are not significant beyond 500mkWh. Economies exist in sales per customer but not in numbers of customers. This study notes the difficulty of using a single year's data to reach conclusions: shocks may have mixed the 'normal' order in the year chosen.

Stewart (1979) estimates a plant level cost function on a sample of 58 new power plants that went into service in 1970–71. The cost function is a translog specification involving the capacity and heat rate of the plant with the dollar cost per kWh as the dependent variable. Stewart then simulates the minimum costs of plants with different capacities and heat rates and load factors. He finds that capacity utilization has a much greater effect on average cost than unit size. This leads him to suggest that the omission of an explicit treatment of load factor from other studies leads to an overstatement of the MES given that larger plants tend to have higher loads. His simulation indicates MES at 250MW for a high load factor plant.

The preceding studies were all cost function based and as such open to serious methodological criticism. In particular, is it reasonable to fit a particular stochastic functional form to firms using differing technologies? The results are still biased by Nerlove type criticisms – the cost function is only being approximated by data which may not be on the cost curve. A U-shaped cost curve remains curious from an engineering point of view: we expect continuously increasing returns to scale. Atkinson and Halvorsen (1984), looking at 123 IOUs operating in 1970, suggest that there is no evidence for decreasing returns in the electricity generating industry if shadow rather than actual prices are used. Non-stochastic techniques do exist to measure efficiency and these can also deal with economies of scale. We shall return to these techniques later but should mention their implications for the question of scale efficiency. An early non-parametric study by Seitz (1971)[23] looks at 181 new power plants built in the USA between 1947 and 1963 and suggests that MES occurs at 250MW. This study is based on very old data but does confirm that plants smaller than MES are at a much bigger relative cost disadvantage than plants larger than MES. Fare et al. (1985a, 1985b) indicate U shaped average cost curves at both the firm (1985a) level for 1970 data and the plant (1985b) level for 1978 data. These studies confirm the results of the parametric studies (where they use actual prices and costs) using a different methodology.

The issue of the optimal structure of the ESI thus raises a lot of issues broadly relating to the degree of competition within the industry and hanging on the characteristics of demand and the nature of production economies. It is a gross simplification to view the electricity generating industry as having one output, in fact it is a multiproduct industry producing a very large number of outputs,[24] each of which gives rise to different costs of production. No one vertical level of the industry can be separated from the rest – upstream costs affect downstream technology and vice versa.[25]

To conclude this discussion we look at two papers which examine the size of vertical economies in generation. Kerkvliet (1991) examines 149 observations on 20 US coal mine mouth plants over the period 1979–87. Seven of the plants are integrated with the mines that supply them. Kerkvliet finds that the non-integrated plants exercise significant monopsony power. The estimated cost function suggests that the non-integrated plants have 28% higher unit costs than comparable integrated plants. The sample is small but does seem to indicate the importance of integration for optimal investment. Kaserman and Mayo (1991) estimate a multistage quadratic cost function for a sample of 74 US utilities operating in 1981. The sample includes generating only, distributing only firms and integrated firms. The results suggest that for an integrated firm of sample mean size disintegration into separate generation and distribution utilities would result in 11.96% higher costs. It is not clear what sample selection biases are present in this analysis: perhaps integrated utilities have been formed by merger or are tolerated by regulators because of higher efficiency. Together these two studies represent strong empirical support for integrated electric utilities, at least in the USA, in spite of the relatively low plant and firm MES estimates from the economies of scale studies.

3.2.3 Regulation in the ESI

We now examine the evidence for how regulation affects productive efficiency. This is important in trying to separate the effect on productive efficiency of ownership per se and of differences in the type of regulation. Some types of regulation have less effect than others on the ability/incentive to minimize costs.[26] We argued in the previous chapter that the nature of the cost objective was unlikely to be affected significantly by the type of regulation. Before looking at the evidence on the costs of different types of regulation there is the related and more fundamental question of whether regulation achieves its objectives.[27] If regulation works, it may be that productive efficiency is not maximized (e.g. A-J, 1962), however if regulation doesn't work then firms may just minimize costs independently unaffected by regulatory rules.

The evidence we present on the effectiveness of regulation draws on work done on several industries quite similar in structure to the ESI. A-J's paper examined the case of AT&T and Bell in the telecoms industry in the 1950s and suggested that rate of return regulation did create a serious incentive to set predatory prices in competitive markets. This they saw as justification of their overinvestment thesis, because predatory prices led to overinvestment (and a consequent rise in the rate base) in competitive services to meet inflated demand. A-J had no evidence on capital investment and the observation of predatory prices in a competitive market is not dependent on the presence of regulation – it may be a legitimate strategy to drive a competitor out of the market.[28] Crain and Zardkoohi (1980) test whether regulated water companies exhibit rent seeking behaviour (see Chapter 2) and thus attempt to refute the A-J thesis. They find managerial income is significantly higher for private firms with lower costs and obtain results consistent with cost minimization for private regulated firms.[29] They use data on 110 firms in 1976. In a further regression they find that in 34 rate hearings in 1974 the change in the rate was significantly affected by the projected costs of production giving evidence that rent seeking actually resulted in higher profits. They introduce a dummy variable to capture the ability to make political donations and find this is significant. This may indicate that a more efficient firm is in a better position to make such donations and to conduct a successful rate hearing. These results strongly refute the A-J thesis in the water industry.

The historical purpose of electric utility regulation in the USA was to prevent the exploitation of monopoly power and hence to reduce prices below the monopoly price. While this premise has been widely accepted doubts have been raised over whether there is any significant monopoly power in the ESI and over the issue of whether price regulation actually has reduced prices below their unregulated levels. These points are related: 'significant' monopoly power cannot be defined independently of the effectiveness of available regulation. Stigler and Friedland (1962)[30] argued that the apparent success of rate hearings in reducing prices in the 1950s simply reflected the rapid growth of productivity in the ESI which would have resulted in falling prices in the absence of regulation. They further contended that the crudeness of regulatory procedures made it difficult to measure costs and that price control resulted in lower standards of service as utilities were unable to charge for such services.[31]

Moore (1970) attempts to measure the success of regulation in reducing prices to residential electricity consumers. He did this using data on 62 IOUs and 7 MUNIs in 1963. His methodology consisted of estimating the marginal cost of each firm and calculating a demand equation for the sales per residential consumer; this he then used to estimate the profit maximizing price for each firm and hence the ratio of this price to the actual price. Prices charged by MUNIs were on average 10–22% below the profit maximizing price, while IOUs were charging within 5% of the monopoly price.[32] A key assumption of the analysis is that short-run marginal costs equal long-run marginal costs. If they do not, then the observed differences in relative prices may simply reflect differences in the relationship between short- and long-run costs between firms.

Stigler, in his famous 1971 paper on the theory of regulation, examines the trucking industry in the USA and finds evidence that freight haulage rates are higher in states with regulation than without. He attributes this to the decline in applications for new licences and the reduction of entry into the industry as a result of regulation. While the trucking industry bears very little relation to the ESI, the results do indicate the potentially damaging link between regulation and new entry, in practice ESI regulation always restricts the entry of new utilities either implicitly[33] or more often explicitly.

Jackson (1969) provides some evidence which seems to back up the Stigler capture theory. He attempts to isolate the effects of regulation in reducing three[34] sets of prices in three years 1940, 1950 and 1960 using data on 80 regulated and 15 unregulated utilities. The technique involves use of an OLS regression, where average revenue per kWh was the dependent variable and a regulation dummy variable appears as a regressor, to test whether regulation has been more successful in reducing prices charged to regulated firms. The effectiveness of regulation rises through time and is much more pronounced for commercial and industrial prices. The regression equation is fairly ad hoc and has no sound basis in economic theory,[35] but the results do reveal that the nature of regulation is changing through time and that updated evidence on the effects of regulation is required.

Primeaux and Nelson (1980), using a sample of 80 IOUs operating in 1973, test whether there is any evidence for the benefit theory of regulation, in which regulators are assumed to set rate structures in order to maximize their political support. They find no evidence for politically motivated rate structures – there was no correlation between the percentage of output going to industrial users and the ratio of industrial to residential prices. However they do find that for their three price classes[36] prices are significantly below marginal costs at the peak period, implying the presence of over capacity to meet the excess demand. By definition this implies higher unit costs than under marginal cost pricing. It is interesting that the pioneers of marginal cost pricing in electricity have been two public companies – EdF of France and the CEGB. Non-marginal cost pricing may be politically motivated in the sense that the biggest users of peak load electricity are being subsidized by off-peak users.[37]

The above conclusion is confirmed by Wenders (1986), for five utilities (in various years from 1978–1984),[38] who finds that all three of his customer classes[39] pay less than marginal cost at peak load. Residential users were only paying an average of 61% of marginal costs at the peak. The question of cross-subsidy can only be answered with reference to whether a customer class is paying more or less than the fraction of total revenues that it would pay under full marginal cost pricing. The conclusion from this analysis is that residential consumers do pay significantly less (74–89%) than efficiency arguments would suggest they should, at the expense of higher prices for industry and commerce. This seems to be evidence against capture theory. The sample is small but to the extent that under-pricing at peak periods leads to over capacity this is evidence for the tendency for regulation to inflate production costs.

Regulation involves resource costs and none of the above studies have taken this cost into account in analysing the effectiveness of regulation in improving social welfare. Evidence on one important aspect of the direct costs of regulation is given by Prager (1989), using data on 100 IOUs in 1979, who suggests that the regulatory process raises the cost of debt to electric utilities by 42–46 basis points. On capital investment of $18–20bn per year in the US ESI this represents a substantial cost. The most important of these costs arise because of the exclusion of work in progress from the rate base, the extent of regulatory delay and the non-provision of interim relief.[40] A rise in the cost of debt financing is not only a direct cost but also imposes allocative losses through the incentive to use less than the socially optimal amount of capital to minimize production costs.

3.2.4 Different Types of Regulation

We conclude this section by consideration of the differential effects of different types of regulation. So far we have only considered rate of return regulation. This is by far the most common type in the USA, and as noted in Chapter 2 this has an analog in price regulation. We note that while 'yardstick' regulation has been proposed (Shleifer, 1985) and the possibilities of its use in the regulation of electricity distribution have been investigated,[41] the empirical effects of implementation have yet to be tested. We will look at two papers: one on environmental regulation and the other on the bureau vs. commission debate.

The ESI is a major producer of environmental pollutants.[42] In some countries the recognition of this fact has led to regulation to force utilities to reduce emissions from power stations. In particular FGDs have been fitted to many fossil fuel stations in the USA, imposing significant capital costs on the utilities involved where retrofitting is required and affecting the choice of technology in new power stations. Fare et al. (1989b) look at a sample of electric power plants in the years 1969 and again in 1977 to assess the impact of the growth of environmental regulation on costs in an attempt to explain the slowdown in the rate of growth of the industry. They find no significant reduction in cost efficiency between the two periods and cannot therefore attribute the productivity slowdown in the industry to environmental regulation. This result however is not particularly useful. It is self-evident that retrofitting of power stations must raise costs and that given the huge sums involved differences in regulatory standards between countries will influence cost differentials. Nuclear power is now being shown to involve substantially larger decommissioning costs than first thought and has experienced a rise in the perceived safety risk: these factors have already brought about changes in the recognized optimal fuel mix,[43] while changing public preferences concerning the environment have begun to make it very difficult to get approval to construct nuclear stations even when justified on the grounds of cost efficiency.[44] While we might argue that environmentally related costs are relatively small as a percentage at the moment, we should expect to see them become more significant in the future.

Eckert (1973) recognizes that the system of costs and rewards facing regulators affects their choices among alternative regulatory policies and market structures. In particular the incentives facing regulators may be such as to encourage the introduction of cartel arrangements. He identifies two different regulatory bodies: the bureau and the commission. The bureau is run by civil servants with incentives to increase its size (Niskanen, 1968) by regulating more firms and bringing in more bureaucratic procedures. Commissions are run by commissioners on fixed salaries and with terms of office fixed by statute. Commissioners' lengths of office are usually fixed and salary rises are difficult to negotiate.[45] This leads to the hypothesis that the rewards from additional regulation cannot be captured as easily by commissioners as by bureaucratic officials. The implication of this should be that commissions more often preside over monopolies arising from entry restrictions designed to reduce the commissioners' workload. Eckert tests these conjectures by examining information from 27 cities in the USA with populations over 250,000. The evidence is that bureaux are significantly more often associated with monopolies than commissions, which indicates that the reward structure is more complicated than the simple theory suggests. If commissioners are elected they may be subject to closer monitoring than bureaucrats. Even if they are not elected, commissioners might be selected on the basis of their desire to pursue the public interest and hence be less subject to capture. Either way it is clear that the type of regulation does influence market structure and hence degree of competition and the ability to achieve economies of scale.

3.3   Ownership and Efficiency: US Studies

There have been a large number of US studies looking more directly at the question of ownership and its effects on productive efficiency. These have been reviewed in DeAlessi (1974a), Yarrow (1986), Vickers and Yarrow (1988a) and Boardman and Vining (1989, 1992).[46] Before examining some of the papers in detail we note the conclusions of these earlier reviews. DeAlessi is highly critical of the methodology used in the early studies and examines closely the theoretical and statistical techniques used in the early studies, reinterpreting the results from some papers. He finds evidence for the A-J thesis and that MUNIs will in general have lower prices and higher operating costs than IOUs. He also finds that levels of significance are often low, while the variables used frequently lack precision and theoretical justification. However the extent to which the various bits of evidence support each other is impressive. The approach of the other three reviews is less rigorous but, as might be expected from their dates, they are broadly in agreement: while the largest number of studies do find IOUs more efficient than MUNIs, the best of the studies find either no significant difference or even that MUNIs are more efficient. General criticisms of the evidence are similar to DeAlessi. However they also note the nature of the joint hypotheses related to legal structure and regulation which any comparison actually tests for and a failure to take account of the effects of lower costs of capital facing public firms. As with all dynamic industries more evidence, better data and more robust techniques of analysis are required.

In general the studies we shall review fall into two broad classes. Firstly, those which examine pricing policy to see whether prices are lower or price structures are more efficient in one ownership type, and secondly the studies which use costs as their basis for comparison. In general the studies use regression techniques with Fare et al. (1985a) and Hausman and Neufeld (1991) as notable exceptions.

We start with a study by DeAlessi (1974b) which does not fall into any of the general classes. The utility maximization hypothesis implies that managers of MUNIs will enjoy longer tenure than those of IOUs, as they will trade political pricing for tenure at the margin. This implies lower propensities to take risks in public firms. This hypothesis was tested using a sample of 100 IOUs and 100 MUNIs. The frequency with which the chief executive was changed over the period 1962–71 was regressed on the size of the firm, the amount of electricity purchased, and a dummy variable for ownership. The results suggested a significantly longer period of tenure for managers of MUNIs. Just what this result implies for efficiency is unclear. It is generally accepted, especially in politics, that the problem with short tenure is the lack of incentive to take a long-term view and this usually results in a tendency to maximize current profits rather than net present value. The link between tenure and performance is complicated: longer tenure might suggest more successful management or managerial ossification; simple tests will not distinguish the two.

The price structure studies examine the idea that managers of IOUs will more fully exploit the possibilities for increasing profits that are realized by tariffs which reflect the demand and cost characteristics of different customer classes. There are at least three reasons for this: firstly, price regulation by commission will in general encourage price discrimination on the grounds of efficiency and fairness,[47] while regulators of MUNIs in bureaucracies may over-engage in price regulation to the detriment of efficiency; secondly, regulators of MUNIs are more subject to political influences and may smooth rate structures in the interest of political expediency (i.e. to buy votes); and finally managers of MUNIs may be subject to less monitoring and be able to reduce their workload by having simpler tariff structures. This suggests that IOUs will have a larger number of customer classes and will exhibit more time of day pricing. These observations are dependent on the characteristics of the costs of metering, the nature of regulation and the preferences of regulators.

Peltzman (1971), using 1966 data for five consumption levels and three consumption groups investigates the vote-buying thesis by testing five hypotheses that follow from it. Firstly, MUNIs should have lower rates. Peltzman finds that this is so. This has little implication for the productive efficiency question as virtually the whole of the difference can be explained by the lower tax rates enjoyed by MUNIs.[48] Secondly, prices will be relatively low to lower income and consumption groups if the income elasticity of demand exceeds the income elasticity of taxes. This is so as to maximize the number of voters receiving a subsidy while still breaking even or hitting a financial target. Peltzman finds no evidence for this. The reason perhaps lies in the fact that receipt of a small subsidy by a low income consumer is not effective in securing his vote. Much more effective is the receipt of a large campaign fund donation from a satisfied industrial consumer. Thirdly, prices should be lower to voters than to non-voters. To test this Peltzman examined the pricing policies of 31 municipal firms which also serve other cities. The rate schedules were identical in 26 cases, for the other five prices charged to the non-voters were indeed higher, thus the evidence was very weak given the possible differences in delivery costs.[49] Fourthly, individual rates should be more highly correlated within MUNIs; this is because managers have less incentive to independently adjust some rates in the face of a change in demand conditions for one group of users. He found this hypothesis strongly supported by the evidence. Finally, tariff structures within MUNIs ought to less closely reflect differences in the costs of serving different consumer classes. Looking at just two consumer classes[50] he found that there was evidence to support the hypothesis that particular costs matter more to IOUs.

DeAlessi (1977), using data on 20 matched pairs of IOUs and MUNIs in 1970, finds that managers of MUNIs adopt fewer peak related schedules and fewer rate schedules in general than managers in IOUs. This implies that managers of MUNIs are failing to take decisions which would reduce costs and raise profitability. This seems to confirm the results of Peltzman's study. The major criticism of this study would seem to be the complete lack of reference to costs: the efficacy of different rate structures is a function of the differences in costs of supplying consumers in different classes; while matching is an attempt to do this the result is to reduce the sample size to 20 pairs from an industry consisting of 607 MUNIs and 210 IOUs in 1970.

Junker (1975), investigates differences in prices and costs using 1969–70 data on 24 MUNIs and 49 IOUs. Junker uses simple t-tests for comparing sample means and finds that MUNIs have significantly lower prices and significantly higher profit rates than IOUs. However he finds that while on average MUNIs have lower unit costs the difference in costs is not significant. Junker obtains similar conclusions when he investigates prices, profits, and costs using simple regression equations including an ownership dummy variable. Junker concludes that there is no evidence of relative cost inefficiency in publicly owned enterprises. The analysis of this paper is very crude: it is not clear whether the sample firms are engaged in the same electricity functions; and straightforward comparison of average costs makes no allowance for the differing operating environments of the firms: in particular the effect of population density on distribution costs.

The majority of the cost based studies compare IOUs and MUNIs by the estimation of a cost function for both types of firms. This is to assume that all firms are actually on the industry cost curve. As a first approximation this analysis is only possible by assuming that firms are presented with the same technological possibilities, purchase inputs at the same prices and attempt to minimize costs for a given level of

output. These assumptions may subsequently be relaxed by the introduction of regressors designed to allow for these differences. Meyer
(1975) fits a simple cost function to a sample of 30 MUNIs and 30
IOUs for the years 1967, 1968 and 1969. The generation cost equation
contains three variables: generation costs, generation costs squared and
generation costs cubed. The pooled data time series and cross-section
equations containing both IOUs and MUNIs, and having an additional
dummy variable for IOUs indicate that MUNIs have significantly lower
costs. For these results to hold the strong assumptions of cost function
analysis must hold. Our firm level dataset in Chapter 5 reveals that
labour costs within the USA vary from $14,000 to $31,000, while there
are wide variations in fuel costs between companies even for the same
type of fuel. This implies that the results can only be treated with
scepticism: MUNIs may have access to cheaper capital, labour and fuel
than IOUs and the technology employed may well be very different –
for example, no allowance is made for differences in the amount of
hydroelectric power produced by the firms.

Neuberg (1977) extends the Meyer analysis by specifying a cost
function which does accommodate differences in the price of factors of
production. Neuberg looks at two large samples of distribution companies in 1972 – one consisting of 185 IOUs and 189 MUNIs, the
other 90 IOUs and 75 MUNIs – and runs separate regressions on
both.[51] The dependent variable was total distribution costs and the
regressors were number of consumers, number of MWh sold to ultimate
consumers, number of miles of distribution line, square miles of service
territory, price of labour and dummy variable for ownership type. The
results indicate that there is no evidence for cost inefficiency in MUNIs
and tend to confirm Meyer's findings that MUNIs exhibit significantly
lower costs than IOUs. Although the cost function specification is an
improvement on that of Meyer it is by no means complete: a major
omission is the lack of accommodation of the differences in distribution
costs arising out of the presence of different customer types and
different voltages.

DiLorenzo and Robinson (1982) fit a cost function to a sample of
18 public and 23 private generating firms for the years 1970–72.
Looking at total annual steam production expenses as a function of
steam generation in kWh, average fuel cost, total generating capacity
and an ownership dummy the authors found that MUNIs had insignificantly lower costs than IOUs. They concluded that political competition (following Stigler, 1973) was at least as effective in controlling
MUNI costs as competition in the private capital market.

Pescatrice and Trapani (1980) [P+T] use a translog cost function to
model costs by taking account of differences in input prices,[52] while

technological differences are controlled for by only looking at fossil fuel generation. They use data from 33 MUNIs and 23 IOUs for the years 1965 and 1970. The results indicate that the cost differential at the sample mean was 23.5% lower for MUNIs in 1965 and 32.9% lower in 1970. It may be that this differential is due to the incentive effects of regulation: following A-J, the internal cost of capital facing a regulated private firm P_K^i is: $P_K^i = P_K - \lambda \cdot (s-r)/(1-\lambda)$, where s is the maximum permitted rate of return, r is the market rate of return and P_K is the external cost of capital and λ lies between 0 and 1. Thus respecifying the translog cost function and allowing λ to vary across its range a value of λ may be selected to minimize residual sum of squares. If the estimated value of λ is non-zero, this provides evidence for the A-J thesis. P+T find evidence that λ is non-zero and thus support for the view that rate of return regulation involves incentives to deviate from cost minimization.

Atkinson and Halvorsen (1986)[53] [A+H] criticize P+T for implicitly assuming that MUNIs minimize costs and attributing all of the observed differences in efficiency to rate of return regulation. They relax these restrictions by using a translog cost function containing shadow prices, $k_i P_i$, for all inputs. The k_i are estimated separately for MUNIs and IOUs as: $k_i = d_i + g_i D$, where D is an ownership dummy. Their sample consists of data for 123 private and 30 public firms in the year 1970. Equal price efficiency for MUNIs and IOUs is tested by imposing the restriction that their g_i are both equal to zero, while absolute price efficiency further requires the d_i to be equal to 1 for both types of firms. The results indicate that IOUs and MUNIs are equally cost efficient given the internal factor prices that they face. However the hypothesis of absolute price efficiency is rejected, i.e. shadow factor prices do not equal actual factor prices for both types of firms. The magnitude of this inefficiency is small, increasing the costs of production by an estimated 2.4%, though this figure masks large induced increases in the quantities of capital and labour demanded.[54]

Both the previous studies usefully extend the cost function studies of efficiency but they also expose their limitations. The idea is that observed differences in costs arise due to the managers acting 'as if' factor prices are lower than they really are. Managers are assumed to be maximizing a utility function, and the above techniques attempt to model this function better than previous studies. However, what if the manager is simply incompetent and failing to calculate the right solution to his optimization problem? In the above models incompetence appears as shadow prices being less than actual prices and differences in managerial ability will be reflected in differences in estimated shadow prices. These studies similarly do not really separate the effects of ownership and regulation on productive efficiency – the finding that managers of IOUs are apparently acting as if the price of capital were lower than the actual price is not only consistent with the A-J thesis but also with a managerial theory of the firm where managers have a preference for size and face weak shareholder control. The results of all these cost based studies should therefore be interpreted with care, although the general picture is clear: there is no evidence for the Alchian hypothesis and any such ownership effect is swamped by the distortions introduced by rate of return regulation.

A cost function study which takes a different approach is that of Cote (1989) who uses panel data to estimate a stochastic cost frontier model for a sample of newly constructed generating plants. The sample contains 37 IOUs, 9 MUNIs and 16 COOPs observed over the period 1965–73. The estimated frontier cost function allows for noise and inefficiency in the variables.[55] The use of panel data allows allocative and technical efficiency to be calculated given the strong assumption that technical efficiency does not vary over the period considered. The small sample of public plants have an average technical inefficiency of 7% against 14% for IOUs. Cost inefficiency is also higher in IOUs by over 6%.

The cost studies we have reviewed so far involve restrictive assumptions on the parameters and functional form of the cost function (especially Cote, 1989). Fare et al. (1985a), using the same data set as Atkinson and Halvorsen, employ a non parametric, linear programming, technique to calculate six different measures of efficiency. As this is the technique we shall be using to analyse our data set, we need only review their results at this stage. They found that although on average IOUs were slightly more efficient than MUNIs, the difference in overall cost efficiency was not significant. There was however some evidence that MUNIs tended to exhibit increasing returns to scale while the generally larger IOUs exhibited decreasing returns to scale. A+H point out that this result is consistent with their finding that the g_i were equal to zero. Thus it would appear that the Fare et al. study confirms the results of the most sophisticated of the parametric studies and suggests that earlier studies failed to take sufficient account of the differences in factor prices facing the firms. Byrnes, Grosskopf and Hayes (1986) using a similar technique obtain almost identical results for 68 MUNIs and 59 IOUs in 1976 in the water industry.

Hausman and Neufeld (1991) conduct a Fare analysis using US generating plant data on 218 IOUs and 97 MUNIs operating in 1897/98. Their analysis is particularly interesting on two counts. This study represents a pure test of ownership in the absence of rate of return regulation and is the only generation study which uses multiple outputs.[56] They find significantly lower costs in MUNIs (average overall productive efficiency is 9% higher in MUNIs) and that scale inefficiency accounts for the major part of technical inefficiency. Hausman and Neufeld attribute the superior MUNI performance to *public spirit* and *esprit du corps* which was widely held at the time to be a significant factor in public utility management. This study raises the question of whether it is bad policy for the government to constantly tell public sector managers that they are less competent or less motivated than private sector managers and thus undermine *public spirit* and *esprit du corps*. The relatively poor performance of MUNIs today may also be related to the growth of bureaucracies over the last 100 years and hence a decline in the accountability of individual public servants.

While the statistical evidence reviewed above has been subjected to considerable criticism the picture that it presents is reasonably consistent. A general criticism that has been made is that most studies fail to take account of the subsidies which many MUNIs receive eg. low interest Federal loans and large tax exemptions for public power production (Edison Electric Institute, 1985).[57] However from the above studies there is little or no evidence for the Alchian view that IOUs are more efficient than MUNIs. Several studies do indicate that MUNIs are more efficient than IOUs, but the more recent and more technically advanced studies suggest that the differences are insignificant at the worst for MUNIs. The detailed evidence seems to suggest that rate of return regulation is responsible for dissipating any of the property rights gain and also that scale inefficiencies are pervasive.

3.4   Ownership and Efficiency: Non-US Studies

The comparative international evidence on the efficiency of electricity generating companies is poor, generally involving a small number of firms compared in very unsophisticated ways. Corti (1976) compares three European firms, two MUNIs – CEGB and the EdF – and an IOU, RWE,[58] on the basis of financial returns and thermal efficiency for the years 1971–73. He finds significantly better performance on these measures from RWE. He uses this evidence to argue that there does not appear to be any justification for the common view that 'bigger is better' in the ESI. While rate of return comparisons are made spurious by the existence of price control in both the UK and France, RWE impressively outperforms the larger utilities on both capital and labour productivity.[59] Lucas (1985) examines the ESI in Germany, France, Italy, Sweden and Denmark using an institutional approach. It is difficult to characterize his findings but in general Denmark and

Germany perform well while Italy does badly. In Denmark and Germany IOUs or mixed enterprises produce most of the power, while in Italy and France production is dominated by one large MUNI. The impression is however that the role of the state is crucial: relative success in Denmark is a function of the encouragement of municipal district heating schemes; the French nuclear power programme has been motivated by a political will to increase energy security and failure in Italy has been the result of the strangulation of the power station construction programme by the political process. An important determinant of capital costs is the construction time of new coal-fired power stations: analysis of these (Yarrow, 1988) reveals that in competitive environments such as Japan, West Germany and the USA these are shorter than in countries such as the UK and Italy.[60] There are exceptions. France is one of the more efficient countries while IOUs in Belgium and Holland are towards the bottom of the league. Helm and McGowan (1988), in their examination of the ESI in Europe, suggest that there exist three working models: a unitary integrated MUNI system (e.g. UK and France), a mixed ownership with dominant state incumbent system (e.g. Sweden) and a decentralized mixed ownership system (e.g. Holland and Germany). They concluded that none of the systems was obviously superior, and that the major sources of inefficiency originated in the nature of government regulation relating to the industry.

BIE (1991) records some very basic comparative performance indicators for an international sample of electric utilities using 1989–90 data – prices, capacity factors, reserve margins, availability, labour productivity and total factor productivity. This study is in the context of comparing the performance of Australian utilities with other OECD utilities. Little can be inferred from the figures: New Zealand and Canada have the lowest electricity prices (due to low fuel costs) but Japan (with high fuel costs) has very low average outage times.

Pollitt (1993) uses Fare methods to compare the productive efficiency of 78 nuclear power stations operating in Canada, Japan, USA, UK and South Africa in 1989. This study finds no significant difference in efficiency between the IOUs and MUNIs in the sample. This is the only study which examines nuclear power station operating efficiency but neglects consideration of the environmental costs of nuclear power (eg. decommissioning) which is now the most important issue facing the industry.

In addition to the above multi-country studies we review a small number of single country studies relating to non-US firms. An Anglo-American study conducted in 1949[61] found that labour productivity was significantly lower in the UK compared with private firms in the USA. The report concluded that comparatively few large differences existed but there was a considerable aggregation of small items; although the report is out-dated many of the 'small items' seem familiar. American electricity workers were recorded as being experimentally minded and keen to try out new ideas, construction of new plant was considerably faster in the USA, while planning and system control were given careful attention. US employees were noticeably keen for the success of their company and there was a regular supply of information to employees particularly on the financial performance of the company. Further historical evidence is provided by Foreman-Peck and Waterson (1985) who examine 171 UK generating plants operating in 1937. They use a translog cost function following P+T (1980) and find that MUNIs selected by the regulated CEB system[62] were as efficient as selected IOUs. However in the unregulated system MUNIs show substantially lower average costs – none of the differences are statistically significant. Scale economies average 21% of costs. Hammond (1992) extends Foreman-Peck and Waterson (1985) using similar 1937 data. He estimates a translog stochastic cost frontier. He finds evidence of scale inefficiency among selected CEB stations and suggests that fewer stations operating at higher load factors would have substantially reduced costs. Hammond detects no evidence for the superior performance of IOUs or of a bias towards selecting MUNIs to supply the CEB.

An interesting debate has arisen in Canada over whether low cost finance available to MUNIs has actually resulted in over-investment in what is apparently one of that country's most successful industries. Jenkins (1985, 1987) has calculated that the welfare losses involved are of the order of 1% of GNP. The key assumption is that these investments should be earning a gross return of 10% to be consistent with returns in the rest of the economy – in 1980 the actual gross return was only 3.8%. These results are disputed by Spiro (1987) who suggests a lower discount rate of 6% and points out that Jenkins only examines average not marginal cost. Higher capital investment in MUNIs may well reflect lower borrowing costs and hence be allocatively efficient.

Hjalmarsson and Veiderpass (1992a) examine the efficiency of a sample of 285 electricity distribution utilities operating in Sweden in 1985. We discuss the non-parametric *DEA* methodology of this paper in Chapter 8. They find no significant effect from ownership (or organization) or service area, though rural utilities did tend to exhibit higher scale inefficiency. Hjalmarsson and Veiderpass (1992b) examined 289 Swedish electricity distribution companies over the period 1970–86 using Malmquist productivity measures (based on non-parametric efficiency scores). Once again they found no significant difference in efficiency due to ownership.

3.5 Conclusion: Observations on Privatization in the UK

In conclusion we turn to the literature on the effects of privatization in the UK where the 'British Electricity Experiment'[63] is underway.[64] The statics are very hard to separate from the dynamics but the general conclusion is that there will be little gain in productive efficiency as a result of privatization. Prior to privatization Bunn and Vlahos (1989) see the major effect as being to raise real prices 33% above their 1988 level in the long run in order to achieve market rates of return. To the extent that market rates of return imply monopoly deadweight losses privatization will result in reduction in social welfare. Helm (1988) sees the major effect of privatization as the freeing of managers from effective control of the decision making process and hence a large increase in their ability to improve their own welfare, at the possible expense of the shareholder. For both these writers improvements in efficiency are a function of the restrictions on the purchasing of foreign coal, to which the comments on the cost of capital debate in Canada apply, and the degree of competition which the privatized structure of the industry encourages. The privatization of the fossil fuel generation component of the UK's CEGB as two companies would seem to be a long way short of optimal, a number between 10 and 20 would be more consistent with the US evidence.[65] Clearly such a radical reorganization would have been incompatible with the government's legislative timetable and the other objectives of privatization (such as revenue raising). Furthermore the extent of restructuring is limited by the costs of privatization[66] and the need to secure managerial co-operation.[67] Green and Newbery (1991) simulate the duopoly structure of generation in the UK ESI and find that compared with quintopoly welfare losses of £262m p.a. are being incurred – this is equivalent to a cost reduction of c.2.5% in generation. Yarrow (1992) finds that electricity prices have actually risen by more since privatization than rises in underlying costs might have suggested. On average prices in 1991 were 25% higher[68] than pre-privatization trends would have predicted in the 1988 base year.[69] Unless such rises can be justified on the grounds that prices were below marginal cost prior to privatization, these figures would seem to imply that privatization needs to yield substantially lower costs to offset the losses in allocative efficiency due to higher prices.

Evidence on the efficiency effects of privatization in the UK is mixed and limited by the short time period since privatization occurred. Yarrow (1989b) found no significant improvement in the productivity performance of British Telecom and British Gas up to 1988. He also examined the performance of seven other privatized firms operating in competitive environments; of these he concluded only three were clear successes.[70] The most spectacular performer, British Steel, achieved its largest productivity gains in the run up to privatization. Yarrow concluded that in the large utilities government discretion had been replaced by managerial discretion rather than tighter monitoring. This led to a risky overseas acquisitions policy and an unwillingness to take difficult cost cutting measures within the domestic business. Yarrow's findings on British Gas are apparently contradicted in a sophisticated study undertaken by Price and Weyman-Jones (1993). After examining output–input data from the regional divisions of British Gas for the period 1977–8 to 1991, they find evidence of significant increases in productivity growth from 1983 (privatization occurred in 1986) and convergence in regional efficiency levels using a Malmquist index.[71] However their conclusion that privatization added 3% to annual productivity growth is surely too strong. The evidence suggests that the reorganization of British Gas *within* the public sector resulted in an increase in productivity growth. Thus the limited evidence on the *post*-privatization performance of large utilities does not indicate any strong improvement in efficiency.

The conclusion of this chapter seems to be that ownership is not a major determinant of differences in productive efficiency, and hence that there is little reason to expect privatization per se to reduce costs. The structural changes associated with privatization may well reduce costs. However it is important to note that the product resulting from these structural changes may not be the same as before, rendering simple cost comparisons invalid e.g. the reduction of reserve margins leads to reduced security of supply associated with any given output. The interesting question arising from the observation of falling production costs in the UK ESI since privatization is whether costs would have fallen as much under more efficient public management, including the necessary structural reorganization, of the old CEGB and area electricity boards.

Notes

1. See Boardman and Vining (1992) for a comprehensive review.
2. Corti (1976), Lucas (1985), Helm (1988), BIE (1991) and Pollitt (1993). Pollitt (1993) uses a sophisticated non-parametric technique.
3. Renewable energy sources should be omitted because unmeasurable factors external to the control of the firm determine the costs of such energy in such a way that is impossible to observe the efficiency of the firm. For instance the presence of favourable geography in Norway allows the production of almost 100% of that country's electricity from hydroelectric schemes. We observe low costs of production, but how can relative

efficiency be compared with the UK? We shall return to this issue in the specific context of the Fare et al. (1985a) methodology.

4. Hjalmarsson and Veiderpass (1992a,b), Weyman-Jones (1992) and Pollitt (1993). Of these Weyman-Jones (1992) and Fare et al.(1989a) do not address the ownership question directly.

5. In his review of Vickers and Yarrow (1988a).

6. Their sample does not include any electric utilities.

7. Public utilities, such as electricity, are explicitly excluded from the dataset.

8. British Coal, Petróleos de Venezuela and Vale do Rio Doce are cited as sample public corporations.

9. Fuel inputs, generation of electricity, national grid cables and wires, local distribution network, billing and metering, appliance sales and servicing (Helm, (1988), p.7).

10. Our earlier comments on the history of the ESI in the UK apply.

11. There are two major sources of vertical economies (Kaserman and Mayo, 1991). First, a downstream monopoly demands an inefficient combination of inputs from upstream suppliers. Second, transaction costs in the absence of integration may be large. This second source is very important in the ESI which is characterized by technological interdependence, idiosyncratic capital, long-term contracting, multiproduct pricing and uncertainty in supply and demand. These features give rise to large scope for ex post exploitation of sunk investments and the need for expensive insurance if surety of supply is to be maintained, in the absence of all available information.

12. Authors often add a fourth business, supply; see Chapter 8 Section 3 for more information on this.

13. Even this is not obviously the case, public firms can choose to co-operate in a power pool to exploit scale economies. This may involve high transactions costs.

14. We attempted to argue in Chapter 2 that there was little difference in the effects on productive efficiency between the available types of utility regulation.

15. Source: *Financial Times* 28 and 30 January,1991 p.11.

16. See Cowling and Smith (1978) for an early review on the nature of the electricity generating production function.

17. This has three elements: firstly, exemption from some taxes, e.g. federal income tax; secondly, interest paid on municipal bonds frequently not subject to federal income tax; and finally, most MUNIs are exempt from regulatory rules governing debt-equity ratios.

18. Greene (1980a) reruns the Nerlove equation using the maximum likelihood gamma *DSA* production frontier technique (see Chapter 4). This produces a firm level estimate of minimum efficient scale of 4753mkWh against the equivalent Nerlove OLS figure of 4429mkWh.

19. Only one firm in the sample produced more than 55,000mkWh (Christensen and Greene (1976): figure 3, p.674.)

20. Generation, transmission, distribution, administrative and general,

customer accounts expense and sales expenses (Huettner and Landon (1977), p.905).

21. By definition, Q=KU.

22. The four inputs used are cost of bulk electricity, labour, capital and other; in the three input model the cost of bulk electricity is dropped. Output and capacity are the two output variables, in the single output case capacity is dropped.

23. Seitz calculates a **K(u,x)** Farrell type measure of technical efficiency.

24. For practical purposes each half-hour of the year defines a distinct commodity (Vickers and Yarrow (1985), p.52). The new UK power pool prices electricity in half-hourly slots.

25. The most important of these level interactions would seem to be between nationally available fuel inputs and the choice of fuel mix in generation. The choice of publicly owned utilities to use non cost minimizing technology and indigenous fuels is often made but rarely justified on welfare grounds (see Rees 1984b). The choice of the CEGB to purchase British Coal at a price much higher than the world price is a source inefficiency which can be attributed to public ownership of the CEGB.

26. E.g. 'yardstick' regulation (Shleifer, 1985) can offer optimal incentives to minimize costs where rate of return regulation cannot.

27. There is another question: is regulation necessary? The suggestion here is that regulation to control prices is unnecessary and reduces incentives to cost minimize. Joskow (1989) presents a review of the possibilities for deregulation among US IOUs. He advocates the creation of pool markets for power. However there is the problem of ensuring that adequate new investment in the industry would occur. Joskow also recommends the vertical separation of the industry as has occurred in the UK.

28. See Tirole (1988), pp.363–84.

29. The dependent variable is ln (total managerial income / total book value of assets), the cost variable is ln (average operating costs / total book value of assets).

30. See Section 3.2.1 for their arguments on the existence of monopoly power in the ESI.

31. A dissertation by Emmons (reviewed 1991) analyses electricity prices in 1930 and 1942 and concludes that MUNIs charged 28% less than IOUs in 1930, only 15% less in 1942. Most of the 1942 difference was due to the lower capital costs facing MUNIs. Emmons argues that rate of return regulation was ineffective prior to New Deal tightening of procedures and yardstick Federal power projects (such as the TVA). Carter (1991) suggests that observed regulatory ineffectiveness was due to small agency budgets and regulatory 'capture'.

32. These results are confirmed by studies on the profitability of MUNIs versus IOUs, such as Shepherd (1966) and Mann (1970) who use 1960 and 1966 data respectively, which find that rates of return are higher in IOUs and exhibit less variability than in MUNIs. These accounting studies are of dubious value from a measurement point of view but do lend credence to Moore's results.

33. The 1983 Energy Act in the UK removed the restriction on the connection of new generators to the national grid, and forced the distribution companies to publish prices at which they would buy electricity from private generating companies. The move failed to attract a single private generator because the Act allowed the incumbent firm, the CEGB, to manipulate prices to force the distribution companies to offer new generators prices below the marginal cost of the electricity they were buying from the CEGB (see Helm, 1988).

34. Average price of total sales per kWh, average price of residential sales per kWh and average price per kWh of commercial and industrial sales.

35. The regressors are population served, income level of population, fuel costs per BTU, proportion of hydro-electric power and the regulation dummy variable.

36. Residential, commercial and industrial.

37. The daily peak loads in the UK occur around 9–10am and again around 5.30–6pm, due to spikes in residential demand. We suggest therefore non-marginal cost pricing represents a subsidy to residential users.

38. The data are calculated using techniques developed by the US National Economic Research Association.

39. Residential, commercial and industrial.

40. Interim rate relief allows companies that have applied for higher rates to collect them, subject to refund, during the course of the regulatory proceedings.

41. Doble and Weyman-Jones (1991) and Weyman-Jones (1992) investigate the ability of yardstick efficiency measures to distinguish efficiency differences in the presence of differing operating environments in the UK electricity distribution industry.

42. See House of Commons Select Committee on the Environment (1989a) for details of the UK position on some of the atmospheric pollutants produced by the ESI.

43. Nowhere has this been more evident than in the UK, where the rise in estimated decommissioning costs resulted in the nuclear power plants being withdrawn from the privatization of National Power and being formed into a new public company – Nuclear Electric.

44. The example of Italy has already been noted. However the recent Swedish referendum on nuclear power has approved the complete phasing out of nuclear energy, and represents the most extreme response to new information on nuclear power so far.

45. Note that in the UK context, the current regulatory arrangement involves the Director General of Electricity Supply (the head of the regulatory agency) acting like a commissioner. He is certainly much more visible and accountable than the unseen bureaucratic monitors responsible for the electricity industry prior to privatization.

46. The 1992 paper is a revision of the 1989 paper, but no additional studies comparing efficiency between IOUs and MUNIs are added under electric utilities.

47. For example OFTEL's encouragement of the rebalancing of BT's telephone charges in the UK, see Hartley and Culham (1988).
48. A partial explanation is also found in the large amounts of purchased power sold on by MUNIs, purchased at below long run marginal cost from private producers.
49. DeAlessi (1974a) in his review of Peltzman, p.26.
50. Residential users consuming 500 kWh per month and Industrial users consuming 100,000 kWh per month.
51. There was extra information available on the smaller sample.
52. The translog cost function contains variables for capital, labour, fuel, factor prices and neutral and non-neutral technological change. P+T use an index of technology which measures the vintage of the firm's generating equipment, computed as the weighted average age of the firm's generating equipment used by the firm where the weights are the percentage of total capacity installed at any given date.
53. See Chapter 5 Section 3 for more details of this paper.
54. Across both types of firms price inefficiency increases the quantity of capital demanded by 23.4% and the quantity of labour demanded by 10.2% for IOUs and 16.9% for MUNIs.
55. See the next chapter for more details of the stochastic cost function.
56. The study specifies three outputs – incandescent lights, arc lights and stationary motors – and six inputs – AC generators, DCCV generators, DCCA generators, coal, waged employees and salaried employees.
57. This criticism cannot be applied to the Fare et al. (1985a) analysis, as factor prices are taken as given.
58. Rheinisch-Westfalisches Elecktritätswerk (RWE) is the largest producer of electricity in Germany.
59. Differences in the basis of calculation, e.g. amount of subcontracted labour, and the technology employed may make simple comparisons invalid.
60. Japan=3 years; UK=6.7 years.
61. Anglo-American Council on Productivity (1950).
62. The CEB (Central Electricity Board) was the forerunner of the CEGB and operated the national grid.
63. See Vickers and Yarrow (1991b) for details of the UK privatization.
64. The 12 regional electricity distribution companies in England and Wales were listed on the stock exchange on 11 December, 1990 and the generating companies – National Power and Power Gen – were listed on 12 March, 1991. The Scottish companies – Scottish Power and Scottish Hydro-Electric – were listed on 18 June, 1991.
65. Though the difference in average costs is likely to be small due to the shallowness of the average cost curve at output levels above the cost minimum. The major advantage of 10–20 companies is likely to be reduced regulatory costs through the easier achievement of allocative efficiency. This optimal number of firms is a declining function of the cost of restructuring.
66. The restructuring costs involved in the setting up of National Power were £491m in the accounting year 1989–90 (National Power, 1990). These

costs contrast with the relatively small resource costs involved in the legal transfer of ownership, see Jenkinson and Mayer (1988).

67. Kay and Thompson (1986) suggest that senior managers in a company are the most effective interest group involved in a privatization.

68. For small industrial consumers prices were 40% higher than trends would predict.

69. Privatization plans were first published in a Government White Paper in February 1988.

70. The seven companies were: British Airways, British Steel, Britoil, Jaguar, National Freight Corporation, Cable and Wireless and Associated British Ports. The last three were the clear successes.

71. See Caves, Christensen and Diewert (1982) for more information on Malmquist indices.

CHAPTER 4

FOUR METHODOLOGIES FOR MEASURING PRODUCTIVE EFFICIENCY

4.1 Introduction

In this chapter we detail the four methodologies for measuring the productive efficiency of individual firms and plants that we use in Chapters 5 to 8. These methodologies will provide the raw efficiency scores which will allow us to test the relative efficiency of the broad classes of privately owned and publicly owned electric utilities. We will develop indices for measuring the efficiency of single output–multiple input production (electricity generation) and multiple output–multiple input production (electricity transmission and distribution). We also compare the theoretical properties of these methodologies and report on several empirical studies of their relative merits. The aim is to introduce a representative range of methodologies for evaluating business unit level efficiency to provide 'methodology cross-checking' of the null hypothesis that ownership does not affect productive efficiency.

The idea of measuring productive efficiency of individual business units is usually traced back to Farrell (1957) who first introduced the concept of a firm/business unit level index of cost efficiency which measured efficiency relative to a best practice isoquant constructed from sample data. Farrell distinguished two mutually exclusive and exhaustive sources of productive inefficiency: technical and allocative inefficiency. Suppose a firm/business unit produces output y^0 with inputs x^0 and the production function is described by $\phi(\cdot)$ then the unit is technically efficient if $y^0 = \phi(x^0)$ and technically inefficient if $y^0 < \phi(x^0)$. Technical inefficiency thus arises due to excessive use of inputs and hence the actual bundle of inputs used lies within the best practice isoquant. Let w_i be the price of input i, the unit is allocatively efficient if

$$\phi_i(x^0) / \phi_j(x^0) = w_i / w_j$$

and allocatively inefficient if

$$\phi_i(x^0) / \phi_j(x^0) \neq w_i / w_j$$

assuming that $\phi(\cdot)$ is differentiable. Allocative inefficiency arises because the ratio of inputs does not reflect the ratio of relative prices and hence total cost could be reduced by employing a different mix of inputs. Given that the unit is technically efficient, allocative inefficiency arises because the unit is producing at the wrong point on the frontier given the relative factor prices that it faces. Both technical and allocative inefficiency involve costs to the unit and thus technical and allocative efficiency are necessary and sufficient conditions for minimizing the costs of producing y^0 at the unit.[1] Both technical and allocative efficiency scores are expressed as ratios between 1 and 0 with a score of 1 indicating 100% efficiency.

In electricity generation the mix of factors is largely determined by the type of fuel technology being employed at the power station (e.g. coal or gas). Thus observed factor mixes are largely a result of investment decision making rather than day-to-day operating decisions. This implies that one way of characterizing allocative productive efficiency is as a measure of the losses arising from poor investment decisions. Technical efficiency, which assumes the factor mix as given, may then be thought of as a measure of operating inefficiency.

The key problem in measuring productive efficiency is the modelling of the best practice production frontier against which each individual unit is to be compared. In their extremely helpful survey articles Forsund, Lovell and Schmidt (1980) and Lovell and Schmidt (1988) identify four major classes of methodologies for modelling the best practice frontier: the non-parametric programming technique (or data envelopment analysis), the parametric programming technique, the deterministic statistical technique and the stochastic frontier method. In what follows we label these techniques: *DEA*, *PPA*, *DSA* and *SFM* respectively.

DEA and *PPA* utilize linear programs to calculate efficiency scores. The *DEA* technique uses a linear program to construct a transformation frontier (an isoquant) and to compute efficiency relative to the frontier. The *PPA* technique also uses a linear program to construct a transformation frontier. However this technique differs from *DEA* in that the linear program actually computes the parameters associated with a particular functional form for the production function and then computes efficiency relative to this frontier. The *DSA* and *SFM* techniques use statistical techniques to estimate a production function and to estimate efficiency relative to this frontier. The *DSA* technique assumes no error in measurement or noise in the variables and hence that all deviation from the estimated frontier is attributable to inefficiency, while the *SFM* technique assumes the presence of some noise or error in the variables and hence that not all deviation from the estimated frontier can be attributed to inefficiency.

The measurement of productive efficiency is a rapidly developing field and the distinctions outlined by Lovell and Schmidt are beginning to be complicated by new hybrid techniques which combine and extend the categories outlined above. Wagstaff (1989) notes recent developments which compare and extend the treatment of the error terms in the *SFM* technique (and also in the *DSA* technique) and the extension to the analysis of panel data rather than just cross-sectional data. Many of the theoretical extensions involve the use of complex maximum likelihood functions. In practice the techniques used in empirical studies on new data have lagged well behind the theoretical developments. Recent theoretical papers by Banker et al. (1991), Banker and Maindiratta (1992) have attempted to combine the *DEA* and *SFM* techniques to incorporate noise in a programming model for efficiency calculation.[2] Banker and Maindiratta reported no empirical test of their model and concluded that the technique was likely to produce increasingly unstable results as the number of data points increased. As the vast majority of empirical studies on interesting data[3] do fall into the methodological categories outlined by Lovell and Schmidt (1988) and we are constrained in the number of methodologies we can implement we retain the classifications and implement fairly standard examples of the four methodologies.

We note here that there are two relevant characteristics of the datasets that we will analyse in the following chapters which constrain the choice of methodologies. Firstly, all of the data we have available are cross-sectional i.e. for a single year. This rules out techniques which require panel data for their implementation. Secondly, we only have information on input prices for some of the generation data. This rules out using techniques which estimate technical and allocative efficiencies simultaneously from a profit or cost function. In particular it turns out that only one of the methodologies, *DEA*, is easily implementable in the multiple output–multiple input context of electricity transmission and distribution. We return to these issues later in this chapter.

The chapter is in six sections. Sections 4.2 to 4.5 introduce the *DEA*, *PPA*, *DSA* and *SFM* methodologies in turn. Section 4.6 compares the theoretical properties of the methodologies and reviews comparative studies using more than one technique on the same dataset.

4.2　The *DEA* Technique

The term 'data envelopment analysis' (*DEA*) was introduced by Charnes, Cooper and Rhodes (1978) [hence CCR] in a paper which reintroduced and extended the work of Farrell (1957).[4] CCR proposed a linear program for measuring the technical efficiency of a multiple input–multiple output individual decision making unit (DMU) which did not require any prior assumptions to be made as to the form of the production function. Simultaneously Fare and Lovell (1978) also reintroduced the ideas of Farrell proposing linear programs to measure technical efficiency developed from an axiomatic treatment of the production function. The Fare and CCR programming approaches to productive efficiency measurement developed separately in subsequent work. The first empirical studies in the two traditions were Charnes, Cooper and Rhodes (1981) who analysed the efficiency of a sample of US schools and Fare, Grosskopf and Logan (1983) who analysed the efficiency of a sample of Illinois electric utilities. CCR developments concentrated on the application to the measurement of the technical efficiency of non-profit or public sector activities where input and output prices were hard to identify. Fare refinements allowed the additional calculation of allocative efficiency if input prices were available (see Fare, Grosskopf and Lovell (1985c) or (1994)). In what follows we adopt the Fare approach and label it *DEA*. The initial reason for using the Fare approach in this book was the early application of Fare linear programs to the measurement of productive efficiency in the electricity industry with Fare et al. (1985a) [hence FGL].

The *DEA* technique of FGL involves a non-stochastic approach to the measurement of productive efficiency which allows the disaggregation of that measure into several mutually exclusive and exhaustive components. The technique is essentially comparative in that the overall efficiency measure compares the average cost of production of a DMU to the average costs of least cost DMUs. A major practical advantage of this technique is that the actual costs incurred by the DMU are not compared against some hypothetical least cost DMU but against best practice (least cost) DMUs in the sample. Indeed it is possible to identify the best practice DMUs against which inefficient (i.e. non least cost DMUs) are being compared and hence to suggest cost reducing changes based on the actual behaviour of 'successful' (i.e. lower cost) DMUs. Note that this does not mean there is no possibility of reducing cost at 'efficient' DMUs. Measured efficiency scores represent upper bounds on actual efficiency scores. *DEA* can also allow for the possibility that some of the variables may not be under the control of the managers of the DMU, what we might call environmental variables. This is particularly true in the electricity transmission and distribution where variables which substantially affect costs such as route km or service area may be determined by statute, regulation or geography.

The remainder of this section is divided into four parts. Part one details six measures of productive efficiency. Part two details the measurement of productive efficiency in the presence of environmental variables. Part three explains how relevant best practice DMUs can be identified for each DMU to be analysed. Part four briefly reviews developments in the *DEA* literature.

4.2.1 *Six Measures of Productive Efficiency*

In the tradition of Koopmans (1951), Shephard (1970) and Afriat (1972) we follow Fare and Lovell (1978) and introduce a piecewise linear technology *L(u)*. *L(u)*, the reference technology, is an input correspondence[5] constructed by taking convex combinations of the observed inputs and outputs. We construct a vector of outputs *U* (in a multiple output context *U* is a matrix and *u* is a vector) whose *n* elements represent the observed outputs of the *n* DMUs and an *n* *f matrix, *X*, whose elements represent the observed quantities of the *f* inputs utilized by each of the *n* DMUs. Given *U* and *X* and a constant returns to scale input correspondence (i.e. *L(ku)=kL(u)*, *k>0*) satisfying strong disposability of inputs (i.e. free disposal of excess inputs is possible) the upper level set of the reference technology is calculated as:

$$L^{+}(u) = \left\{ x \in R_{+}^{n} : u \le zU,\ zX \le x,\ z \in R_{+}^{n} \right\} \qquad (4.2.1)[6]$$

Where $z = (z_1, z_2, ..., z_n) \in R_{+}^{n}$ denotes the intensity parameters which are used to allow for the convex combinations of observed inputs and outputs.

In modelling electricity generation we assume that a single output (electric energy) is produced by three inputs – capital (or capacity), labour and fuel. As we noted in Chapter 1, this inadequately captures the multi-dimensional nature of electricity production, however it is the standard characterization used in the literature (we discuss the modelling of electricity transmission and distribution in Chapter 8). In what follows we illustrate the calculation of the efficiency measures with reference to two inputs (K and L) and one output. Consider Figure 4.1, taken from FGL, where the piecewise linear curve II represents an isoquant of the upper level set $L^{+}(u)$ of the reference technology.

Essentially $L^{+}(u)$ is the isoquant – the boundary set of input combinations which can be combined to produce a given output – defined by the best practice DMUs at the output actually produced by the DMU whose efficiency is being evaluated. If the DMU being analysed (at R) were on the isoquant (e.g. at B) it would be 100% technically efficient. The pp line corresponds to the price vector of input prices faced by the DMU being analysed at R. Introducing input prices means that we can identify the point on the isoquant where the

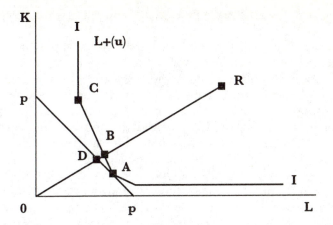

Figure 4.1: Overall, Allocative and Technical Measures of Productive Efficiency

DMU should be producing (A above). A corresponds to the point at which the DMU at R should be producing, given the input prices that it faces (pp in Figure 4.1), if it is to minimize costs. If the DMU were at this point it would be said to be 100% overall productively efficient. The *DEA* technique provides a method for identifying the isoquant and measuring the 'distance' of an individual DMU from the 100% efficient points.[7]

Thus given the available production technology, which defines the position of $L^+(u)$, and input prices, pp, efficient (minimum cost) operation occurs at A.[8] The distance ratio *OD/OR*, following FGL, denotes the measure of overall efficiency, **O(u,p,x)**,[9] by which we can compare different DMUs in the sample. We can think of this as the ratio of actual to potential input usage. This definition avoids problems of comparison and allows the interpretation of **1−O(u,p,x)** as the percentage amount by which inputs could be proportionately reduced if the DMU were operating efficiently with respect to input prices and available technology. **O(u,p,x)** can be further disaggregated into two major components: overall technical efficiency **K(u,x)** and allocative (or price) efficiency **A(u,p,x)**. A DMU is technically efficient if it is working on the isoquant, e.g. in the diagram both A and B are technically efficient but R is technically inefficient. **K(u,x)**=*OB/OR*. Allocative efficiency attempts to capture the inefficiency arising solely from the wrong choice of technically efficient combinations given input prices, thus for a DMU at R, **A(u,p,x)**=*OD/OB*.

We can see that: $\quad OD/OR = OB/OR \cdot OD/OB \quad$ (4.2.2)

or $\qquad$ $$O(u, p, x) = K(u, x) \cdot A(u, p, x) \qquad (4.2.3)$$

Note the radial nature of the efficiency measures and the limitations this introduces. Consider points on $L^+(u)$ to the north of C, these points are technically efficient on a radial measure of efficiency but inefficient in a Paretian sense: they involve producing the given output with strictly more of at least one output than at the efficient point C. This point has been recognized in the CCR literature by the development of a non-Archimedian approach to ensure 'Pareto-Koopmans efficiency' (see for example Charnes and Cooper, 1985). This approach complicates the linear programs required and has its own problems.[10] Fare and Lovell (1978) also suggest the use of a non-radial measure of technical efficiency – the Russell measure. Neither of these non-radial approaches is capable of the same convenient decomposition that we will go on to detail below.

The calculation of the above efficiency measures involves the use of linear programming methods. Instead of imposing a functional form and estimating cost and production functions, as in parametric studies, the observed inputs and outputs of the DMUs are used to construct a piecewise linear reference technology. Linear programs may then be used to calculate the efficiency measures for each DMU.[11]

The assumptions of constant returns to scale of the frontier efficient DMU[12] and free disposal of inputs allow the calculation of $O(u,p,x)$ and $K(u,x)$ and following the identity in (4.2.3) we can also obtain $A(u,p,x)$.

Overall efficiency, $\qquad O(u,p,x) = Q(u,p)/px \qquad (4.2.4)$

where $Q(u,p) = \min\{px : x \in L^+(u)\}$ and px = observed total cost

$Q(u,p)$ is the cost of the cost minimizing input combination for producing the given output valued at the given input prices facing the DMU. It may be calculated as the solution to the following linear program:

min px

$\qquad$ (4.2.5)

s.t. $u \le zU, zX \le x, z \in R^n_+$.

Note here that p can be scaled for an individual DMU making efficiency dependent on relative not absolute prices. In an international context this eliminates a need for choosing an appropriate exchange rate to facilitate comparison. This represents a major technical advantage of *DEA* use in an international context against straightforward comparisons of the financial costs of production.

Technical efficiency is defined as:

$$K(u,x) = \min\{\lambda : \lambda x \in L^+(u)\} \tag{4.2.6}$$

The λ parameter is used to determine the amount by which observed inputs can be proportionally decreased if they are utilized efficiently (hence the efficiency measures we calculate are input-based). **K(u,x)** may be calculated as the solution to the following linear program:[13]

$$\min \lambda$$
$$s.t. \ u \leq zU, zX \leq \lambda x, z \in R_+^n. \tag{4.2.7}$$

The linear program, (4.2.7), can be transformed into a maximization problem[14] where $z_0 = 1/\lambda$, $\mu_i = z_i/\lambda$:

$$\max z_0$$
$$s.t. \ uz_0 \leq \mu U, \mu X \leq x, z \in R_+^n. \tag{4.2.8}[15]$$

Allocative efficiency is then calculated from (4.2.3) as:

$$\mathbf{A(u,p,x) = O(u,p,x)/K(u,x)} \tag{4.2.9}$$

K(u,x) is a measure of aggregate efficiency loss due to non price related mistakes. FGL decomposes this measure exhaustively into three further measures:

$$\mathbf{K(u,x) = F(u,x) \cdot C(u,x) \cdot S(u,x)} \tag{4.2.10}$$

  F(u,x) = pure technical efficiency.
  C(u,x) = congestion efficiency.
  S(u,x) = scale efficiency.

The calculation of these three measures is illustrated in Figure 4.2 (which is taken from FGL). The assumptions of strong disposability (i.e. free disposability) of inputs and constant returns to scale which were present in the linear program (4.2.7) have been dropped to identify isoquant II. This allows the isoquant to bend backwards, indicating that as the quantity of one input (K) is increased the output produced falls. Purely technical efficiency, **F(u,x)**, is then defined as the measure of how much inefficiency is solely due to production within the isoquant defined by best practice DMUs.

  In the diagram **F(u,x)** measured as:

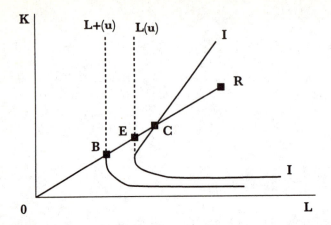

Figure 4.2: Pure Technical, Congestion and Scale Measures of Productive Efficiency

$$\mathbf{F(u,x)} = OC/OR \tag{4.2.11}$$

C falls on a backward bending section of the isoquant. Inputs are said to be congesting.[16] We can measure the loss of efficiency due to congestion as:

$$\mathbf{C(u,x)} = OE/OC \tag{4.2.12}$$

where $L(u)$, going through **E**, represents the closest non-congested technology to that represented by II.

This leaves $\mathbf{S(u,x)}$, the measure of scale efficiency. In the long run in competitive equilibrium the DMU should be operating at a minimum of the U shaped average cost curve. The DMU could adjust its scale and produce its current output level with fewer inputs. The best practice isoquant $L^+(u)$ is the relevant isoquant for comparison as it incorporates the twin assumptions of strong input disposability and constant returns to scale.

$$\mathbf{S(u,x)} = OB/OE \tag{4.2.13}$$

The details of the linear programs required for the above three measures of technical efficiency are given below.[17] It is also possible to identify whether a DMU exhibiting scale inefficiency is exhibiting constant, increasing or decreasing returns to scale and thus assign it as CRS, IRS or DRS.[18]

F is yielded as a result of placing a restriction on $x \geq zX$ such that:

Min λ

$s.t.\ u \leq zU,\ zX = \delta\lambda x,\ z \in R_+^k,\ \sum_i z_i = 1,\ 0 < \delta \leq 1.$ (4.2.14)

where **F**=λ.

Moving to **C** it is necessary to define **W**:

Min λ

$s.t.\ u \leq zU,\ zX \leq \lambda x,\ z \in R_+^k,\ \sum_i z_i = 1.$ (4.2.15)[19]

where **W**=λ.

From **F** and **W** we then calculate, **C=W/F** and thus **S=K/W**.

S=1 implies constant returns to scale, decreasing/increasing returns to scale are indicated by calculation of **W***:

Min λ

$s.t.\ u \leq zU,\ zX \leq \lambda x,\ z \in R_+^k,\ \sum_i z_i \leq 1.$ (4.2.16)

where **W***=λ.

If **S**≠1 and **W=W*** this implies decreasing returns to scale, if **S**≠1 and **W≠W*** this implies increasing returns to scale.

4.2.2 Productive Efficiency with Environmental Variables

The formula for calculating efficiency in the presence of environmental variables is taken from Weyman-Jones (1992). The idea of incorporating environmental variables into the linear programs of *DEA* first appears in Banker and Morey (1986). They distinguish between controllable and uncontrollable inputs and outputs: uncontrollable variables are environmental variables.

Efficiency with environmental variables is calculated by the following linear program:[20]

Min λ

$s.t.\ u \leq zU,\ zX_1 = x_1,\ zX_2 \leq \lambda x_2,\ \sum_i z_i = 1,\ z \in R_+^k.$ (4.2.17) where X_1 is the set of input quantities associated with inputs which are considered to be environmental variables, X_2 is the set of input quantities associated with the inputs which are free to vary. The crucial set of constraints $zX_1 = x_1$ ensures that the DMU is compared to an efficient frontier where the values of the environmental variables have the same values. The $\sum z_i = 1$ constraint imposes variable rather than constant returns to scale. We label environmental efficiency scores as **KENVx(u,x)** where **x** is the number of environmental variables. Thus in (4.2.17) **KENVx(u,x)=λ**.

We note here the connection between the calculation of environmental variables and input subvector measures of efficiency calculated in Brynes (1985). In electricity generation capital may be regarded as a sunk input, it can be varied *ex ante* but not *ex post*. Thus the six measures of productive efficiency in Section 4.2.1 are *ex ante* efficiency scores. When we consider the issue of privatization involving a change in ownership of existing power stations *ex post* measures of efficiency would seem to be important. Input subvector measures of efficiency fix some of the inputs to allow *ex post* technical efficiency measures to be calculated. The linear program required to calculate these measures is similar to (4.2.17). The only difference is in the second constraint restricting the constrained inputs which is $\leq$ in the subvector measure and is $=$ in the environmental variables. This implies that in the environmental variables efficiency measure the unit is only compared to a constructed frontier along which the values of the environmental variables are equal to those of the unit being analysed. In the case of the input subvector the constructed frontier has the same or less of the environmental variables. Thus the environmental efficiency measures must be greater than or equal to equivalent input subvector efficiency measures. Pollitt (1993) gives further details of input subvector efficiency measures and uses them to analyse a sample of nuclear electric power plants. In this book we do not calculate subvector measures of efficiency in order to simplify presentation and because there are no comparable measures in the three non-*DEA* methodologies. Fare's measure of pure technical efficiency, **F(u,x)**, is close to an *ex post* measure of efficiency for generation in that the DMU is assumed not to be able to alter its scale of production (measured in output rather than capital).

4.2.3   Identifying Reference DMUs

One of the major advantages of *DEA* efficiency measures is that it is possible to obtain the referent frontier efficient DMUs to which an individual DMU is being compared. This is very important when conducting a *DEA* study in order to give advice to the manager/owner of specific DMUs. In the context of this book, the identification of referent DMUs provides an opportunity to check the accuracy of the data and the plausibility of frontier efficiency scores. *DEA* is highly data dependent; if we can identify the referent units we can re-check the data for just the frontier DMUs in order to reduce the risk that errors in the data simultaneously bias the efficiency scores of large numbers of the DMUs. Even if the data are correct we might be hesitant about basing policy conclusions on efficiency scores calculated relative to 'unusual' units, such as DMUs with unique designs.

We briefly outline how referent DMUs used within the linear programs can be identified. Look again at Figure 4.1. The DMU being analysed is actually at R (constant returns to scale is assumed). The frontier DMUs to which it is being compared are represented by C and A, the points determining the limits of the relevant frontier line segment through which *OR* passes. B is a linear combination of C and A. B can be thought of as the position that the DMU represented by R would occupy if it were frontier efficient (assuming fixed factor proportions). It is possible to use the $K(u,x)$ linear program to identify C and A and the weights necessary to define B. We could also locate the frontier DMUs used in the $F(u,x)$, $C(u,x)$, $S(u,x)$ and $KENVx(u,x)$ measures in a similar way.

Consider (4.2.8) the linear program which calculates $K(u,x)$. For each DMU in a three input–one output case a maximum of three DMUs can be in the basis which defines the efficient frontier. These DMUs have non-zero z_i weights in the final iteration of the linear program when solved by the simplex method (Dantzig (1963).[21] These DMUs are the frontier efficient DMUs such as C and A in Figure 4.1. The z_i are the weights required to define B from C and A. These weights may sum to more than one in the linear program (4.2.8) so they need to be scaled so that they sum to 1. In summary, once the $K(u,x)$ linear program has been solved, the basis variables represent the frontier efficient DMUs to which R is being compared and the values of the basis variables represent the weights of these basis variables in the location of the frontier efficient linear combination B. Standard linear programming packages allow for easy extraction of the required information.

The identification of referent DMUs for each DMU allows the calculation of an additional measure of scale: the Proximity Scale Factor (PSF) (Macmillan, 1987). As noted earlier the computer program used to calculate the above measures is based on the simplex method. The PSF is calculated from the basis variables in the final simplex tableau in the $K(u,x)$ linear program. The non-zero units in the basis represent frontier efficient DMUs to which the DMU being analysed is being compared. The values attached to these basis variables represent the proximity of the basis DMUs to the analysed unit. Taking the ratio of each basis variable measure to the sum of the basis variables we obtain a proximity measure attached to each basis variable. Calculation of the PSF involves multiplying the capital of the basis units by the proximity measures and summing them to obtain an estimate of the size of operation to which the units being analysed are being compared. The ratio of the capitals provides the measure of the PSF.[22] We use this measure in Chapter 5.

4.2.4 A Review of the DEA Literature

Since 1978 over 400 articles have appeared applying the *DEA* methodology to numerous productive activities (Seiford, 1990). The *Journal of Econometrics* devoted a special issue to *DEA* in 1990 and Leibenstein and Maital (1992) argued in the *American Economic Review* that '*DEA* merits consideration as a primary method for the measuring and partitioning of X-inefficiency' (p.428). Surveys of the *DEA* methodology are contained in Charnes and Cooper (1985) and Seiford and Thrall (1990). The CCR tradition was extended by Banker, Charnes and Cooper (1984) who dropped the constant returns to scale assumption in favour of variable returns to scale in their BCC model. BCC and Fare et al. (1983) introduced the less restrictive variable returns to scale technology which overcame one of the major shortcomings of the 1978 papers (see Grosskopf, 1986). Linear programmes have been developed which calculate efficiency in the presence of discrete or so called categorical variables (Banker and Morey (1986), Kamakura (1988), Rousseau and Semple (1993)). Several papers have attempted to model non-linear line segments along the frontier (eg. Charnes, Cooper, Seiford and Stutz (1982)).

The empirical literature has used *DEA* to investigate many industries. Several papers using CCR have examined the efficiency of non-profit organizations. For example CCR (1981) examined the efficiency of a sample of US schools; Banker, Conrad and Strauss (1986) looked at US hospital efficiency and Ali et al. (1992) examined the efficiency of inter-government revenue transfers in Massachusetts. Among the private sector (or market) industries to be analysed using *DEA* are coal (Brynes et al. (1984, 1988)), water (Brynes (1985) and Brynes et al. (1986)), farming (Grabowski and Paskura, 1988), banking (Rangan et al. (1988), Aly et al. (1990), Berg, Forsund and Jansen (1991) and Fukuyama (1993)) and electricity (Fare et al. (1983, 1985a, 1985b and 1989b) and Hausman and Neufield (1991)). Most of the published studies involve US data and relatively few examine UK data. One of the first UK studies was a comparison of the efficiency of the rate collection function of metropolitan district councils in Thanassoulis, Dyson and Foster (1987) while Weyman-Jones' (1992) study of the efficiency of UK electricity distribution companies is one of the most recent. In their review of the UK efficiency studies using *DEA* Norman and Stoker (1991) cite four other published UK public sector applications and devote a chapter to seven case studies, including a comparison of the efficiency of UK water companies and an analysis of the efficiencies of the branches of a national building society. In another review of the British literature, Button and Weyman-Jones (1992) cite a further two *DEA* studies on UK building societies.

4.3 The *PPA* Technique

The parametric programming approach is closely related to the *DEA* methodology. The major difference between the two approaches is that the production frontier has a specific parametric functional form. Like *DEA* however the *PPA* method makes no allowance for errors and the calculated frontier is highly sensitive to outliers. The *PPA* technique was first proposed by Farrell (1957), who suggested computing a parametric convex hull of the observed input-output ratios using the Cobb-Douglas functional form. Aigner and Chu (1968) were the first to implement Farrell's suggestions with subsequent developments appearing in Forsund and Jansen (1977) and Forsund and Hjalmarsson (1979a,b). A key advantage of this technique over *DEA* is the relatively little computer time required to generate the efficiency scores: only one linear program needs to be solved per dataset rather than one per DMU under *DEA*.

This section is in three parts. Part one details the formulation of the linear program required to estimate translog production frontier and hence to calculate measures of overall technical efficiency ($\mathbf{K(u,x)}$). Part two discusses the calculation of allocative and overall measures of productive efficiency. Part three reviews the literature.

4.3.1 *Calculating $K(u,x)$ using PPA*

In this part of the section we follow the outline given in Lovell and Schmidt (1988). Lovell and Schmidt describe the calculation of a *PPA* frontier with a Cobb-Douglas functional form; we however describe the calculation of *PPA* efficiency scores relative to a translogarithmic (translog) functional form.[23] The translog functional form is a flexible functional form which relaxes the constant elasticity of substitution and the invariant returns to scale assumptions implicit in Cobb-Douglas and is in fact a second order approximation to any arbitrary functional form. We note that the Cobb-Douglas form is nested within the translog functional form.

The input set is defined relative to a production function, $\phi(x)$:

$$L(u) \equiv \left\{ x : u \leq \phi(x) \right\} \tag{4.3.1}$$

The translog production function may be written as (see Griliches and Ringstad, 1971):

$$\ln u = a + \sum_{i=1}^{n} \alpha_i \ln x_i + \tfrac{1}{2} \sum_{i=1}^{n} \sum_{j=1}^{n} \gamma_{ij} \ln x_i \ln x_j, \tag{4.3.2}$$

where $\gamma_{ij} = \gamma_{ji}$, $x_i = $ *input* i, $n = $ *number of inputs.*

Note that if all γ_{ij} are set equal to zero, translog reduces to Cobb-Douglas. We rewrite (4.3.1) as:

$$L(u) = \left\{ x : \ln u \leq a + \sum_{i=1}^{n} \alpha_i \ln x_i + \tfrac{1}{2} \sum_{i=1}^{n} \sum_{j=1}^{n} \gamma_{ij} \ln x_i \ln x_j, \right.$$
$$\left. a \text{ unrestricted}, \ \alpha_i \geq 0, \ \gamma_{ij} \geq 0, \ i = 1, ..., n, \ j = 1, ..., n \right\} \tag{4.3.3}[24]$$

If there are K DMUs in the sample, the parameters in $\phi(x)$ (a, α_i and γ_{ij}) are computed by solving the following linear program:

$$\min \left\{ \sum_{k=1}^{K} \left[a + \sum_{i=1}^{n} \alpha_i \ln x_i^k + \tfrac{1}{2} \sum_{i=1}^{n} \sum_{j=1}^{n} \gamma_{ij} \ln x_i^k \ln x_j^k - \ln u^k \right] \right\}$$

s.t.

$$\left[a + \sum_{i=1}^{n} \alpha_i \ln x_i^k + \tfrac{1}{2} \sum_{i=1}^{n} \sum_{j=1}^{n} \gamma_{ij} \ln x_i^k \ln x_j^k - \ln u^k \right] \geq 0, \quad k = 1, ..., K. \tag{4.3.4}[25]$$

a unrestricted, $\alpha_i \geq 0$, $\gamma_{ij} \geq 0$, $i = 1, ..., n$, $j = 1, ..., n$.

This linear program is equivalent to minimizing the sum of the absolute residuals subject to the constraint that each residual be non-positive.

It is a relatively straightforward matter to calculate $\mathbf{K}(\mathbf{u},\mathbf{x})$ measures of technical inefficiency from the residuals in the constraints in (4.3.4). Define for the kth DMU ε^k:

$$\varepsilon^k = a + \sum_{i=1}^{n} \alpha_i \ln x_i^k + \tfrac{1}{2} \sum_{i=1}^{n} \sum_{j=1}^{n} \gamma_{ij} \ln x_i^k \ln x_j^k - \ln u^k \tag{4.3.5}$$

which is the deviation of $\ln u^k$ from its optimal value. Hence:

$$\mathbf{K}(\mathbf{u}^k,\mathbf{x}^k) = e^{-\varepsilon^k} \tag{4.3.6}$$

4.3.2 *Calculation of Overall and Allocative Efficiency*

Once the parameters of the efficient frontier have been calculated it is straightforward to write down the problem which solves for $\mathbf{O}(\mathbf{u},\mathbf{x})$ and $\mathbf{A}(\mathbf{u},\mathbf{x})$. Define $Q(u^k,p^k)$ as the minimum cost of producing unit k's output given the input prices faced by unit k and the frontier technology:

$$Q(u^k, p^k) = \min\left\{ p^{kT} x : \begin{bmatrix} a + \sum_{i=1}^{n} \alpha_i \ln x_i^k \\ + \tfrac{1}{2} \sum_{i=1}^{n} \sum_{j=1}^{n} \gamma_{ij} \ln x_i^k \ln x_j^k - \ln u^k \end{bmatrix} \geq 0, \right. \tag{4.3.7}$$
$$\left. a \text{ unrestricted}, \; \alpha_i \geq 0, \; \gamma_{ij} \geq 0, \; i = 1,\ldots,n, \; j = 1,\ldots,n \right\}$$

which allows us to calculate overall and allocative efficiency as follows:

$$\mathbf{O}(\mathbf{u}^k,\mathbf{p}^k,\mathbf{x}^k) = Q(u^k, p^k) / p^{kT} x^k \tag{4.3.8}$$

$$\mathbf{A}(\mathbf{u}^k,\mathbf{p}^k,\mathbf{x}^k) = \mathbf{O}(\mathbf{u}^k,\mathbf{p}^k,\mathbf{x}^k) / \mathbf{K}(\mathbf{u}^k,\mathbf{x}^k) \tag{4.3.9}$$

Looking at (4.3.7) we can see that at the optimum the constraint will bind and the problem becomes one of constrained optimization. If $\phi(x)$ is Cobb-Douglas this gives rise to a straightforward solution via the Lagrangian method (which we solve in Chapter 7, Section 3). In the case of the translog production function the Lagrangian system becomes non-linear and is not straightforwardly solvable. Thus when we come to calculate allocative efficiencies we restrict ourselves to a

Cobb-Douglas functional form for the parametric production frontier. In Chapters 6 and 7 however the problem did not arise as even when we postulated a translog functional form, the γ_{ij} were all calculated to be zero which restricts the frontier to be Cobb-Douglas.

4.3.3   A Review of the PPA Literature

The initial advantages of the *PPA* technique over *DEA* were seen to be its ability to provide a mathematical specification of the production frontier and its easy handling of non-constant returns to scale (Forsund et al. 1980). However as we have noted there are difficulties in implementing flexible functional forms and empirical work using *PPA* has tended to use relatively simple functional forms. The *PPA* approach is difficult to implement in the presence of multiple outputs. One method, proposed by Lovell and Schmidt (1988), involves specifying a cost function and minimizing the deviations from this cost frontier by choosing the values of the cost function parameters. This allows the calculation of overall efficiency for each unit. However the decomposition of overall efficiency requires the application of the Kopp-Diewert-Zieschang algorithm following Kopp and Diewert (1982) and Zieschang (1983). Although this method is feasible the major problem with it is that it requires input price data to calculate even the technical efficiency measures. This makes the method unsuitable for our study of transmission and distribution in Chapter 8 as we have no data on input prices.

Although the *PPA* technique looked like a promising new technique in the 1970s, rapid advances in *DEA* following 1978 led to criticism of the need to specify a functional form and its inability to handle errors in data. Forsund et al. (1980) note that although the *PPA* technique produces estimates of the parameters of the frontier production function, it does not produce standard errors for those estimates and hence does not allow inferences to be made about the parameter values. This amounts to saying that the technique has the disadvantage of a specific functional form without the advantage of standard errors for the estimated parameters. Forsund and Jansen (1977) noted that the basic Aigner and Chu formulation uses a sample maximum output to estimate the population maximum output and hence the best practice frontier may be pessimistically biased in each dimension. They propose a linear program for the derivation of maximum likelihood estimates of the parameters of the production function. Fare, Grosskopf and Li (1992) note that the *PPA* technique generates an 'industry' frontier since only one set of parameters is estimated from 'firm' level data. This means that inputs can be reallocated between DMUs in order to maximize industry output. *DEA* measures however generate DMU level efficiency measures and no reallocation of the resources available to the industry is considered. Fare, Grosskopf and Li therefore suggest a hybrid model where some of the inputs can be reallocated within the industry and some are DMU specific.

Relatively few empirical studies have been based on the *PPA* method. Forsund and Hjalmarrson (1979a,b) investigated the efficiency of milk processing DMUs in Sweden using *PPA*. Technical efficiency was measured in a dynamic setting relative to a homothetic production function allowing for variable scale elasticity. Kopp and Smith (1980) calculate *PPA*, *DSA* and *SFM* production frontiers for a sample of US coal-fired steam electric generating DMUs using Cobb-Douglas, CES and translog functional forms. Al-Obaidan and Scully (1991) compared the efficiencies of private and state-owned DMUs in the international oil industry using the *PPA*, *DSA* and *SFM* techniques. Their *PPA* technique involved the straightforward implementation of a reparameterized version of a constant returns to scale, two-input Cobb-Douglas function.

4.4 The *DSA* Technique

The *DSA* technique differs sharply from the programming techniques outlined in the previous sections. This approach uses statistical techniques to estimate the frontier and can be easily estimated using standard statistical packages. This technique was first proposed by Afriat (1972) and extended by Richmond (1974) and Greene (1980a,b). As in the *PPA* technique a specific functional form for the production frontier must be specified. In the exposition below we assume a translog functional form.

This section is in two parts. In part one we derive the efficiency measures and in part two we discuss the *DSA* literature.

4.4.1 *Calculating the DSA Measures*

We loosely follow the exposition in Lovell and Schmidt (1988). As in (4.3.1) the input set is defined relative to a production function, $\phi(x)$:

$$L(u) \equiv \left\{ x : u \leq \phi(x) \right\} \tag{4.4.1}$$

Actual output deviates from frontier output by ε, hence for a translog functional form we can write:

$$\ln u = a + \sum_{i=1}^{n} \alpha_i \ln x_i + \tfrac{1}{2} \sum_{i=1}^{n} \sum_{j=1}^{n} \gamma_{ij} \ln x_i \ln x_j + \varepsilon \tag{4.4.2}$$

where $\gamma_{ij} = \gamma_{ji}$, $x_i = $ *input* i, $n = $ *number of inputs.*

$\varepsilon \leq 0$ is a one-sided disturbance and represents the technical inefficiency relative to a deterministic production frontier. As in the *PPA* methodology the frontier is deterministic i.e. measured without allowance for noise or measurement error. However the *DSA* frontier is estimated rather than computed.

The most straightforward way to estimate the parameters in (4.4.2) is by corrected ordinary least squares (COLS) introduced by Richmond (1974). If μ is the mean of ε then we can rewrite (4.4.2) for the kth DMU as:

$$\ln u^k = (a+\mu) + \sum_{i=1}^{n} \alpha_i \ln x_i^k + \tfrac{1}{2} \sum_{i=1}^{n} \sum_{j=1}^{n} \gamma_{ij} \ln x_i^k \ln x_j^k$$

$$+ (\varepsilon^k - \mu), \quad k = 1,\dots,K \tag{4.4.3}$$

where $\gamma_{ij} = \gamma_{ji}$, $x_i = $ *input* i

This equation can then be estimated by OLS to obtain best linear unbiased estimates of $(a+\mu)$, α_i and γ_{ij}. The next step is to obtain separate measures of μ and a. The easiest way to do this is to increase the production frontier until it just envelops the data and so estimating μ as:

$$\hat{\mu} = -\min\Big\{ \ \mu : \mu \geq 0, \ (\hat{a}+\mu) + \mu + \sum_{i=1}^{n} \hat{\alpha}_i \ln x_i^k$$

$$+ \tfrac{1}{2} \sum_{i=1}^{n} \sum_{j=1}^{n} \hat{\gamma}_{ij} \ln x_i^k \ln x_j^k - \ln u^k \geq 0, \tag{4.4.4}$$

$$k = 1,\dots,K, \ \gamma_{ij} = \gamma_{ji}, \ x_i = \textit{input } i \ \Big\}$$

(4.4.4) provides a consistent estimate of $\hat{\mu}$ for any one sided distribution of ε with a positive density. This avoids having to specify a density function for ε. (4.4.4) allows an estimate of $\hat{a}$ to be calculated from the estimate of $(a+\mu)$ in (4.4.3).The individual unit level errors, ε^k, can then be estimated via the equivalent of (4.3.5) and technical efficiency measures calculated from (4.3.6). Lovell and Schmidt (1988) note that maximum likelihood estimation (MLE) methods can also be used to estimate the parameters of $\phi(x)$ and $f(\varepsilon)$, however the above COLS approach is much more straightforward.

There are three ways to generate the overall and allocative efficiency measures in the *DSA* methodology: firstly, by calculating deviations of the actual input proportions from optimal input proportions using a derived cost frontier (Schmidt and Lovell, 1979); secondly, by minimizing costs subject to the production frontier and the input prices as in Section 4.3.2; or thirdly, by estimating the deterministic cost frontier and applying the Kopp-Diewert-Zieschang decomposition algorithm. As we noted in Section 4.3.3 the Kopp-Diewert-Zieschang is undesirable in that it cannot generate technical efficiency measures in the absence of input prices. Both the derived cost frontier approach and the cost minimization approach are difficult to implement with technologies more complicated than Cobb-Douglas. A derived cost frontier may not be known and a non-linear algorithm may be required to solve the cost minimization problem. To maintain consistency and simplicity across approaches we calculate *DSA* measures of overall and allocative efficiency from a Cobb-Douglas production function using the cost minimization approach outlined in Section 4.3.2 and detailed in Chapter 6 Section 3.

4.4.2 A Review of the DSA Literature

The *DSA* method has the advantage over the two previous approaches of being relatively straightforward to implement: our exposition was based on an application of OLS and simple manipulation of the residuals. The method allows statistical inference but suffers from the need to specify specific functional forms for the production function and optionally for the errors. Greene (1980b) proposed the use of a gamma distribution for $f(\varepsilon)$ for use in maximum likelihood estimates of the parameters of $\phi(x)$ and $f(\varepsilon)$. MLE allows direct estimation of the constant term and is more efficient since it uses all information on the density $f(\varepsilon)$. As for the programming approaches no allowance is made in the *DSA* method for errors in variables. The technique is not easily extendible to the handling of multiple outputs: independent calculation of technical inefficiency in this case requires the construction of an index of aggregate output.

The *DSA* method forms the starting point for the *SFM* technique. Thus compared to the *SFM* technique relatively few empirical studies have employed the methodology. Richmond (1974) reports efficiency calculations using a Cobb-Douglas form of the *DSA* on a sample of

Norwegian manufacturing data for different functional forms for $f(\varepsilon)$. Banker, Conrad and Strauss (1986), in a comparison of the *DEA* and *DSA* methods, report the calculation of a *DSA* frontier cost function for a sample of US hospitals using the COLS approach and a translog system of equations. The study assumes that all cost inefficiency is technical inefficiency. Wagstaff (1989) also implements the *DSA* and *SFM* approaches for a hospital production function using both cross-sectional and panel data for a sample of Spanish hospitals. Chen and Tang (1987) use the *DSA* and *SFM* techniques to analyse the relative efficiency of export and import oriented DMUs in the Taiwanese electronics industry in 1980. Perelman and Pestieau (1988) measure the relative performance of a sample of international railroads and postal services. This study just uses a Greene (1980a,b) MLE gamma *DSA* approach on panel data. They calculate technical efficiency measures for the DMUs in each industry and surmount the problem of multiple outputs by constructing an aggregate index of output for each industry. Al-Obaidan and Scully (1991) also use a Greene (1980a,b) frontier to calculate efficiency scores in their study of the international petroleum industry.

4.5   The *SFM* Approach

The previous three sections detailed approaches to the measurement of productive efficiency which made no allowance for stochastic errors due to noise or measurement error. All deviations from the frontier were labelled as inefficiency. This is clearly an unsatisfactory characteristic of deterministic frontiers. The stochastic frontier method extends the *DSA* method in an attempt to incorporate random errors into a parametric frontier estimated by statistical methods. This technique was first proposed by Aigner, Lovell and Schmidt (1977) [hence ALS] and Meeusen and van den Broeck (1977). Jondrow, Lovell, Materov and Schmidt (1982) [hence JLMS] provided the developments which first allowed the calculation of unit level efficiency scores from the stochastic frontiers proposed in the earlier papers. Since then many papers have appeared extending the technique and applying it to a wide variety of industries. To keep matters fairly simple we follow the ALS and JLMS papers.

This section is in two parts. In part one we discuss the derivation of efficiency scores for individual units. In part two we review some of the large theoretical and empirical literature using this method.

4.5.1 Calculating the SFM Measures

We again start from the exposition in Lovell and Schmidt (1988). In contrast to (4.4.1) we define the input set relative to a production function, $\phi(x)$, which incorporates a two-sided random error, ε_1:

$$L(u) \equiv \left\{ x: u \leq \phi(x) \exp\{\varepsilon_1\} \right\} \tag{4.5.1}$$

The random error captures the effects of noise, measurement error and exogenous shocks beyond the control of the production unit. We specify a translog functional form as in (4.4.2) and eliminate the inequality by introducing the one sided error, ε_2, which arises due to technical inefficiency:

$$\ln u = a + \sum_{i=1}^{n} \alpha_i \ln x_i + \tfrac{1}{2} \sum_{i=1}^{n} \sum_{j=1}^{n} \gamma_{ij} \ln x_i \ln x_j + (\varepsilon_1 + \varepsilon_2) \tag{4.5.2}$$

where $\gamma_{ij} = \gamma_{ji}$, $x_i = $ *input i*

The *DSA* method appears as a special case of the *SFM* where $\varepsilon_1 = 0$.

It is necessary to select a density function for ε_2. ALS and JLMS consider both the half-normal and exponential densities. The truncated normal (Stevenson, 1980) and the gamma density (Greene, (1980b, 1990)) are other suggested possibilities. We use the half-normal density for ε_2, while ε_1 is distributed as a random normal:

$$\varepsilon_1 \sim \mathcal{N}(0, \sigma_{\varepsilon_1}^2), \; \varepsilon_2 \sim \left| \mathcal{N}(0, \sigma_{\varepsilon_2}^2) \right| \tag{4.5.3}$$

ALS[26] note that the distribution of the sum of a symmetric normal random variable and a truncated half normal random variable is:

$$f(\varepsilon) = \frac{2}{\sigma} f * \left(\frac{\varepsilon}{\sigma} \right) \left[1 - F * (\varepsilon \lambda \sigma^{-1}) \right], \quad -\infty \leq \varepsilon \leq +\infty,$$

where $\sigma^2 = \sigma_{\varepsilon_1}^2 + \sigma_{\varepsilon_2}^2$, $\lambda = \sigma_{\varepsilon_2} / \sigma_{\varepsilon_1}$, $\varepsilon = \varepsilon_1 + \varepsilon_2$, $\qquad$ (4.5.4)

and $f * (\cdot)$ *and* $F * (\cdot)$ *are the standard normal density and distribution functions*

From (4.5.2) and (4.5.4):

$$\varepsilon = \ln u - (a + \sum_{i=1}^{n} \alpha_i \ln x_i + \tfrac{1}{2} \sum_{i=1}^{n} \sum_{j=1}^{n} \gamma_{ij} \ln x_i \ln x_j)$$

(4.5.5)

where $\gamma_{ij} = \gamma_{ji}$, $x_i = $ *input* i, $n = $ *number of inputs*

where a, α_i *and* γ_{ji} are the parameters to be estimated by maximum likelihood. The likelihood function is:

$$\ln L(u / a, \alpha_i, \gamma_{ji}, \lambda, \sigma^2) = N \ln \frac{\sqrt{2}}{\sqrt{\pi}} + N \ln \sigma^{-1}$$
$$+ \sum_{i=1}^{N} \ln\left[1 - F * (\varepsilon \lambda \sigma^{-1})\right] - \frac{1}{2\sigma^2} \sum_{i=1}^{N} \varepsilon^2$$

(4.5.6)

The parameters of the production function estimated by (4.5.6) can be used in (4.5.5) to yield estimates of ε for each unit. As ALS demonstrated the parameters estimated by (4.5.6) can only be used to calculate a sample average measure of efficiency as we do not have separate estimates of ε_1 and ε_2.[27] JLMS demonstrate the decomposition of each ε via a conditional density function.[28] One can use either the mean or the mode of this conditional density function. The mode is more straightforward to estimate by the formula:

$$M(\varepsilon_2 / \varepsilon) = -\varepsilon(\sigma_{\varepsilon_2}^2 / \sigma^2) \quad if \ \varepsilon \le 0$$
$$= 0 \qquad\qquad if \ \varepsilon > 0$$

(4.5.7)

(4.5.7) is easily solved from the formulae under (4.5.4) as:

$$M(\varepsilon_2 / \varepsilon) = -\varepsilon\left[\frac{\lambda^2}{1+\lambda^2}\right] \quad if \ \varepsilon \le 0$$
$$= 0 \qquad\qquad if \ \varepsilon > 0$$

(4.5.8)

For each unit we substitute the result in (4.5.8) in (4.3.6) to obtain the estimate of $\mathbf{K(u,x)}$. Note here that the availability of panel data means that unit level inefficiency can be entered into the cost equation as a variable rather than as an error term. This allows direct estimation of inefficiency and eliminates the need to make distributional assumptions about inefficiencies. Many of the papers on the *SFM* only obtain unit specific efficiency measures at the expense of requiring panel data.

4.5.2 The Calculation of O(u,p,x) using the SFM

The estimation of allocative and overall productive efficiency within the *SFM* technique is a complicated process. In his recent review, Bauer (1990) notes that the usual cost system approaches to stochastic inefficiency measurement, where cost is a function of both technical and allocative inefficiency and input share equation errors represent allocative inefficiency, give rise to complex relationships between the errors which usually require arbitrary assumptions and complex likelihood functions in order to generate results. In such a cost function system it is necessary to model the relationship between the non-negative allocative inefficiency in the cost function and the two-sided allocative inefficiency disturbances in the input share equations (the 'Greene' problem[29]). The most advanced methods require panel data and few empirical studies have attempted to produce separate technical and allocative efficiency scores for cross-sectional data. It is a much more straightforward matter to produce an overall efficiency score calculated from deviations from an estimated stochastic frontier cost function than it is to decompose these deviations in order to produce separate allocative and technical efficiency measures. We therefore propose to calculate overall efficiency scores only in the case of *SFM* in Chapter 7. This will greatly ease exposition and does not substantially affect our ability to draw conclusions regarding the relative allocative and overall productive efficiency of publicly owned and privately owned electric power plants.

The estimation of stochastic cost frontier proceeds in a similar way to the estimation of the stochastic production function except that the one-sided error, ε_2, representing inefficiency is greater than zero rather than less than zero (i.e. gives rise to higher cost rather than lower output). We follow the same notation as in equations (4.5.1) to (4.5.8). For a translog cost function and following (4.5.2) we can write:

$$\ln c = a + \alpha_1 \ln u + \beta_1 (\ln u)^2 + \sum_{i=1}^{n} \gamma_i \ln w_i$$

$$+ \frac{1}{2} \sum_{i=1}^{n} \sum_{j=1}^{n} \delta_{ij} \ln w_i \ln w_j + \sum_{i=1}^{n} \rho_i \ln u \ln w_i + (\varepsilon_1 + \varepsilon_2) \qquad (4.5.9)$$

where $\delta_{ij} = \delta_{ji}$, w_i = *price of input i.*

In order to maintain linear homogeneity in prices we need to impose the following restrictions on the parameters:[30]

$$\sum_{i=1}^{n} \gamma_i = 1, \ \sum_{i=1}^{n} \delta_{ij} = 0 \ \text{ for each } j, \ \sum_{i=1}^{n} \rho_i = 0. \tag{4.5.10}$$

We can write the cost function equivalent of (4.5.5):

$$\varepsilon = \ln c - \left\{ \ a + \alpha_1 \ln u + \beta_1 (\ln u)^2 + \sum_{i=1}^{n} \gamma_i \ln w_i \right.$$

$$\left. + \tfrac{1}{2} \sum_{i=1}^{n} \sum_{j=1}^{n} \delta_{ij} \ln w_i \ln w_j + \sum_{i=1}^{n} \rho_i \ln u \ln w_i \ \right\} \tag{4.5.11}$$

Following (4.5.6) and noting the change of sign in ε, we can then estimate the cost function parameters by maximum likelihood:

$$\ln L(u \ / \ a, \alpha_1, \beta_1, \gamma_{ji}, \delta_i, \rho_i, \lambda, \sigma^2) = N \ln \frac{\sqrt{2}}{\sqrt{\pi}} + N \ln \sigma^{-1}$$

$$+ \sum_{i=1}^{N} \ln \left[F*(\varepsilon \lambda \sigma^{-1}) \right] - \frac{1}{2\sigma^2} \sum_{i=1}^{N} \varepsilon^2 \tag{4.5.12}$$

We again the use the mode of the conditional density function (due to JLMS) to calculate the individual overall efficiency scores.

$$M(\varepsilon_2 / \varepsilon) = \varepsilon(\sigma_{\varepsilon_2}^2 / \sigma^2) \quad \text{if } \varepsilon \geq 0$$

$$= 0 \quad \text{if } \varepsilon < 0 \tag{4.5.13}$$

(4.5.13) can be converted to (4.5.14) by the same method by which (4.5.7) converts to (4.5.8). This gives us:

$$M(\varepsilon_2 / \varepsilon) = \varepsilon \left[\frac{\lambda^2}{1 + \lambda^2} \right] \quad \text{if } \varepsilon \geq 0$$

$$= 0 \quad \text{if } \varepsilon < 0 \tag{4.5.14}$$

Then we use (4.3.6) to calculate the individual unit measure of $O(\mathbf{u},\mathbf{p},\mathbf{x})$.

We note that the translog cost function in (4.5.9) can be substituted for the production function in (4.4.3) under the *DSA* and used to give overall efficiency scores under the COLS-*DSA* technique. The calculation of these efficiency scores is a by-product of estimating the *SFM* cost frontier where we use OLS estimates of the parameters as starting values for the maximum likelihood estimates. The cost equivalent of (4.4.4) involves reducing the intercept in the cost function until it just envelops the data. We report the resulting translog *DSA* overall efficiency scores in our analysis in Chapter 7 in addition to the Cobb-Douglas measures detailed in Section 4.4.

4.5.3 A Review of the SFM Literature

The literature on the *SFM* technique is large and growing rapidly. Theoretical advances in the properties of the frontiers to be estimated coupled with advances in the speed and power of computer processing have allowed this theoretically and practically complex technique to become more suitable for general use. However the technique remains difficult to implement in practice because of lengthy algorithms and suffers from a lack of transparency in the derivation of the results. An excellent survey of the *SFM* literature is contained in Bauer (1990).

Early *SFM* developments investigated the role of the functional form of the distribution of the efficiencies. ALS and Meeusen and van den Broeck (1977) considered exponential and half-normal distributions for ε_2. These suffer from the disadvantage of having modes at zero. Stevenson (1980) developed more generalized likelihood functions incorporating truncated normal and gamma densities for ε_2. These densities may have non-zero modes. This results in biasing measured inefficiency downwards and may explain the tendency in some studies for *SFM* to give rise to surprisingly little measured inefficiency (e.g. Weyman-Jones, 1992).

Later developments began to focus on the possibilities for separating allocative and technical inefficiency. Bauer (1990) identifies three major approaches to the calculation of separate, unit specific measures of allocative and technical efficiency. These approaches are based on the estimation of a cost function system consisting of the cost function and a set of input share equations (e.g. for translog functional forms) or input demand functions (e.g. for a Cobb-Douglas functional form). Each approach involves a different solution to the Greene problem which we noted above. We briefly examine each approach in turn.

Firstly, Schmidt and Lovell (1979) suggest calculating the deviations of the actual input proportions from optimal input proportions using a derived cost frontier. The Greene problem is solved by functionally mapping (i.e. solving via analytic optimization) the errors in the factor demand equations (when considering Cobb-Douglas) into the allocative inefficiency term in the cost function. We first suggested this method for the *DSA* technique in Section 4.4.1; Schmidt and Lovell (1979) actually derive the appropriate formulae for a *SFM* Cobb-Douglas production frontier, the application to *DSA* being a special case where ε_1 is set equal to zero. We note again that the explicit form of the cost frontier may not be derivable for technologies more complicated than Cobb-Douglas. Some more complicated functional forms have been used in the literature to analytically derive *SFM* efficiency scores. Kumbhakar (1988) uses the generalized production function (GPF) – a more general form of Cobb-Douglas which allows scale elasticity to vary across units – to derive technical and allocative efficiency measures. Kumbhakar (1989) uses a generalized-McFadden (SGM) cost function to derive measures of technical and allocative efficiencies using panel data.

Secondly, the relationship between the allocative efficiency errors in the input share equations and the allocative inefficiency in the cost function is assumed to have a specific functional form. This approach has been developed by Schmidt (1984), Melfi (1984) and Bauer (1985). A major drawback of this approach is that there turns out to be a large number of parameters to be estimated. It is also highly questionable whether imposing a relationship between the errors which is almost certainly wrong is better than ignoring the relationship altogether.

Thirdly, we can estimate the stochastic cost frontier, ignoring the relationship between the disturbances in the cost and input share equations. The one-sided disturbance in the cost function is assumed to be a combination of technical and allocative inefficiency and is estimated via a JLMS approach. The DMU specific one-sided errors so obtained are then decomposed by the Kopp-Diewert-Zieschang decomposition algorithm to generate the separate measures of $\mathbf{A(u,p,x)}$ and $\mathbf{K(u,x)}$. This method would allow the estimation of more complicated functional form (eg. a translog cost function) and also extension to multiple outputs. As noted in Section 4.3.3 this solution method means that the calculation of technical efficiency measures requires the availability of input price data. This approach has been developed by Bauer (1985).

We now go on to briefly review some of the empirical situations to which *SFM* analysis has been applied. The literature is very large and this review does not pretend to be comprehensive, merely representative.

The majority of published empirical applications of *SFM* involve the application of an ALS-type production function. Early studies could not produce unit-specific efficiency measures without panel data. Meeusen and van den Broeck (1977) compared the efficiency of a sample of French manufacturing companies. This study estimated a Cobb-Douglas production function and assumed an exponential distribution for the inefficiency term. Kopp and Smith (1980) estimated Cobb-Douglas, CES (constant elasticity of substitution) and translog production frontiers using ALS-half normal for a sample of coal-fired electric power plants. Pitt and Lee (1981) estimated an ALS-truncated normal production function for a sample of Indonesian weaving firms operating in the early 1970s. Their approach required panel data in order to generate firm-specific inefficiency measures. Chen and Tang (1987) estimated an ALS-half normal production function for a sample of Taiwanese electronics firms.

The majority of later ALS studies of technical efficiency made use of JLMS to obtain unit-specific inefficiencies. Danilin et al. (1985) examined technical efficiency in a sample of Soviet cotton refining enterprises using an ALS-half normal production function. Wagstaff (1989) examined efficiency in a sample of Spanish hospitals. He estimated an ALS-half normal production function examining both cross-section data and panel data. Green et al. (1991) estimated an ALS production function assuming both half-normal and truncated normal distributions for the inefficiencies for a sample of Australian and British manufacturing firms. Al-Obaidan and Scully (1991) estimated an ALS-half normal production function for a sample of international petroleum companies. Kalirajan (1991) examines technical efficiency in Philippine rice farms.

A smaller number of studies attempt to measure cost inefficiency. We note a few of these studies. Hammond (1992) examines the cost efficiency of pre-war electric power plants in the UK using an ALS-gamma and ALS-truncated normal multi-output cost function and JLMS. Weyman-Jones (1992) estimates a translog cost function using an ALS-half normal technique and calculates efficiency scores using JLMS. Relatively few papers have attempted a decomposition of cost efficiency into technical and allocative efficiency. Kumbhakar (1988) [see Section 4.5.1 above] examines technical efficiency in a sample of US railroads using an analytically derived cost frontier. Ferrier and Lovell (1990) follow a Schmidt (1984)-type multiple-output translog cost function decomposition in order to measure allocative and technical efficiency for a sample of US banks. Kumbhakar (1991) follows the decomposition method suggested by Schmidt (1984) to obtain estimates of firm technical and allocative inefficiency for a sample of US airlines using panel data. Kalirajan and Yong (1993) use an analytic approach to decomposing allocative and technical efficiency using a Cobb-

Douglas production function for a sample of Chinese iron and steel enterprises.

4.6 A Summary of the Relative Merits of the Four Methodologies

In this section we summarize the comparative theoretical and empirical performance of the four methodologies outlined in the previous sections. Helpful reviews of the relative strengths of the *DEA* approach can be found in Sexton et al. (1986) and Seiford and Thrall (1990). The starting point for comparison is to distinguish the programming – *DEA* and *PPA* – and statistical techniques – *DSA* and *SFM*.

In the two programming approaches efficiency measures are computed, not estimated. The *DEA* technique allows easy calculation of allocative and technical efficiencies. A further decomposition of technical efficiency into three mutually exclusive and exhaustive components is possible. Unlike *PPA*, the *DEA* technique does not require the specification of a functional form for the production frontier and no distribution need be specified for the inefficiencies. The choice of functional form for the production function in the *PPA* may give rise to difficulty in calculating allocative efficiency if the functional form is complex. The estimation of parameters for a production function may be considered desirable. However these parameters are estimated without standard error. The *PPA* technique requires only one linear program per dataset rather than one per DMU for *DEA*. Depending on the number of units to be analysed this may be an important resource cost advantage of *PPA* over *DEA*. Both of the programming techniques are highly sensitive to measurement error in the frontier efficient units. *DEA* is also sensitive to specification error – the choice of inputs and outputs – and variable selection – the choice of measured variables. In particular changing the number of inputs and outputs may substantially affect the number of units appearing to be frontier efficient and the actual efficiency scores. More inputs and outputs result in non-negative changes in unit level efficiency. This is true also for *PPA* but not to the same extent. *DEA* is easily extendible to multiple outputs while *PPA* is not.

In the *DSA* and *SFM* techniques efficiency scores are estimated not computed. Both require the specification of a functional form for the production/cost function. The *SFM* technique admits the possibility of stochastic error in the measurement of efficiency while the *DSA* technique (like *DEA* and *PPA*) assumes all deviations from the frontier should be attributed to inefficiency. The *DSA* technique for production functions is straightforward to implement via COLS and requires no assumptions to be made about the distribution of the inefficiencies. *SFM* technical efficiency – when measured relative to a production rather than cost function – requires an assumption to be made about the form of the inefficiency error distribution. The choice of error distribution will have an effect on the measured inefficiencies and the parameters of the production function. The estimation of allocative inefficiency is straightforward for simple functional forms using *DSA*. For more complicated functional forms such as translog the separation of allocative and technical inefficiency based on the estimation of a frontier cost function requires substantial effort. The calculation of allocative efficiency remains easier for *DSA* due to the simplifying assumption of zero stochastic error. However for both *DSA* and *SFM* formidable likelihood functions need to be estimated with many parameters. Several formulations of the *SFM* require panel data or even more assumptions to extract DMU specific rather than average inefficiency measures. For the *SFM* approach in particular, complex functional forms and stochastic errors would seem to bias measured inefficiency downwards. If there were no stochastic error in a sample of data, the allowance made for noise in *SFM* techniques would result in some inefficiency being considered as noise. We therefore expect that in general *SFM* efficiency measures will be higher than *DSA* measures for given DMUs in a dataset. The likelihood that some inefficiency will be wrongly classified as noise is a real problem for efficiency measurement: this is the heart of the moral hazard problem for principals (owners, regulators etc.) in relation to their agents.[31]

We now compare the programming and statistical techniques: in particular we compare *DEA* and *SFM*. The *DEA* technique does not require the specification of a functional form for the production function. This would not be a serious problem for the *SFM* technique if a suitable production function can be estimated. Flexible functional forms can provide adequate approximations to underlying production functions; however they may involve large numbers of variables and give rise to serious problems for the calculation of allocative efficiency. The *DEA* technique is non-stochastic and makes no allowance for errors, unlike the *SFM* technique. This is a major potential drawback of the programming approach. Empirical work always involves some degree of measurement error, data handling errors, stochastic shocks etc. However the ability of the *SFM* technique to handle errors comes only at the expense of the imposition of a functional form for the errors or the use of panel data. It is also true that *DEA* scores are highly susceptible to specification and variable selection errors. *SFM* frontiers give rise to standard errors for each of the parameters, this allows the contribution of individual variables in the production function to be evaluated. Sophisticated sensitivity analysis of *DEA* scores is a possible solution to this problem, but it is complicated and time consuming relative to the analysis of standard errors in an *SFM* frontier.

Both techniques are potentially computationally expensive. However as a general rule the *SFM* technique requires more preparation than *DEA* but less time to implement. This is because while *SFM* may require complex likelihood functions against the simple linear programs for *DEA*, *SFM* requires only one statistical estimation per dataset to generate the frontier against which inefficiencies are measured whereas *DEA* requires one linear program to be solved per DMU. *DEA* allows easy extension to multiple outputs in a production frontier context and can also incorporate environmental variables into the analysis in a straight-forward way. *SFM* can only be extended to multiple outputs in the context of a cost frontier. This makes *DEA* particularly suitable for the analysis of inefficiency in non-profit organizations or for measuring technical inefficiency when input and output prices are not available (e.g. electricity distribution in this book). Ferrier and Lovell (1990) note that while many variables can be considered using *DEA* this rapidly gives rise to an excessive number of efficient units. This may result in a tighter constraint on the number of input and output variables which can be used in *DEA* relative to *SFM*.

Finally, we examine some of the empirical studies that have been conducted on data using two or more of our chosen methodologies in order to compare the performance and properties of the techniques. We report a couple of papers which use simulated Monte Carlo data produced from a known production frontier in order to analyse the properties of the methodologies. Banker et al. (1988) compared the *DEA* and *DSA* techniques using data generated from a two input–one output translog production function. They concluded that the *DEA* technique produced substantially better results; this conclusion was stronger the smaller the dataset. Gong and Sickles (1992) compared *DEA* and *SFM* techniques on data generated from several different functional forms of the production frontier. In general *SFM* outper-formed *DEA* but for some underlying forms *DEA* outperformed *SFM* (including translog). The relative ability of *DEA* improved as the sample size was increased.

There have been more comparative studies using real data. Banker et al. (1986) compare hospital efficiency using *DEA* and *DSA*. Their *DSA* method assumes no allocative inefficiency in hospital costs and is thus highly suspect. Kopp and Smith (1980) compare *PPA*, *DSA* and *SFM* using electric power plant data. They conclude that the form of the production function is more important than the measurement technique. Al-Obaidan and Scully (1991) use the same three techniques on oil companies and obtain similar estimated frontiers. Chen and Tang (1987) use *DSA* and *SFM* to calculate the relative efficiency of a sample of import-oriented and export-oriented firms. Both approaches showed export-oriented firms to be more efficient, however the average technical efficiencies were higher under the *SFM* technique. Wagstaff (1989) compares *DSA* and two *SFM* approaches on hospital data. The *DSA* indicated substantially higher average inefficiency than the cross-sectional *SFM* (though the panel data *SFM* inefficiency was higher than for the others). However the rank correlation between the two cross-sectional measures was high at 0.9. Ferrier and Lovell (1990) use *DEA* and *SFM* on panel data on US banking. They found that the *DEA* frontier was more flexible than a translog *SFM* frontier and that correlations between the technical efficiencies generated by the two methodologies were not statistically significant. Weyman-Jones (1992) examined overall cost efficiency in electricity distribution using *DEA* and *SFM* techniques. He found that *SFM* showed relatively little inefficiency compared with *DEA*.

The comparative studies suggest that the *SFM* efficiency scores will in general be higher than the non-stochastic methodologies would suggest. Choice of functional form for the production function would seem to be an important factor in determining the value and the accuracy of efficiency scores under the *DSA* and *SFM* techniques. The two Monte Carlo studies we report suggest the superiority of *DEA* and *SFM* over *DSA* and suggest that *SFM* may perform better in general than *DEA*.

If this author was to have to judge the relative merits of the techniques he would favour *DEA* over *SFM* (and *PPA* and *DSA*) for practical application because of the relative ease of extension to allocative efficiency, multiple outputs and environmental variables and the lack of restrictive distributional assumptions and complex likelihood functions.

Notes

1. Forsund et al. (1980) point out that profit maximization occurs in the presence of technical, allocative *and* scale efficiency. Production is scale inefficient if $p \neq c_y(p,w)$ where $c(\cdot)$ is the differentiable cost function and p is the output price vector. In this book we are only concerned with constrained cost minimization i.e. the minimization of production costs given the actual output. The reasons for this are two-fold: firstly, we wish to confine our study to the supply side and abstract from demand side effects and secondly we have no data on output prices. Scale efficiency in this sense will not concern us.

2. Banker et al. (1991) introduces the term stochastic data envelopment analysis (SDEA) to describe a linear program for measuring inefficiency which incorporates noise in the variables.

3. Most of the papers which introduce new empirical techniques with an example do not explicitly set out to test an empirical hypothesis concerning an industry or country. In fact many simply produce efficiency scores for a sample of US electric power plants.

4. Farrell (1957) was largely ignored in the literature until 1978. Farrell and Fieldhouse (1962) attempted to relax the constant returns to scale assumption, unsatisfactorily. Seitz (1971) is a rare example of published empirical work during this period (on steam electric plants) using a Farrell linear program.

5. $L(u) = \left\{ all\ input\ vectors, x \in R_+^n, yielding\ at\ least\ output\ rate\ u \in R_+^n \right\}$

6. We drop DMU specific superscripts for u, x and p in this section.

7. The idea of measuring inefficiency as a 0 to 1 coefficient is traced through Farrell to Debreu's (1951) concept of a coefficient of resource utilization. Both CCR and Fare et al. (1985a) credit Shephard (1970) for the introduction of the idea of a 'distance function' to measure inefficiency.

8. Note that minimum cost operation will always occur at a facet on the frontier corresponding to at least one frontier efficient firm.

9. Where u = output, p = input prices and x = the vector of inputs.

10. An infinitesimal e is introduced into the linear programs to ensure that Pareto inefficient DMUs do not appear to be efficient. Fare and Hunsacker (1986) demonstrate that even this does not guarantee Pareto efficiency. Ali (1990) points out that *DEA* scores can be sensitive to the value of the infinitesimal used in the linear programs and that the value is rarely reported in empirical work.

11. Sueyoshi (1992) presents an effectively designed algorithm for measuring technical and allocative efficiencies using *DEA* which helps illuminate the implementation of the linear programs in the text.

12. See Byrnes (1985) for more details of this assumption.

13. We utilitized an Apple Macintosh computer program called FARE/MAC1 written by the Author. Commercial packages are readily available such as LINGO from LINDO SYSTEMS INC. P.O.B.148231, Chicago, IL 60614, USA.

14. In our linear programming package we utilized equivalent maximizations of all the linear programs in this section. We do not include the equivalent maximizations in the other cases to save space but the change of variables required is similar to that which changes (4.2.7) to (4.2.8).

15. This linear program is a reparameterization of program (3) in Charnes, Cooper and Rhodes (1978), pp.431–2. Links between the CCR (1978) and Fare et al. (1985a) approaches are explored in Fare and Hunsacker (1986).

16. Fare and Svensson (1980) introduce an axiomatic characterization of the

concept of congestion. Congestion is not distinquished in the CCR literature.

17. We use the input-based (rather than output-based) measures of **F(u,x)**, **C(u,x)** and **S(u,x)**. Our measures give the % of the actual inputs per unit output that could be used if the DMU were to become frontier efficient. For the distinction between input and output based measures see Fare and Hunsacker (1986).

18. The linear programs required to calculate the **F(u,x)**, **C(u,x)** and **S(u,x)** measures were evaluated using a program called FARE/MAC2I written by the author.

19. (4.2.15) is program (19) in Banker, Charnes and Cooper (1984), p.1084.

20. We utilize a program called FARE/DIST.ENV written by the author to calculate these measures.

21. See Macmillan (1986, 1987) for more information on the use of the simplex method in the context of *DEA*.

22. Macmillan (1987), pp.1518–9, provides further details on the proximity measures.

23. Translog functional forms were first introduced in Christensen, Jorgenson and Lau (1971,1973). Using Monte Carlo experiments Guilkey, Lovell and Sickles (1983) compare three flexible functional forms – translog, generalized Leontief and generalized Cobb-Douglas – and conclude that the translog form performs at least as well as the other two and 'provides a dependable approximation to reality provided reality is not too complex' (p.614).

24. Note that in order to keep the computation reasonably straightforward and to ensure a plausible frontier we restrict all of the parameters to be positive. In Sections 4.4 and 4.5 the estimated translog frontiers have unrestricted parameters.

25. If we convert (4.3.4) to a maximization problem by multiplication by -1 then for frontier efficient firms the constraint in (4.3.4) binds and the corresponding slack variables are zero. We solve (4.3.4) using the simplex method, this means that all the slack variables are in the initial basis and that in the final basis the number of basic primal variables corresponds to the number of zero-valued slacks. Hence the number of frontier efficient firms equals the number of non-zero parameters in the production function.

26. ALS, p.26, credit Weinstein (1964) with the first derivation of this result.

27. The mean of $f(\varepsilon)$ is $E(\varepsilon) = E(\varepsilon_2) = -\sigma_{e_2} \sqrt{2}/\sqrt{\pi}$. From this and the definitions of σ^2 *and* λ ALS solve for the average value of inefficiency. Using (4.3.6) an average measure of **K(u,x)** can be estimated.

28. Lovell and Schmidt (1988) note that one drawback of these estimates is that they are not consistent. The variance of the conditional distribution remains the same no matter how large the sample.

29. See Greene (1980b), pp.104–5.

30. We ignore the input share equations which can be jointly estimated with the cost function. The estimation of a translog cost function system would improve the efficiency of the estimates of the parameters. However the

associated increase in complexity involved in translog system estimation and the possibility that the translog functional form may not be the most suitable form mean that undue concern for statistical efficiency is spurious.

31. Weyman-Jones (1992) makes this point in an article which investigates the best way for regulators to monitor the performance of UK electricity distribution companies.

CHAPTER 5

PRODUCTIVE EFFICIENCY IN ELECTRIC UTILITIES

5.1 Introduction

This chapter has two distinct goals. Firstly, it seeks to analyse the effect of ownership on the productive efficiency of an international sample of electric utilities. Secondly, it analyses the effects of ownership using two distinct methodological approaches applied to a common dataset in order to compare and evaluate the relative performance of the methodologies.

The analysis is conducted using new data collected on an international sample of electric utilities operating in 1986. The sample contains data from 95 firms operating in nine countries. The majority of the data used in the previous studies of relative performance which we discussed in Chapter 3 were for the 1970s or earlier and included data only from the USA. The two methodologies used are those of Fare et al. (1985a) [FGL] and Atkinson and Halvorsen (1986) [A+H]. These methodologies are of interest because, as explained Chapter 3, they represent the most recently developed techniques in both the parametric (A+H) and the non-parametric (FGL) approaches to the testing of the effects of ownership on productive efficiency. The A+H approach estimates a translog shadow cost function for the data and allows the calculation of the effects of ownership on both allocative and technical productive efficiency within the two ownership classes. The FGL approach, which we detailed in the previous chapter, calculates the relative technical and allocative (price) efficiency scores of each firm relative to the best practice firms within the sample. Firm level results can then be aggregated for each ownership class to test for the effects of ownership on technical and allocative efficiency.

The use of two methodologies applied to the same dataset addresses some of the problems in evaluating the validity of the majority of previous studies which applied a single, new methodology to a new dataset. In particular it is not possible to distinguish whether differences in the results depend on data or methodological differences. If two different methodologies applied to the same dataset were to yield similar results we could perhaps be more confident in using our results as a basis for policy proposals. Such an argument has been called the 'methodology cross-checking principle' by Charnes, Cooper and Sueyoshi (1988). The original A+H and FGL papers did use the same dataset and arrived at broadly similar results: there is little significant difference in performance between the two ownership types. In this chapter we apply the original analysis to a new and more modern dataset and suggest that the results in the original FGL methodology cannot be validly compared with the A+H results without a change to the FGL methodology. We amend the FGL methodology to facilitate a more legitimate comparison.

We demonstrate that there are significant differences in the quantity and quality of information that is produced under the two techniques. We find evidence from both the methodologies for no significant differences in technical efficiency between the two ownership types, once scale effects have been taken into account. On allocative (price) efficiency the A+H approach finds no evidence of significant differences while the FGL approach finds mixed evidence of superior efficiency in private firms.

This chapter is in seven sections. Section 5.2 introduces the dataset. Section 5.3 contains the details of the A+H methodology. Section 5.4 compares the FGL and A+H methodologies following the presentation in Chapter 4 and Section 3 of this chapter. Sections 5.5 and 5.6 give the FGL and A+H results of the analysis. Section 5.7 is a conclusion.

5.2   The Dataset

The dataset consists of a sample of 95 firms from the USA (73), Australia (5), Japan (9), UK (3), France (1), Italy (1), Denmark (1), Canada (1) and Ireland (1) operating during the accounting year ending in 1986.[1] A listing of the sample companies is in Appendix 2.1. For each firm there are seven variables: output, three inputs – capital (or capacity), labour and fuel – and three input prices. The data are for thermal power production only: hydroelectric, nuclear and renewable power statistics have not been included. Both the FGL and A+H methodologies would suggest that it is more reasonable to restrict the analysis to just thermal production.[2]

An underlying assumption of the FGL linear programming technique is that factor prices are fixed. This is not true if alternative technologies can be used to adjust factor mixes in order to lower factor prices. For example if substituting nuclear for thermal power reduces the average price of fuel (per heat unit) at the cost of higher capital input this may well be efficient in a cost minimizing sense but would show up as a move to more inefficient production using the linear programs outlined above. Another example of where the technique breaks down might be the extra capital costs incurred in order to build a coal-fired power station on top of a coal mine – this reduces fuel costs at the expense of higher capital costs.

The common dataset used in FGL and A+H looked at thermal production (i.e. coal, oil and gas) only. This assumes that firms cannot reduce average factor prices by changing the thermal technology employed – it is not clear that this assumption is reasonable. If power station level data were used it might be possible to eliminate many of the above problems by matching public and private plants by type and age. The A+H methodology fits a cost function to the data which plays a similar role to the reference isoquant in FGL. Clearly nuclear and hydro production of electricity is likely to involve very different functional forms. In the case of hydroelectric even the nature of the inputs differs (there is no easily measurable fuel input), so the three input formulation used in A+H to model thermal power production is inappropriate. Once again it is noted that the restriction of the scope of the analysis to thermal power production is a convenient simplification: within the class of thermal power production there are many different technologies and hence many different cost functions.

The data for non-US firms were collected from company accounts and from data provided by the companies and national associations of electricity producers. The US data were collected from US Energy Information Agency (USEIA) publications: *Financial Statistics of Selected Electric Utilities 1986* and *Historical Plant Cost and Annual Production Expenses For Selected Electric Plants 1986*. Output is measured as millions of kilowatt-hours generated in the accounting year 1986. Inputs include labour, capital and fuel. Labour is measured as the number of employees employed at power stations, fuel is measured in TBTU (BTU*10^{12}) and capital is measured MW of nameplate (gross) capacity. The rental cost of capital is calculated following Christensen and Jorgenson (1969) and represents the real historic cost of capital.[3] The price of labour is derived from the total labour costs in each utility where these were available, and otherwise from labour costs in other firms within the state (for US MUNIs). Fuel prices were calculated as the result of fuel costs divided by fuel input. All prices were measured in millions of US dollars. Purchasing Power Parity exchange rates[4] were used to convert the non-US data to common currency units. A more detailed account of the data sources and derivations is given in Appendix 1.1.

5.3   The A+H Methodology

A+H criticized previous parametric studies on the grounds that they simply attempted to test hypotheses concerning the joint effects of ownership and regulation. A+H then developed a model which attempted to investigate the relative cost efficiency of privately owned and publicly owned electric utilities while allowing for the effects of regulation. Their empirically testable model is developed from the theoretical model of utility maximizing behaviour of a manager subject to rate of return regulation. Starting from this model it can be shown that the behaviour of firms is equivalent to cost minimization subject to appropriately defined shadow, rather than market, prices. Given an appropriate form for the shadow cost function it is possible to derive an estimateable cost function which links actual costs with actual quantities and estimateable shadow prices. A+H use the flexible translog cost function to model costs within their sample of firms. The shadow prices facing the different ownership classes in the sample can be distinguished and tested for significant relative and absolute price inefficiency. Differences in technical inefficiency between the two ownership types can also be tested for even after allowing for possible differences in technology used by the two ownership types.

In this section we will sketch the derivation of the A+H model. The model used in their 1986 paper is developed more fully in their 1984 paper which just examined price efficiency within the privately owned electric utilities in their 1986 dataset. We refer to these papers as is appropriate.

We start from A+H (1986), p.282, by defining a managerial utility function, in which utility is the function of both profit and the quantities of inputs used by the firm:

$$U = U(\pi, X). \tag{5.3.1}$$

$U = U(.)$ is a twice continuously differentiable concave utility function, p is profit and X is an n-component vector of inputs. We further assume that $\delta U/\delta \pi > 0$. This functional form may be rationalized as the outcome of a principal–agent relationship where the manager's incentive scheme provides an imperfect but monotonically increasing relationship between profit and managerial reward, such that the manager still has an incentive to pursue non-profit objectives such as the number of employees or the size of the firm's output.

The manager maximizes his utility subject to a demand constraint and a regulatory constraint. The demand constraint arises from a downward sloping demand curve, while the regulatory constraint limits profits in relation to input quantities. For private firms the regulatory constraint may take the form of explicit rate of return regulation while for public firms implicit constraints are imposed by the requirement to minimize prices while maintaining an adequate bond rating.

The Lagrangian for the manager's constrained optimization problem is:

$$L = U(\pi, X) - \lambda \left[\pi - R(X) + \sum_i P_i X_i \right]$$
$$- \sum_k \theta_k \left[R(X) - \sum_i P_i X_i - G_k(K^{G^k}) \right]$$

(5.3.2)

The first constraint is the demand constraint such that profit is a function of $R(.)$, the twice continuously differentiable revenue function, and of input costs, where P_i represents the market price of input i. The second constraint is the regulatory constraint which effectively restricts each input according to the function $G(K^{G^k})$, where θ_k is the Lagrange multiplier for the regulatory constraint on input k. For example under rate of return regulation there is one input constraint on capital of the form:

$$R(X) - \sum_{i=1}^n P_i X_i \le (\overline{P}_K - P_K) X_K,$$

(5.3.3)

where $\overline{P}_K$ is the allowed rate of return.

Differentiating eq. (5.3.2) and noting that $\lambda = \delta U / \delta \pi$, we obtain the first order necessary condition for an interior solution for input i:

$$\frac{\partial R}{\partial X_i} = P_i - \frac{(\delta U / \delta X_i) + \sum_k \theta_k (\delta G^k / \delta X_i)}{(\delta U / \delta \pi) - \sum_k \theta_k}.$$

(5.3.4)

This equation says that the manager should set the marginal revenue product of each input equal to its shadow price, where the shadow price differs from the market price due to the combined effects of utility maximizing behaviour and regulation. In the absence of regulation and managerial non-profit maximization each θ_k would be equal to 0 and the $\delta U / \delta \pi = 0$, leaving marginal revenue products equal to market prices as under unconstrained profit maximization.

Defining the shadow price of input i, P_i^*, as equal to the right hand side of eq. (5.3.4) we can define:

$$\frac{\delta R/\delta X_i}{\delta R/\delta X_j} = \frac{P_i^*}{P_j^*} \quad i,j = 1,...,n .$$

(5.3.5)

and via the product rule of differentiation we can then write:

$$\frac{\delta R/\delta X_i}{\delta R/\delta X_j} = \frac{\delta Q/\delta X_i}{\delta Q/\delta X_j},$$

(5.3.6)

where Q is the quantity of output. The right hand side of eq. (5.3.6) is equal to the MRTS_{ij}, thus using the definition in eq. (5.3.5) we have shown that utility maximizing behaviour under regulation can be modelled as cost minimization subject to appropriately defined shadow prices. Looking at eq. (5.3.4) , we see that the weaker the relationship between profit and managerial utility the higher will be the ratio of $\delta U/\delta X/\delta U/\delta \pi$ and – all other things being equal – the lower the cost efficiency of the firms. It is harder to generalize about the effects of deviations between shadow and market prices, as deviations from cost efficiency depend on deviations in relative and not absolute shadow prices. Under rate of return regulation the A-J effect (in the presence of simple profit maximization) leaves $P_l = P_l^*$ and $P_f = P_f^*$ but $P_k > P_k^*$ thus causing the relative shadow price of capital to fall below its relative market price and create the incentive for inefficient overuse of capital.

We now proceed to derive an estimateable cost equation which seeks to estimate shadow prices and model their effects on cost efficiency. Here we follow A+H (1984), p.650. Lau and Yotopolous (1971) suggested that shadow input prices could be approximated by:

$$k_i P_i,$$

(5.3.7)

where k_i is a factor of proportionality, k is input and firm specific. Our analysis above allows us to assume that the firm behaves in such a way as to seek to minimize total shadow costs i.e. the dual objective function to that in eq. (5.3.2) above. Applying Shephard's Lemma (1970) to the shadow cost function we can write:

$$\frac{\delta C^S}{dk_i P_i} = X_i ,$$

(5.3.8)

where C^S is the shadow cost function. This allows us to substitute for X_i in the actual cost function and so derive:

$$C^A = \sum_i P_i X_i = \sum_i P_i \frac{\delta C^S}{dk_i P_i} \tag{5.3.9}$$

We now define M^S as the shadow input cost share:

$$M_i^S \equiv \frac{k_i P_i X_i}{C^S}. \tag{5.3.10}$$

Rearranging eq. (5.3.10) we get:

$$X_i = M_i^S C^S (k_i P_i)^{-1}, \tag{5.3.11}$$

and substituting in eq. (5.3.9), the actual cost function may be rewritten as:

$$C^A = C^S \sum_i k_i^{-1} M_i^S \qquad i = 1,\ldots,n \tag{5.3.12}$$

taking logs we get:

$$\ln C^A = \ln C^S + \ln \sum_i k_i^{-1} M_i^S. \tag{5.3.13}$$

In order to derive an estimateable equation we need to find C^S and M^S for appropriate functional form for the shadow cost function. We use the popular flexible translog functional form to model the shadow cost function:

$$
\begin{aligned}
\ln C^S = {}& \alpha_0 + \alpha_Q \ln Q + \frac{1}{2} \gamma_{QQ} (\ln Q)^2 \\
& + \sum_i \gamma_{iQ} \ln Q \ln(k_i P_i) + \sum_i \alpha_i \ln(k_i P_i) \\
& + \frac{1}{2} \sum_i \sum_j \gamma_{ij} \ln(k_i P_i) \ln(k_j P_j) \qquad i,j = 1,\ldots,n.
\end{aligned}
\tag{5.3.14}
$$

Total shadow cost should increase proportionally when all shadow prices increase proportionally. Linear homogeneity of eq. (5.3.14) implies the following relationships among the parameters:

$$\sum_i \alpha_i = 1$$

$$\sum_i \gamma_{iQ} = 0 \tag{5.3.15}$$

$$\sum_i \gamma_{ij} = \sum_j \gamma_{ij} = \sum_i \sum_j \gamma_{ij} \;.$$

Logarithmic differentiation of eq. (5.3.14) gives rise to the following expression for shadow cost shares:

$$\frac{\delta \ln C^s}{\delta \ln(k_i P_i)} = \frac{k_i P_i}{C^S} \frac{\delta C^s}{\delta k_i P_i} = \frac{k_i P_i X_i}{C^S} = M_i^S$$

$$= \alpha_i + \sum \gamma_{ij} \ln(k_i P_j) + \gamma_{iQ} \ln Q \quad i,j=1,...,n. \tag{5.3.16}$$

Substituting eq. (5.3.14) and eq. (5.3.16) into eq. (5.3.13) we arrive at the following expression for the actual cost function:

$$\ln C^A = \alpha_0 + \alpha_Q \ln Q + \frac{1}{2} \gamma_{QQ} (\ln Q)^2 + \sum_i \gamma_{iQ} \ln Q \ln(k_i P_i)$$

$$+ \sum_i \alpha_i \ln(k_i P_i) + \frac{1}{2} \sum_i \sum_j \gamma_{ij} \ln(k_i P_i)\ln(k_j P_j) \tag{5.3.17}$$

$$+ \ln\left(\sum_i k_i^{-1}(\alpha_i + \sum \gamma_{ij} \ln(k_i P_j) + \gamma_{iQ} \ln Q) \right)$$

$$i,j=1,...n.$$

The actual cost share equations are derived in the following way:

$$M_i^A = \frac{P_i X_i}{C^A}. \tag{5.3.18}$$

We can then substitute for X_i and C^A using eq. (5.3.11) and eq. (5.3.12):

$$M_i^A = \frac{M_i^S k_i^{-1}}{\sum_i M_i^S k_i^{-1}} \qquad\qquad i=1,...,n. \tag{5.3.19}$$

Finally using eq. (5.3.16) we can substitute in eq. (5.3.19) to get the following set of actual cost share equations:

$$M_i^A = \frac{\left[\alpha_i + \sum \gamma_{ij} \ln(k_i P_j) + \gamma_{iQ} \ln Q\right] k_i^{-1}}{\sum_i \left[\alpha_i + \sum \gamma_{ij} \ln(k_i P_j) + \gamma_{iQ} \ln Q\right] k_i^{-1}} \qquad i,j = 1,...,n. \qquad (5.3.20)$$

As the cost share equations sum to 1, one of them can be dropped in estimating the translog system of cost equations derived above. A+H (1984) estimated a three input – capital, labour and fuel – translog cost function system using eq. (5.3.17) and two (labour was dropped in both A+H papers) input share equations, (5.3.20). This allowed them to estimate the shadow prices and test for significant deviations from absolute and relative price efficiency. A+H (1984) did so for a sample of private firms; it is however possible to amend the analysis in order to further incorporate and estimate the effects of ownership on price efficiency and on technical efficiency (A+H, 1986).

Both A+H and FGL suggest that scale effects are important. Scale effects can actually be calculated for each firm using FGL, and this provides an important point of comparison between the two methodologies. The elasticity of actual cost with respect to scale is:

$$\frac{\delta \ln C^A}{\delta \ln Q} = \alpha_Q + \gamma_{QQ} \ln Q + \sum_i \gamma_{iQ} \ln(k_i P_i)$$

$$+ \frac{\sum_i k_i^{-1} \gamma_{iQ}}{\sum_i k_i^{-1} M_i^S} \qquad i = 1,...,n. \qquad (5.3.21)$$

This is obtained by differentiation of eq. (5.3.17). Scale economies, *SE*, can then be calculated as unity minus the right hand side of eq. (5.3.21):

$$SE^A \equiv 1.0 - \frac{\delta \ln C^A}{\delta \ln Q}, \qquad (5.3.22)$$

multiplying by 100 we can express scale economies as a percentage.

We now return to A+H (1986), p.289,[5] to complete the derivation of the set of equations to be estimated in order to incorporate the effects of ownership on technical and price efficiency.

The above derivation requires three sets of amendments before the performance of both public and private can be reasonably estimated. The first amendment allows for possible differences in technology between the two ownership types. Technological differences are modelled by incorporating dummy variables in the linear terms in the shadow cost function:

$$\alpha_i^r = \alpha_i + b_i D^r,$$

$$\alpha_Q^r = \alpha_Q + b_Q D^r, \qquad\qquad i = 1,\dots,n, \tag{5.3.23}$$

$$\sum_i b_i = 0,$$

where $r = P$ for privately owned utilities and $r = G$ for publicly owned utilities. $D^P = 0$, $D^G = 1.0$ and α_i, α_Q, b_i and b_Q are the parameters to be estimated. $\sum b_i = 0$ ensures linear homogeneity for public firms in the presence of the restrictions in (5.3.15).[6] The second amendment allows for the possibility that public and private firms may face different shadow prices. In the theoretical model each firm has its own set of shadow prices with the k_i in eq. (5.3.7) being input and firm specific. However it is not possible to estimate a different set of shadow prices for each firm, so that a convenient simplification is to assume that all firms in the same ownership group face the same shadow prices. The k_i are defined by the equation:

$$k_i^r = d_i + g_i D^r, \qquad\qquad i = 1,\dots,n, \tag{5.3.24}$$

where r, D^P and D^G are defined as in eq. (5.3.23) and d_i and g_i are the parameters to be estimated. The actual total cost eq. (5.3.17) and the share equations (5.3.20) are homogeneous of degree zero in the k_i^r. Thus one of k_i^r should be set to 1 to normalize the estimated values of the other k_i^r. Following A+H (1986) we normalize k_L^r, the labour input shadow price vector. The final amendment to the cost equation allows for possible differences in technical efficiency between the two types of utilities by including a dummy variable in the intercept term:

$$\alpha_0^r = d_0 + g_0 D^r. \tag{5.3.25}$$

If we make the substitutions outlined in equations (5.3.23), (5.3.24) and

(5.3.25) in eq. (5.3.17) and incorporate the linear homogeneity relationships in eq. (5.3.14), then for the three inputs eq. (5.3.17) and two of the input share equations in (5.3.20) represent the system of equations to be estimated. Together these three equations form a non-linear system of equations which can be estimated by full information maximum likelihood.[7] Restricted versions of the full system were also estimated by full information maximum likelihood.

5.4 A Comparison of the A+H and FGL Methodologies

The FGL methodology contrasts sharply with that of A+H which we outlined above. We have outlined this approach in detail in the previous chapter. We can use the FGL linear programs to calculate six measures of productive efficiency for each firm in a sample. The measures were $O(u,p,x)$, overall efficiency, which can be decomposed into $A(u,p,x)$, allocative or price efficiency, and $K(u,x)$, overall technical efficiency such that:

$$O(u,p,x) = A(u,p,x) \cdot K(u,x)$$

$K(u,x)$ can be further decomposed into pure technical, $F(u,x)$, congestion efficiency, $C(u,x)$ and scale efficiency, $S(u,x)$, such that:

$$K(u,x) = F(u,x) \cdot C(u,x) \cdot S(u,x)$$

The linear programs needed to calculate these measures and their interpretation were discussed in the previous chapter.

One difference between this approach and that of A+H is that the relative efficiency of each firm is calculated directly. The A+H technique assumes that public and private firms are equally price (in)efficient within their ownership classes. In order to generate parametric measures of individual firm level efficiency scores we would need to adopt a parametric cost frontier approach (such as the *PPA*, *DSA* and *SFM* techniques in Chapter 4).

Both techniques can be used to estimate technical and price efficiency. However the FGL methodology does allow a more satisfactory modelling of technical inefficiency in that the $K(u,x)$ measure can be decomposed into three further measures in order to help identify sources of inefficiency (such as suboptimal scale or backward bending isoquants). A+H only models relative technical inefficiency as a shift in the cost function, but such a characterization of technical inefficiency especially for a flexible functional form is unsatisfactory. It is interesting to note the differences in degrees of freedom between the two techniques. There are 18 free variables (including the constant) in the full A+H (1986) system of equations.[8] The FGL approach involves a maximum of three referent firms leaving only three degrees of freedom. This is a drawback of flexible functional forms: underlying differences may be masked by the fitting of a large number of variables to a relatively small dataset.

An important advantage that FGL has over A+H lies in the handling of the input prices. The FGL technical efficiency measures require no information on prices in order to be calculated. The A+H methodology does require input prices in order to estimate the relative effects of ownership on technical efficiency (A+H model differences in technical efficiency effects very simply using eq. (5.3.25)). As the input price data are subject to a wide margin of error the relative independence of the FGL methodology to input price data is a distinct advantage of the technique.[9]

Further major differences in the two techniques centre round their parametric versus non-parametric nature. The FGL approach has the advantage of not imposing any, possibly wrong, prior assumptions about the distribution of the errors or about the form of the cost function. However A+H do use a very flexible functional form which can be a second order approximation to any arbitrary function. This would seem to go some way to reducing the apparent restrictiveness embodied in favouring one functional form over another. Allowance for some errors would seem to be desirable in a world characterized by shocks and errors in data measurement. In the FGL methodology all shocks and errors are incorporated as differences in efficiency. The most worrying way in which this affects the results is when a shock or error makes one firm a referent firm for a large number of others and hence biases the results not only for itself but for other firms. The potential seriousness of these problems for the current analysis will be discussed later in this chapter.

As mentioned in Section 5.1, FGL does not provide strict comparison with A+H (1986). A key feature of the A+H paper was the introduction of dummy variables to incorporate differences in technology between the two firms (eq. (5.3.23) above). FGL calculated their efficiency measures for a pooled sample of public and private firms. This implicitly assumes that the two ownership types have access to the same technology as they are compared to the same set of referent firms. Brynes (1985) points out that the way to control for technology differences within the FGL methodology is to split the data into public and private firms and calculate separate efficiency measures for each subset of the data. Thus public firms have their efficiency measured relative to other public firms and private firms relative to other private firms. Pooling the data instead will bias the results by attributing as inefficiency all differences in performance between the best practice public and private firms (although this is plausible). For instance FGL's original results suggested that public firms were more efficient on the **O**, **A** and **K** measures than private firms. If private firms can be considered to use different technology then splitting the data might have changed the nature of this result. In our analysis we split the data and calculate the efficiency measures in this way in order to incorporate differences in technology.

In addition to the six FGL efficiency measures we also calculate and report the PSF capital measure and the likely returns to scale under the FGL methodology. These measures allow further investigation of the nature of returns to scale within the sample. Both of these measures were discussed in the previous chapter. The six efficiency measures and the two returns to scale measures were calculated by Fortran 77 programs written by the author.[10] The programs were run using a Fortran compiler[11] on an Apple Macintosh LCII computer.

5.5   FGL Results

The summary results for the FGL methodology are recorded in Table 5.1 below. Summary statistics are reported for the total number of firms in the dataset as well as for MUNIs and IOUs separately. They

Table 5.1:   Summary Results for Firm Sample

	O(u,p,x)	A(u,p,x)	K(u,x)	F(u,x)	C(u,x)	S(u,x)
AV TOTAL	0.7662	0.8723	0.8641	0.9468	0.9723	0.9355
AV PRIVATE	0.8268	0.9065	0.9092	0.9457	0.9809	0.9810
AV PUBLIC	0.6623	0.8136	0.7867	0.9487	0.9576	0.8575
SD PRIVATE	0.2623	0.2257	0.2543	0.0701	0.0277	0.0185
SD PUBLIC	0.3255	0.3100	0.1743	0.0996	0.0973	0.1893
MAX PRIVATE	1.0000	1.0000	1.0000	1.0000	1.0000	1.0000
MAX PUBLIC	1.0000	1.0000	1.0000	1.0000	1.0000	1.0000
MIN PRIVATE	0.4382	0.5512	0.7950	0.8447	0.8092	0.7950
MIN PUBLIC	0.0573	0.2428	0.0825	0.6222	0.4821	0.1710
MED PRIVATE	0.8302	0.9253	0.9094	0.9483	0.9974	0.9959
MED PUBLIC	0.7374	0.9034	0.8297	1.0000	0.9996	0.9204

Av = Average, Max = Maximum, Min = Minimum and Med = Median.

show that IOUs on average outperform MUNIs on five out of six of the efficiency measures.

Average overall efficiency is 0.7662 for the whole sample. Decomposing overall efficiency into its two component measures – allocative efficiency and overall technical efficiency – it appears that each contributes fairly equally to overall efficiency. High levels of allocative inefficiency are not unexpected in any given year as short-run variations in fuel and other factor prices are likely to leave firms looking as if they have chosen the wrong factor proportions. If regulatory effects are significant then firms may be acting in response to shadow rather than the actual (market) prices used in our analysis – this would show up as allocative inefficiency. For instance a strong A-J effect would lead to a low shadow price for capital. Differences in environmental regulations could lead to measured technical inefficiency as firms use additional inputs to meet the regulations (see Fare et al., 1989). There is a large difference in overall efficiency between public and private firms (public=0.6623, private=0.8268).

The differences between IOUs and MUNIs in average allocative and overall technical efficiency are of fairly equal size (around 10%) with a large difference in average scale efficiency. These summary statistics would seem to suggest that suboptimal choice of scale may be a major cause of the relative inefficiency of public firms.

Table 5.2:   Returns to Scale: Firm Sample

| | *Likely DRS* | | *Likely CRS* | | *Likely DRS* | |
	psf>1	*Fare RTS*	*psf=1*	*Fare RTS*	*psf<1*	*Fare RTS*
Total	23	17	9	12	63	66
Public	4	4	3	6	28	25
Private	19	13	6	6	35	41

Turning to Table 5.2 scale inefficiency appears to be pervasive with 69% – on the Fare measure (66% on the PSF measure) – of firms exhibiting increasing returns to scale. MUNIs seem to be more likely to be operating at too small a scale with 80% exhibiting IRS – on the PSF measure – against 58% for IOUs (71% and 68% respectively on the Fare measure). FGL found significant scale effects[12] but they were not the most dominant determinant of overall efficiency. This may have been due to the shorter tail of low output US MUNIs in their sample compared to this study[13] and the better sample matching, by output, of the FGL study. Indeed FGL's smallest firms do exhibit very

Table 5.3: Summary of Tests of the Effect of Ownership on Efficiency: Firm Sample

Efficiency Measure	Analysis of Variance F $(Prob>F)$	Kruskal-Wallis χ^2 $(Prob>\chi^2)$	Median Scores (points above median) χ^2 $(Prob>\chi^2)$	Van der Waerden (1-way) χ^2 $(Prob>\chi^2)$	Savage (exponential) χ^2 $(Prob>\chi^2)$
O(u,p,x)	16.543 (0.0001)	6.2681 (0.0123)	3.3353 (0.0678)	7.292 (0.0069)	1.7901 (0.1809)
A(u,p,x)	9.294 (0.003)	4.0861 (0.0432)	3.3353 (0.0678)	4.7494 (0.0293)	1.7938 (0.1805)
K(u,x)	18.217 (0.0001)	5.4579 (0.0195)	1.9688 (0.1606)	6.2644 (0.0123)	0.4045 (0.5248)
F(u,x)	0.038 (0.8462)	4.9254 (0.0265)	5.7857 (0.0162)	2.8841 (0.0895)	7.3984 (0.0065)
C(u,x)	2.721 (0.1024)	0.0001 (0.9936)	0.0838 (0.7722)	0.0626 (0.8025)	0.1325 (0.7159)
S(u,x)	24.211 (0.0001)	6.3789 (0.0115)	1.9688 (0.1606)	6.9604 (0.0083)	0.658 (0.4173)

low efficiencies,[14] in several cases lower than the lowest values recorded in this study.

Table 5.3 lists a battery of one-tailed statistical tests on the efficiency measures.[15] The null hypothesis is that there is no significant difference in the efficiency of public and private firms. Apart from the analysis of variance tests the tests are non-parametric in keeping with the non-parametric nature of the Fare analysis. The median scores test is a test of central tendency and the other three tests are rank order tests.[16] A value of less than 0.05 in the bracket below each test statistic indicates rejection at the 5% level of the null hypothesis of no difference in efficiency.

Table 5.3 indicates that it is difficult to generalize about the significance of differences in efficiency between the two ownership classes. We might have expected a more convincing confirmation of the relative efficiency of private firms from the summary statistics in Table 5.1. However Table 5.3 shows that while private firms appear to be relatively more efficient on the **O(u,p,x)**, **A(u,p,x)**, **K(u,x)** and **S(u,x)** measures of efficiency only three out of the five test statistics are significant for each of these measures. On the other two measures the evidence shows three rejections in favour of the alternative hypothesis that public firms are more efficient for $F(u,x)$ – and the null hypothesis is not rejected by any of the five statistics for $C(u,x)$.

We now review the unreported results for the individual firms – the codes refer to the firm listings in Appendix 2.1. The non-US firms perform very well in comparison to the US firms. In particular the eight Japanese utilities (I2-I9) have very high technical efficiency arising from very high comparative thermal efficiencies at Japanese power plants and the very low capital-labour ratios (Shikoku Electric Power has the lowest at 0.9426). The low capital-labour ratios here are the result of contracting out of maintenance jobs to sub-contractors (usually utility company subsidiaries);[17] this tends to make the firms frontier efficient in the technical sense but unreported detailed results suggest that their output to labour ratios are not exceptionally high.

The five publicly owned thermal Australian utilities (M1-M5) perform relatively well within the sample of public utilities with $K(u,x)$, overall technical efficiency, in the range 0.7219 (QEC – Queensland Electricity Commission) to 1.0 (SECWA – State Electricity Commission of Western Australia). Two of these utilities, ECNSW (M1) and QEC (M3), have relatively low fuel costs (<$1m per TBTU compared to $1.5m+ in most US utilities), but seem to have adjusted their input mix in a relatively efficient way in the presence of 'unusual' relative prices. The Danish utility in the sample, Elsam (I1), poses another problem for the technique – joint production of heat via a combined heat and power (CHP) scheme. To count production as equivalent to electric power production would have made Elsam frontier efficient, however as the relative valuation of different outputs is difficult and complicated by large public subsidies to the CHP distribution system the heat production is excluded from the measured thermal power output. Non-inclusion of CHP is to under-represent efficiency because of the inclusion of power station inputs required to deliver heat. The French utility, EdF (M11), performs relatively poorly with $O(u,p,x) = 0.7481$ and $K(u,x) = 0.8983$ – it has the lowest overall efficiency of all of the non-US MUNIs. This is due to the fact that thermal production in France represents a small and declining percentage of production, thermal power plants tend to be used as peaking plant and have low capacity utilization rates. Of the UK utilities, the CEGB (M6) exhibits high overall efficiency, (0.9801) and high overall technical efficiency (0.9941), this results from high capacity utilization and reasonable thermal efficiency. High capacity utilization is, perhaps, a function of underinvestment in new plant and hence declining reserve margins – there had been very little new capacity added in the CEGB since the mid-1970s.[18] All of the technical inefficiency originates in suboptimal scale with the PSF (=16.297) suggesting that for a public firm the

CEGB was 16 times larger than optimal scale. The SSEB (M7) exhibits lower overall and technical efficiency at 0.9183 and 0.9545 respectively due to a lower load factor and lower thermal efficiency. Interestingly, in view of claims to the contrary the CEGB exhibits 100% purely technical and congestion efficiency at its thermal plants. All technical inefficiency at the CEGB's thermal plants originates from suboptimal scale. The CEGB and SSEB also exhibit high allocative efficiency at their thermal plants at 0.9859 and 0.9621 respectively. The major British firms perform very well against the competition in the sample. Looking at the US firms, the most efficient private firms are Duke Power (I15) and Arkansas Power and Light (I27) ($O(u,p,x)$ = 1.0000). Both these firms have high load factors and labour productivity. Duke Power has lower capital and labour productivity than Arkansas Power and Light but higher thermal efficiency.

Allocative and overall efficiency measures need to be viewed with some caution as data availability forced us to measure price of capital using original and not current cost. This introduces a problem: differing age profiles of power stations and differing national inflation rates may distort comparisons of the capital employed to make a firm *appear* to be performing well e.g. relatively inefficient stations in high inflation countries may have artificially low prices of capital and hence appear to be efficiently substituting into (artificially) cheap capital. If the age profiles of the assets of the companies are similar and the inflation rates convergent then problems of asset comparison are unlikely to arise. The problem is essentially that we are comparing historic accounting costs not economic costs. This may increase the allocative efficiency of non-US utilities relative to the US utilities.

Another capital problem centres round the measurement of the quantity of capital. FGL measure capital input using nameplate capacity rating. This is clearly problematic: the capital employed in thermal stations using different fuels (e.g. a coal-fired and a gas-fired station) is not the same per unit of output capacity. The FGL technique also fails to recognize that a lot of the small public firms (mostly single-plant) are constrained by lack of demand from exploiting plant economies of scale, they carry fixed costs but are only connected to the load for a few hours a year. To eliminate this problem one should only compare plants connected to the load for similar time periods; this requires power station level data. Finally, the characteristics of the downstream production process – the electricity transmission and distribution systems – may be significant determinants of generation costs and thus the observation of inefficient low output firms may be a function of high transmission costs to remote consumers.[19]

5.6 A+H Results

As we explained in Section 5.3 the final stage of the implementation of an A+H study involves the estimation of a translog cost function system of three equations: the actual cost equation (5.3.17) and two input share equations (5.3.20). Following A+H we dropped the labour share equation and normalized k_L^r to unity by setting $d_L=1.0$ and $g_L=0.0$ and estimated the system of equations by full information maximum likelihood. We then proceeded to test the efficiency hypotheses using likelihood ratio tests for parameter restrictions[20] – these tests involve χ^2 tests (with degrees of freedom equal to the number of the restrictions) of the null hypothesis that equations incorporating the parameter restrictions cannot be rejected at the 5% significance level.

We began by testing for price (allocative) efficiency with respect to all inputs. For privately owned utilities this involves the restriction:

$$d_K = d_F = 1.0, \tag{5.6.1}$$

and for publicly owned utilities the restriction:

$$d_K + g_K = d_F + g_F = 1.0. \tag{5.6.2}$$

These restrictions are equivalent to restricting the shadow price to be equal to the market price (they set the factor of proportionality equal to 1). Equal price (in)efficiency between the two ownership types is tested for by imposing the restriction $g_K = g_F = 0$. Equal technical efficiency is tested for by the restriction $g_0 = 0$ from eq. (5.3.25).[21] A joint test of equal price and technical efficiency tests the hypothesis of equal cost efficiency. Equal cost efficiency is accepted at the 5% level.[22] This implies that the A+H methodology finds no difference in overall efficiency between the two ownership types. This seems to confirm the results from the FGL methodology in the previous section.

The above finding that public and private firms are equally cost efficient does not indicate whether the firms in the sample are actually price efficient. The test for absolute price efficiency given no overall difference in cost efficiency involves re-estimating the system of equations after incorporating the restrictions $g_0 = 0, g_K = g_F = 0$ and $d_K = d_F = 1.0$. The hypothesis of absolute price efficiency is comfortably accepted at the 5% level.

The final equation system estimated is the cost equation (5.3.17) and the share equations (5.3.20) incorporating the five restrictions tested above. This system represents a simple translog actual cost function system with technology dummies from eq. (5.3.23).[23] The final equation

Table 5.4: The Estimated A+H Cost Function

	Parameter Estimates (standard errors in parentheses)		
α_0	3.4260 (0.6981)**	γ_{KQ}	-0.0164 (0.0054)**
α_Q	0.1385 (0.1500)	γ_{LQ}	-0.0230 (0.0042)**
b_Q	0.0314 (0.0548)	γ_{FQ}	0.0394 (0.0055)**
γ_{QQ}	0.0682 (0.0186)**	γ_{KK}	0.1263 (0.0132)**
α_K	0.8510 (0.0837)**	γ_{LL}	0.0500 (0.0363)
b_K	0.0176 (0.0701)	γ_{FF}	0.1293 (0.0262)**
α_L	0.3982 (0.1282)**	γ_{KL}	-0.0235 (0.0150)
b_L	0.0549 (0.1175)	γ_{KF}	-0.1028 (0.0163)**
α_F	-0.2492 (0.1304)*	γ_{LF}	-0.0265 (0.0285)
b_F	-0.0725 (0.1080)		

** significant at 5%, * significant at 10%

is given in Table 5.4. The generalized R^2 for this equation is 0.99997.[24] There are 19 variables in this equation of which 10 are significant at 5% and a further 1 at 10%.[25]

We conclude that, after allowing for differences in technology, there is no difference in the cost (overall), price (allocative) or technical efficiency of public and private firms.

The finding that absolute as well as relative price efficiency cannot be rejected is different from the result of A+H who were able to reject this hypothesis for their data. A+H then proceeded to test for price efficiency between pairs of inputs. They were able to use their actual cost equation to evaluate the effect of price inefficiency on production costs for each firm. They also examined the effect of price inefficiency on the demand for each input. We do not do this as we found that the hypothesis of absolute price efficiency could not be rejected.

From eq. (5.3.21) and eq. (5.3.22) (with all $k_i = 1$) we can use the estimated equation reported in Table 5.5 to calculate the scale effect for each firm. The unreported firm level results show that scale effects are pervasive – the codes refer to the firm listings in Appendix 2.1.

Twenty-two firms exhibit DRS and 73 firms exhibit IRS. Only six public firms exhibit DRS, and of these only the CEGB (M7) and ENEL (M10) exhibit decreasing returns to scale above 10%. The CEGB has a potential scale economy of 20.6% of actual costs. All other firms exhibit increasing returns to scale. On average private firms have potential scale economies of 4.3% compared to 20.3% for public firms. The results confirm the significant effect of sub-optimally low scale among public firms identified by the results in Section 5.5. Optimal scale appears to be somewhere between 20,000 and 30,000mkWh for IOUs[26] (considering those IOUs with scale economies in the region of 0.0%) with scale inefficiency increasing much more rapidly for each unit of output below this range compared with unit rises in output above this range.

5.7 Conclusions

The results reported in Sections 5.5 and 5.6 indicate that for two very different methodologies there is no significant difference in the productive efficiency of the public and private firms, after appropriate allowance has been made for differences in technology. The results from the FGL analysis show some weak evidence that private firms outperform public firms on allocative and scale efficiency and that this leads in turn to, again weakly supported, outperformance on overall and overall technical efficiency. Public firms have significantly better performance on the congestion measure of efficiency. The A+H results more strongly support the null hypothesis of no difference in performance between the two ownership types. Equal cost (overall), price (allocative) and (technical) efficiency are jointly tested and cannot be rejected.

The results on the presence of scale inefficiency are really very similar across the two techniques. The FGL results suggest average losses due to suboptimal scale are around 2% of total costs for IOUs and around 14% for MUNIs. These figures compare with the A+H estimates of 4% and 20% respectively. The detailed firm level results for both methodologies reveal a long tail of small US MUNIs with substantial scale inefficiencies. Large non-US MUNIs tend to be suboptimally large e.g. CEGB and ENEL. However the methodologies differ sharply on the size of this scale effect: for the ENEL and CEGB, A+H suggest scale losses of 15.0% and 20.6% of average costs while FGL suggests losses of 0.0% and 0.6%. This leads us to suggest that while the methodologies may be used to make general statements about the relative efficiency of IOUs and MUNIs, firm specific measures should be treated with caution.

We note the effects of the allowance for technology differences on both sets of results. This allowance, while appealing on the grounds that we are taking more factors into account, is problematic. It may be that such an allowance masks the general under-performance of even the best MUNIs. This reduces the FGL methodology to a comparison of the distributions of efficiency scores. In subsequent chapters we do not undertake separate *DEA*s on IOUs and MUNIs but analyse pooled samples only. The theoretical justification for this is that all firms do have access to the same technology set: the choice of MUNIs to restrict the choice set, e.g. by investing in a domestic technology which the government prefers, is not something we should allow for in our comparison of relative efficiency – if such behaviour reduces the relative efficiency of MUNIs this is a legitimate cost of the public ownership form and a potential argument for privatization. With respect to this sample, earlier pooled sample *DEA* runs (e.g. Pollitt, 1992) do not change the general results of this chapter. The effect of the technology dummies in the A+H analysis may also mask legitimate differences in costs between IOUs and MUNIs. Attempts to remove the dummy variables led to difficulty in reaching a final estimated equation and hence it was decided to stick with the original A+H equation. In both methodologies adjustments for technology differences lead to differences in optimal scale between IOUs and MUNIs which are not valid if we assume no difference in technology between the two ownership forms.

This chapter confirms the results of both the earlier papers by A+H and FGL. Given scale effects, there is no significant evidence for the superior performance of IOUs over MUNIs. There is strong evidence that substantial economies of scale exist for small single-plant firms. This suggests that many small US MUNIs could be merged. There is weaker evidence that very large utilities such as the CEGB exhibit diseconomies of scale and hence should be divided into several smaller companies. Before either of these observations could become policy recommendations we would need further information on the costs of integrating small isolated systems in the USA and the benefits of vertical integration within a large utility, such as the CEGB. In the absence of significant vertical economies, the finding that optimal scale for a privately owned generation utility lies in the range 20,000 to 30,000mkWh suggests that the thermal part of the CEGB should have been split into 5–10 firms on privatization.

Notes
1. The end of the accounting year is: 31 December, 1986 for the firms from the USA, Italy, France, Denmark, Canada and Ireland; 31 March, 1986 for firms from the UK and Japan; and 30 June, 1986 for Australia.
2. Pollitt (1991) and Pollitt (1993) report results from the FGL methodology for a sample of nuclear power plants.
3. The measurement of the quantity and price of capital in this study is different from that in Pollitt (1991) and Pollitt (1992). In these previous studies the author used historic cost of capital as the measure of quantity and a nominal interest rate adjusted for depreciation as the measure of price. The current study represents a return to the method used in FGL and A+H to handle capital measurement. Early calculations for this study using the FGL methodology suggested that there was little difference in the results generated under the two alternative ways of handling capital.
4. Taken from IEA (1990).
5. Note that the ½s in front of the γ_{QQ} and $\sum\sum\gamma_{ij}$ terms are mistakenly dropped in equations (8) and (9) of A+H (1986), pp.288–9.
6. A+H do not make this relationship specific in their paper, though their results indicate that they have incorporated it.
7. We used the FIML procedure in the TSP package on the Oxford University VAX network to perform the estimation.
8. 24 variables are listed in the full model but there are 6 linear homogeneity restrictions in eq. (5.3.15) and eq. (5.3.23).
9. Note that both the A+H and FGL methodologies do not require information on exchange rates. The A+H methodology imposes linear homogeneity in prices. FGL requires only relative prices to calculate the optimal production point (see Figure 4.1 in Chapter 4). We do convert the prices used in this chapter to US dollars – this is not necessary for the analysis.
10. Three separate programs were used: FARE/MAC1 calculated **O**, **A** and **K**. FARE/MAC2 calculated **F**, **C**, **S** and the likely returns to scale according to FGL; and FMPSF calculated the proximity scale factor measure discussed in Chapter 4.
11. The compiler used was MacFortran V2.4 by Absoft Corporation.
12. 66% of IOUs exhibited DRS and 80% of MUNIs exhibited IRS (FGL., p.97).
13. Only 9 MUNIs (out of 30) produced less than 500mkWh (5 less than 200mkWh) in Fare (p. 105) compared with 19 in this study (15 less than 200mkWh).
14. For example OBS 8 in the FGL data set has output of 14mkWh and the lowest overall efficiency rating of 0.0096 (p.103).
15 .These tests were conducted using the NPAR1WAY procedure in the computer program SAS available on the Oxford University Computing Service VAX network.
16. For more information see Appendix 3.
17. This information was conveyed to the author in communications with

some of the Japanese electric power companies (EPcos). Comparison of Maintenance and Labour costs suggests they are of similar magnitude and hence that the true capital-labour ratio is less than half that suggested by the company accounts.

18. National Power which inherited 30,000MW of CEGB capacity had only just over 2000MW of post 1974 capacity operational in 1991. Source: 'A powerful reckoning' *Financial Times*, 28 January 1991, p.11. PowerGen which inherited 18,000 MW of CEGB capacity had only 3000MW of post 1974 capacity operational in 1991. Source: 'Why price will be the ultimate determinant.' *Financial Times*, 30 January 1991, p.11.

19. See our review of Roberts (1986) in Chapter 3, Section 2.2.

20. These tests involve calculating the test statistic $-2(L_1 - L_2)$ where L_1 is the log likelihood of the restricted system and L_2 is the log likelihood of the unrestricted system.

21. Note this is a test of equal technical (in)efficiency. The formulation of the problem does not allow testing of absolute technical efficiency.

22. We note here the difficulty experienced in estimating an equation system incorporating these restrictions. Convergence was not achieved by the full information maximum likelihood technique but the likelihood ratio was relatively high enough to accept the parameter restrictions.

23. A test of the significance of the technological dummies is not appropriate as differences in technologies need to be modelled in order to provide valid comparison with the results from the A+H (1986) paper and the FGL results in Section 5.5.

24. The generalized R^2 is calculated using the formula in footnote 11 p.292 A+H (1986). The formula is $1 - \exp\{2(L_1 - L_2)/T\}$, where L_1 is the logarithm of the likelihood function when all the constrained variables are set to zero and L_2 is the maximum when the coefficients are included in the model. L_1 is calculated from the reported log likelihood from the first iteration of the full information maximum likelihood with starting values of zero. L_2 is the reported log likelihood from the estimation of the final equation reported above.

25. Regularity conditions for the shadow cost function are that it be monotonically increasing and concave in shadow prices. Montonicity is checked by determining if the calculated values of the shadow cost shares are positive and concavity is checked by observing whether the principal minors of the Hessian matrix have the correct alternating signs (in this case negative-positive-negative). All the shadow cost shares are positive for all but two labour shares. The Hessian reveals that the function is neither concave nor convex as the principal minors are positive-negative-negative in shadow prices.

26. On a smaller sample size, the optimal scale range is 13,000–24,000mkWh for MUNIs.

CHAPTER 6

TECHNICAL EFFICIENCY IN ELECTRIC POWER PLANTS

6.1 Introduction

This chapter seeks to extend the firm level analysis of the previous chapter by analysing the technical productive efficiency of an international sample of electric power plants. The analysis of the previous chapter is extended in four ways. Firstly, efficiency analysis is applied to a new dataset collected from published and unpublished sources. This dataset is drawn from a wider sample than that used in Chapter 5 and contains data from a different year: 1989. Secondly, the analysis of efficiency is tested at the plant rather than the firm level. This extension tests the importance of the nature of the business unit used in the analysis i.e. electric utility versus power plant. Thirdly, three further methodologies are recruited to be used in the analysis to provide extensive 'methodological cross-checking' of the results. Fourthly, regression analysis of the efficiency scores is undertaken in order to attempt to explain the plant level results.

The analysis is conducted using new data from a sample of 768 thermal electric power plants operating in 14 countries in 1989. For the purpose of providing more meaningful comparisons between plants the full sample is further divided into four subsamples on the basis of theoretical load factors (LFs): LF>60%, 60%>LF>30%, 30%>LF>15% and LF<15%. The rationale for these divisions is that they roughly correspond to three shift (base), single and double shift (mid-merit) and peaking plants. This division provides subsamples of 213, 318, 129 and 108 units. In what follows the datasets will be referred to as BASE60, MID60, MID30 and PEAK15 respectively.

Four methodologies are used to analyse the data: ff. Fare et al. (1985a), Aigner and Chu (1968), Afriat (1972) and Aigner, Lovell and Schmidt (1977). These methodologies represent each of the major approaches to productive efficiency: non-parametric programming, parametric programming, deterministic statistical frontier and stochastic frontier: hence *DEA*, *PPA*, *DSA* and *SFM*. This study is the only one we have seen which uses all four of these methodologies on the same dataset. The details of these methodologies were discussed in Chapter 4.

The results confirm the conclusions of Chapter 5 and suggest that the null hypothesis of no difference in technical productive efficiency between public and private firms holds at the plant level. This conclusion is demonstrated to be robust with respect to both load factor and to methodology employed. Plausible results are obtained under all methodologies but the degree of measured plant level inefficiency appears to be substantially lower under the *SFM* approach relative to the other methodologies. The two programming approaches are shown to produce highly correlated plant level efficiency scores as do the two statistical approaches. Regression analysis of the efficiency scores shows that the available data on plant characteristics can explain 40-60% of the variation in plant efficiency scores.

The chapter is in eight sections. Section 6.2 introduces the dataset. Sections 6.3 to 6.6 contain details of the analysis of each of the four datasets in turn. Section 6.7 details the regression/Tobit analysis of the efficiency scores obtained for the BASE60 dataset. Section 6.8 is a conclusion.

6.2 The Dataset

This section describes the nature of the datasets used in the analysis in the following sections of this chapter. The full dataset consists of 768 power plants from the USA (606), Denmark (2), Germany (4), Japan (24), Taiwan (7), Australia (20), Canada (20), Hong Kong (1), Ireland (6), Greece (8), New Zealand (3), South Africa (13), Thailand (6) and the UK (48) operating during the accounting year ending in 1989. Together these power plants produced around 40% of the world output of electricity generated in thermal[1] power stations in 1989. The sample plants are listed in Appendix 2.2. The dataset consists of information on four variables for each plant: output and three inputs – capital (or capacity), labour and fuel. We also have information on the ownership (C=COOP, I=IOU, M=MUNI), location, fuel type, load factors and single factor efficiency measures of the sample plants. This provides the raw data for the calculation of efficiency scores in each of the four methodologies employed for measuring productive efficiency. Additional data on plant age is used in the regression/Tobit analysis of the BASE60 dataset in Section 6.7.

The data are collected from a number of sources. The US data are collected from a database compiled from US Energy Information Agency source material. Data for Germany, Thailand, Taiwan and the UK were kindly supplied by London Economics[2] from industry sources; Japanese data were supplied by the Japan Electric Power Information Centre (JEPIC)[3] and the electric power companies themselves. Other non-US data were collected from company accounts and from communications with the companies. Output is measured in millions of kWh produced in the accounting year 1989. Capital is measured in MW of nameplate (gross) capacity, labour is measured as the number of employees employed at the power station site and fuel is measured in TBTU (BTU*10^{12}). The age of the 213 base plants is measured in years since average commissioning date of generator units. A more detailed account of the data is contained in Appendix 1.2.

The full dataset is divided into the four subsamples (subsample plants are listed in Appendix 2.2) on the basis of theoretical load factor (LF). The theoretical load factor is the ratio of actual output produced to the maximum output of electricity that a plant could produce if it were to be operated continually at maximum capacity. It is calculated as follows:[4]

$$LF = \frac{Y}{K \times 8.76}$$

$Y = output \left(millions\ of\ kWh\right)$

$K = nameplate\ capacity\ (MW)$

None of the power stations in our sample could be expected to have a load factor of 100% as we use figures for net output which includes station losses. The highest load factor we report is 92.2%.[5] In theory LF is heavily correlated with productive efficiency: it measures the efficiency with which capital is being used at a power plant and plants with low load factors may demonstrate lower fuel efficiency as a result of more fuel intensive start-ups relative to plants being operated continuously. However low load factors may be the result of poor availability (due to unplanned outages[6]) or low efficiency causing other plants connected to the electricity grid to be called on to supply power instead of the inefficient plant. Of course, measured LF may be low because of major repair work on the boilers or generators at a plant: we recognize this but have no access to information on planned outages; we assume these outages are stochastic and that in a large sample they will not bias efficiency comparisons between ownership types.

It would therefore seem to be invalid to compare the productive efficiency of plants with very different load factors. Thus we divide the data into four subsamples on the basis of measured LF. If the highest measured LF in the full sample is 92.2% and this plant is a three shift base plant then subdivisions at 30% and 60% might correspond to the maximum LF one and two shift plants respectively. A further division is introduced at 15% below which genuine peak load only plants might be thought to operate. Thus we generate four data subsets: BASE 60, MID60, MID30 and PEAK15. Table 6.1 gives more details of these datasets. While the division of the full dataset is fairly arbitrary, the BASE60 dataset contains genuine base load plants and provides a robust dataset on which further analysis (regression and Tobit) can be conducted.

Table 6.1: Plant Data Subset Characteristics

	PEAK15	*MID30*	*MID60*	*BASE60*
USA	87	107	254	158
Canada	2	5	7	6
Denmark	1	0	1	0
Germany	0	0	0	4
Hong Kong	0	0	0	1
Japan	2	6	9	7
Taiwan	0	0	2	5
Australia	0	2	14	4
Greece	1	0	4	3
Ireland	1	1	3	1
New Zealand	1	1	1	0
South Africa	1	2	6	4
Thailand	0	0	0	6
UK	12	5	17	14
Total COOPs	3	2	17	11
Total IOUs	62	92	220	148
Total MUNIs	43	35	81	54
Totals	108	129	318	213

6.3 Analysis of the PEAK15 Dataset

The summary results for the four methodologies – *DEA, PPA, DSA* and *SFM* – are recorded in Table 6.2 for the PEAK15 analysis. Summary results are reported for the total number of firms as well as for COOPs, IOUs and MUNIs separately. IOUs outperform MUNIs on average in all but one of the seven reported efficiency measures. The COOPs perform well but as their scores refer to only three plants we will not discuss their performance in what follows in this section.

Looking at the *DEA* averages the divergence between the overall technical efficiency scores is matched by the divergence in scale efficiency scores suggesting that the results may be influenced by small peak load plants in the USA connected to isolated systems.

Table 6.2: Summary Results for PEAK15

	K(u,x) DEA	F(u,x) DEA	C(u,x) DEA	S(u,x) DEA	K(u,x) PPA	K(u,x) DSA	K(u,x) SFM
AV TOTAL	0.7759	0.8577	0.9709	0.9360	0.7790	0.7490	0.8790
AV COOP	0.8349	0.9087	0.9833	0.9331	0.8167	0.8092	0.9381
AV PRIVATE	0.7933	0.8617	0.9674	0.9536	0.7955	0.7571	0.8899
AV PUBLIC	0.7465	0.8484	0.9749	0.9107	0.7527	0.7330	0.8591
SD COOP	0.1071	0.0815	0.0150	0.0647	0.0695	0.0363	0.0553
SD PRIVATE	0.1233	0.1123	0.0572	0.0766	0.1009	0.0920	0.0840
SD PUBLIC	0.1485	0.1500	0.0420	0.1240	0.1363	0.1083	0.1039
MAX COOP	0.9213	0.9963	0.9959	0.9828	0.8968	0.8510	0.9989
MAX PRIVATE	1.0000	1.0000	1.0000	1.0000	1.0000	1.0000	1.0000
MAX PUBLIC	1.0000	1.0000	1.0000	1.0000	1.0000	0.9768	1.0000
MIN COOP	0.7151	0.8350	0.9667	0.8600	0.7726	0.7851	0.8909
MIN PRIVATE	0.4390	0.6219	0.6704	0.5303	0.4608	0.5050	0.6164
MIN PUBLIC	0.4832	0.5240	0.7889	0.5169	0.5218	0.5399	0.6397
MED COOP	0.8683	0.8949	0.9873	0.9565	0.7807	0.7915	0.9244
MED PRIVATE	0.7810	0.8818	0.9882	0.9842	0.7987	0.7572	0.9016
MED PUBLIC	0.7473	0.8682	0.9944	0.9601	0.7529	0.7313	0.8687

The *DEA*, *PPA* and *DSA* average scores look very similar with **K(u,x)** averages of 77.59%, 77.90% and 74.90%. The two programming approaches – *PPA* and *DEA* – produce very similar results, as expected: average efficiency scores are within 0.5% for the total, IOUs and MUNIs. The correlation matrix in Table 6.3 shows a high correlation[7] between the *DEA* and *PPA* results and between the *SFM* and *DSA* results. In Table 6.2 we also observe a large divergence between the three non-stochastic methodology results and the *SFM* results. The average efficiency under the *SFM* measure being around 10% higher. This is what we would expect: a large part of measured inefficiency under the non-stochastic approaches is attributed to shocks and statistical noise by the stochastic approach.

Table 6.4 indicates that scale inefficiency is pervasive as measured by the Fare RTS method. 97 out of 108 plants exhibit increasing returns

Table 6.3: Correlation Table: PEAK15

	DEA	PPA	DSA	SFM
DEA	1.0000			
PPA	0.8525	1.0000		
DSA	0.5724	0.8349	1.0000	
SFM	0.6421	0.8757	0.9586	1.0000

Table 6.4: Fare Returns to Scale: PEAK15

	Likely DRS	*Likely CRS*	*Likely IRS*
Total	6	5	97
COOPs	0	0	3
IOUs	2	4	56
MUNIs	4	1	38

to scale. This is not a surprising result as all the plants are operating at very low load factors.

Table 6.5 lists a battery of one-tailed statistical tests on the efficiency measures. For the purposes of these tests the co-operatives are dropped. The null hypothesis is that there is no difference in efficiency between publicly owned and privately owned electric utilities. The tests are the same as those used in the previous chapter. The results in Table 6.3 are fairly conclusive: all four of the overall technical efficiency measures indicate that the null hypothesis of equal efficiency cannot be rejected. 20 out of 20 tests on the measures of **K(u,x)** fail to reject the null hypothesis. Looking at the detailed *DEA* results for **F(u,x)**, **C(u,x)** and **S(u,x)**: four out of five statistics indicate rejection of the null for **S(u,x)** in favour of the alternative hypothesis that privately owned firms are

Table 6.5: Summary of Tests of the Effect of Ownership on Efficiency – IOUs vs. MUNIs: PEAK15 (62 IOUs, 43 MUNIs).

Efficiency Measure	Analysis of Variance F $(Prob>F)$	Kruskal-Wallis χ^2 $(Prob>\chi^2)$	Median Scores (points above median) χ^2 $(Prob>\chi^2)$	Van der Waerden (1-way) χ^2 $(Prob>\chi^2)$	Savage (exponential) χ^2 $(Prob>\chi^2)$
K(u,x) DEA	3.091 (0.0817)	2.6969 (0.1005)	0.8221 (0.3646)	3.2334 (0.0721)	1.4136 (0.2345)
F(u,x) DEA	0.269 (0.6051)	0.0598 (0.8068)	0.2618 (0.6089)	0.248 (0.6185)	0.3036 (0.5816)
C(u,x) DEA	0.538 (0.4651)	0.8002 (0.371)	1.1416 (0.2853)	0.8893 (0.3598)	0.9866 (0.3206)
S(u,x) DEA	4.807 (0.0306)	4.8089 (0.0283)	4.3757 (0.0365)	4.8485 (0.0277)	3.1806 (0.0745)
K(u,x) PPA	3.427 (0.067)	3.401 (0.0652)	2.879 (0.0897)	2.941 (0.0864)	0.148 (0.7004)
K(u,x) DSA	1.502 (0.2231)	1.8726 (0.1712)	2.879 (0.0897)	1.7272 (0.1888)	0.4637 (0.4959)
K(u,x) SFM	2.802 (0.0972)	2.231 (0.1353)	.4.3757 (0.0365)	1.9007 (0.168)	0.2249 (0.6354)

more efficient while the five statistics for $\mathbf{C(u,x)}$ test the null against the alternative hypothesis that publicly owned firms are more efficient.

We now look at the unreported detailed plant level results: the codes refer to the plant listings in Appendix 2.2.1. The firms that demonstrate high efficiency scores tend to be those with high load factors, though a frontier efficient firm, Lavrio (M8, PPC of Greece) has a load factor of less than 1%.[8] The *DEA* measures report that five plants are 100% efficient. The *PPA* measures are generated from a translog frontier estimated to have four non-zero coefficients and hence four plants which are frontier efficient.[9] The *DSA* measures are calculated on the most efficient outlier and so only one plant is frontier efficient. The *SFM* measures indicate that 13 plants are frontier efficient. Of the efficient plants the two Japanese plants, the Greek plant and two US plants are efficient on two of the efficiency measures: Kudamatsu (I18, Chugoku Electric Power) is efficient on the *DEA* and *SFM* measures; Toyama Shinko (I19, Hokuriku Electric Power) is efficient on the *DEA* and *DSA* measures; Lavrio (M8, PPC of Greece) is efficient on the *DEA* and *PPA* measures; Blackstone Street (I30, Cambridge Electric Light) is efficient on the *DSA* and *SFM* measures; and Canaday 1 (M20, Central Nebraska Public Power) is efficient on the *PPA* and *SFM* measures. Looking at the single factor efficiency measures for these efficient plants: the Japanese plants have high fuel and capital efficiency; the Greek plant has the highest fuel efficiency of any plant in the sample; Canaday 1 performs well on all three of the single factor efficiency measures; the surprise result is Blackstone Street, a plant which does not perform well on any of the single factor efficiency measures. The statistical approaches could give rise to frontier firms which are difficult to justify as the position of the frontier is equally determined by efficient and inefficient outliers: the programming frontiers are only affected by efficient (not inefficient) outliers. No plant is efficient on three or more of the measures. The two other efficient plants on the *DEA* measure perform above averagely well on the *PPA* measures but below average on the *SFM* and *DSA* measures: Saguaro (I4, Arizona Public Service Company) has an un-usually low number of employees (high labour productivity) as does Wilkes (I54, Southwestern Electric Power Company). Most of the other plants that are efficient on the non-*DEA* measures are plausibly so, however 4 of the 13 plants that are efficient on the *SFM* measure do not perform notably well on any of the single factor efficiency measures: Arsenal Hill 5 (I28, Southwestern Electric Power), Blackstone Street (I30, Cambridge Electric and Light), J.D. Kennedy (M7, Jacksonville Electric Authority) and Coffeyville (M11, Coffeyville Municipal Light). In general the detailed results indicate the weaknesses of both the programming and statistical approaches: programming approaches give too much weight to efficient outliers and the statistical approaches can give rise to apparently inefficient firms appearing on the frontier.

6.4 Analysis of the MID30 Dataset

The summary results for the analysis of the 129 plants in the MID30 dataset are recorded in Table 6.6. The summary results indicate a similar pattern to that noted in the last section. Privately owned plants outperform publicly owned plants on all of the efficiency measures, though it is very close for the $C(u,x)$ measure. The two co-operatives in the sample do notably less well than the average.

Table 6.6 suggests that average efficiency for the plants in the MID30 dataset is higher than for those in the PEAK15 dataset, the lowest average for $K(u,x)$ being 82.65%, under the *PPA* measure. The stochastic method has the highest average efficiency and this is 3.60% above the next highest average for *DEA*. Although the average for IOUs is higher than for MUNIs, for all seven measures of efficiency, the medians are much closer: the $F(u,x)$, $C(u,x)$, *SFM* and *DSA* medians are actually higher for MUNIs than for IOUs. The standard deviation is higher for MUNIs than for IOUs in all seven measures suggesting the best public plants may be just as efficient as the best private plants.

Table 6.6: Summary Results for MID30

	$K(u,x)$ DEA	$F(u,x)$ DEA	$C(u,x)$ DEA	$S(u,x)$ DEA	$K(u,x)$ PPA	$K(u,x)$ DSA	$K(u,x)$ SFM
AV TOTAL	0.8626	0.9282	0.9781	0.9514	0.8265	0.8390	0.8985
AV COOP	0.6789	0.8781	0.9866	0.7805	0.6746	0.7730	0.8262
AV PRIVATE	0.8780	0.9303	0.9782	0.9653	0.8465	0.8416	0.9045
AV PUBLIC	0.8326	0.9254	0.9772	0.9247	0.7827	0.8359	0.8872
SD COOP	0.1694	0.0567	0.0190	0.1603	0.1568	0.0828	0.1170
SD PRIVATE	0.0865	0.0785	0.0379	0.0433	0.0942	0.0713	0.0712
SD PUBLIC	0.1284	0.0922	0.0513	0.1193	0.1303	0.0782	0.0842
MAX COOP	0.7987	0.9182	1.0000	0.8938	0.7855	0.8315	0.9089
MAX PRIVATE	1.0000	1.0000	1.0000	1.0000	1.0000	1.0000	1.0000
MAX PUBLIC	1.0000	1.0000	1.0000	1.0000	1.0000	0.9703	1.0000
MIN COOP	0.5591	0.8380	0.9732	0.6671	0.5637	0.7144	0.7435
MIN PRIVATE	0.5295	0.5944	0.8371	0.7831	0.4733	0.5478	0.5783
MIN PUBLIC	0.5519	0.7156	0.7933	0.5519	0.5635	0.6944	0.7258
MED COOP	0.6789	0.8781	0.9866	0.7805	0.6746	0.7730	0.8262
MED PRIVATE	0.8767	0.9453	0.9958	0.9842	0.8501	0.8425	0.9062
MED PUBLIC	0.8618	0.9620	0.9970	0.9746	0.7898	0.8525	0.9125

The **S(u,x)** measure under *DEA* suggest that much of the measured divergence between average public and private plants may be due to scale inefficiency.

Table 6.7: Correlation Table: MID30

	DEA	PPA	DSA	SFM
DEA	1.0000			
PPA	0.8696	1.0000		
DSA	0.6470	0.6069	1.0000	
SFM	0.7808	0.7200	0.9476	1.0000

The correlation matrix in Table 6.7 reveals the high correlation between the efficiency scores under the two programming methodologies (0.8696) and also a very high correlation between the *SFM* and *DSA* measures (0.9476). The correlation between the programming and statistical methodologies is substantially less than that within methodological class correlations: this suggests that the two broad approaches do yield differing results.

Table 6.8: Fare Returns to Scale: MID30

	Likely DRS	Likely CRS	Likely IRS
Total	21	13	95
COOPs	0	0	2
IOUs	17	10	65
MUNIs	4	3	28

Table 6.8 suggests that increasing returns to scale is pervasive among power plants in this sample, though it is more marked among publicly owned plants: 80% of MUNIs exhibit IRS against 71% of IOUs. We note that the percentage of plants exhibiting IRS in the MID30 sample is much less than the percentage in the PEAK15 dataset (74% against 90%). As load factors increase, and capital is used more efficiently, we would expect the percentage of plants operating in the range of increasing returns to scale to fall.

Table 6.9 reports a battery of one-tailed statistical tests on the efficiency measures; once again we exclude co-operatives from this analysis. The null hypothesis is that there is no difference in efficiency between the two ownership types. The results suggest a general inability to reject the null hypothesis. There is no significant difference in

Table 6.9: Summary of Tests of the Effect of Ownership on Efficiency – IOUs vs. MUNIs: MID30 (92 IOUs, 35 MUNIs).

Efficiency Measure	Analysis of Variance F (Prob>F)	Kruskal-Wallis χ^2 (Prob>χ^2)	Median Scores (points above median) χ^2 (Prob>χ^2)	Van der Waerden (1-way) χ^2 (Prob>χ^2)	Savage (exponential) χ^2 (Prob>χ^2)
$K(u,x)$ DEA	5.264 (0.0234)	2.2509 (0.1335)	0.8735 (0.35)	3.2509 (0.0714)	0.7824 (0.3764)
$F(u,x)$ DEA	0.089 (0.7656)	0.0027 (0.9584)	0.4199 (0.517)	0.032 (0.8581)	0.0006 (0.9802)
$C(u,x)$ DEA	0.016 (0.9002)	0.38 (0.5376)	0.0637 (0.8008)	0.1728 (0.6777)	0.3176 (0.5731)
$S(u,x)$ DEA	7.978 (0.0055)	1.2854 (0.2569)	1.7695 (0.1834)	2.1038 (0.1469)	0.5253 (0.4686)
$K(u,x)$ PPA	9.329 (0.0028)	6.1342 (0.0133)	2.9786 (0.0844)	6.836 (0.0089)	2.144 (0.1431)
$K(u,x)$ DSA	0.154 (0.6952)	0.0111 (0.9162)	0.0637 (0.8008)	0.1807 (0.6707)	0.0164 (0.8981)
$K(u,x)$ SFM	1.35 (0.2475)	0.7132 (0.3984)	0.0637 (0.8008)	1.246 (0.2643)	0.3947 (0.5298)

efficiency between the two ownership types. Twenty tests are performed on the four measures of $K(u,x)$: the null is rejected four times at the 5% level, three of the rejections are by the *PPA* measure. The detailed *DEA* measures surprisingly yield only one rejection on the ANOVA statistic for $S(u,x)$: this probably reflects the fact that the median efficiency scores for $S(u,x)$ are much closer than the average efficiency scores.

We now turn to the unreported plant level efficiency scores – the codes refer to the plant listings in Appendix 2.2.2. We find that efficient plants tend to be those with high load factors. The *DEA* measure of $K(u,x)$ shows that nine plants are 100% efficient compared with four under *PPA*,[10] 1 under *DSA* and 7 under *SFM*. A Japanese plant, Shiriuchi (I33, Hokkaido Electric Power) is 100% efficient under the *DEA*, *PPA*, *DSA* and *SFM* measures. Robinson 1 (I78, Carolina Power and Light) is efficient on the *DEA*, *PPA* and *SFM* measures of $K(u,x)$. A further two plants are fully efficient on two of the measures: Akita (I37, Tohoku Electric Power, Japan) and Peterhead (M33, Hydro Electric, UK) are both efficient on the *PPA* and *DEA* measures. The above four plants have high fuel efficiencies and high load factors. A suspicious data point is the very low fuel efficiency at Estevan (M9, SaskPower, Canada) which is substantially below the average. In spite of this the plant has a high subsample load factor of 28.5%: this may reflect the very low cost of coal facing SaskPower.[11] The results for the five UK plants in the sample are generally good: the high load factor plants – Peterhead (M33, Hydro Electric), Ferrybridge B (M31, CEGB) and Tilbury (M32, CEGB) – show efficiencies in excess of 93% on all four measures; Fawley (M29, CEGB) with a load factor of just 16.7% has efficiencies scores around the average for each of the four measures; only Meaford (M30, CEGB) with a load factor of 17.0% performs substantially below average.

6.5 Analysis of the MID60 Dataset

The MID60 dataset is the largest dataset we analyse in this book; it contains 318 power plants. The summary results for the four methodologies are given in Table 6.10. The results show a similar pattern to the results reported in Sections 6.3 and 6.4: privately owned plants outperform publicly owned plants on six of the efficiency measures (not the *DSA* measure) but the difference between averages is well within one standard deviation. The *SFM* average efficiency measure again indicates substantially lower inefficiency than under the other three measures.

Table 6.10:   Summary Results for MID60

	$K(u,x)$ *DEA*	$F(u,x)$ *DEA*	$C(u,x)$ *DEA*	$S(u,x)$ *DEA*	$K(u,x)$ *PPA*	$K(u,x)$ *DSA*	$K(u,x)$ *SFM*
AV TOTAL	0.8838	0.9126	0.9879	0.9805	0.8621	0.7743	0.9425
AV COOP	0.8672	0.9011	0.9991	0.9645	0.8560	0.7767	0.9447
AV PRIVATE	0.8893	0.9136	0.9909	0.9825	0.8670	0.7726	0.9431
AV PUBLIC	0.8729	0.9126	0.9777	0.9786	0.8505	0.7780	0.9403
SD COOP	0.0687	0.0715	0.0023	0.0494	0.0642	0.0602	0.0514
SD PRIVATE	0.0704	0.0626	0.0219	0.0347	0.0701	0.0497	0.0457
SD PUBLIC	0.0819	0.0725	0.0373	0.0381	0.0846	0.0646	0.0526
MAX COOP	0.9581	1.0000	1.0000	1.0000	0.9410	0.8746	1.0000
MAX PRIVATE	1.0000	1.0000	1.0000	1.0000	0.9970	0.9124	1.0000
MAX PUBLIC	1.0000	1.0000	1.0000	1.0000	1.0000	1.0000	1.0000
MIN COOP	0.7290	0.7768	0.9920	0.8132	0.7342	0.6683	0.8496
MIN PRIVATE	0.6210	0.7546	0.8356	0.6210	0.4961	0.5647	0.6741
MIN PUBLIC	0.6266	0.7291	0.8087	0.8066	0.5302	0.6212	0.7848
MED COOP	0.8542	0.9179	1.0000	0.9894	0.8526	0.7815	0.9573
MED PRIVATE	0.8958	0.9148	0.9985	0.9937	0.8788	0.7741	0.9510
MED PUBLIC	0.8700	0.9182	0.9921	0.9930	0.8559	0.7758	0.9449

The 17 co-operatively owned plants in the sample perform very well against the other ownership types. On average the COOPs outperform MUNIs on two of the four measures of **K(u,x)** and outperform the IOUs on the *SFM* measure. Comparing MUNIs and IOUs the averages and the medians are very close for *DSA* measure of **K(u,x)**, **F(u,x)**, **C(u,x)** and **S(u,x)**. The largest of the divergences on the detailed *DEA* measures is in **C(u,x)** rather than in **S(u,x)**: indeed the median **S(u,x)** is higher for MUNIs than for IOUs. This suggests that operating on backward bending sections of the isoquant rather than at inefficient scale *per se* is the likely cause of differences in **K(u,x)** between the two ownership types. The most efficient plant under the *DSA* measure (which generates only one efficient plant) is a publicly owned firm. The *PPA* and *DEA* results again show very similar summary statistics, while the *DSA* averages are substantially below the figures for the programming approaches. The correlations in Table 6.11 indicate high correlation between *DEA* and *PPA* and between *DSA* and *SFM*.

Table 6.11: Correlation Table: MID 60

	DEA	*PPA*	*DSA*	*SFM*
DEA	1.0000			
PPA	0.8196	1.0000		
DSA	0.7499	0.7621	1.0000	
SFM	0.8007	0.8517	0.9357	1.0000

Table 6.12 reports the Fare measures of returns to scale. Increasing returns is much less common (57%) than in the two previous samples. There is a difference in the figure for MUNIs (46%) and that for IOUs (57%). Median scale efficiency scores are very high: 99.37% and 99.30% for IOUs and MUNIs respectively.

Table 6.13 contains the battery of one-tailed statistical tests on the efficiency measures. We drop the 17 co-operative plants from the statistical analysis as they are all US plants and their ownership form

Table 6.12: Fare Returns to Scale: MID60

	Likely DRS	*Likely CRS*	*Likely IRS*
Total	119	21	178
COOPs	2	2	13
IOUs	79	14	125
MUNIs	38	5	40

finds no parallel in the rest of the countries in the sample. The null hypothesis is that there is no difference in efficiency between privately owned and publicly owned electric utilities. The results indicate that in general we cannot reject the null hypothesis. Twenty out of 20 tests performed on the 4 **K(u,x)** measures indicate that it is not possible to reject the null hypothesis at the 5% significance level. The detailed *DEA* measures show that all five tests on **C(u,x)** do reject the null hypothesis confirming the significance of the difference in average efficiencies noted in Table 6.10.

We turn now to the unreported plant level results – the codes refer to the plant listings in Appendix 2.2.3. 11 plants are 100% efficient on the *DEA* measure of **K(u,x)**, 4 are efficient on the *PPA* measure[12] and 37 are efficient on the *SFM* measure. Three power stations are efficient on three of the measures of **K(u,x)**: Coleson Cove (M21, New Brunswick) and North Wall (M27, ESB) are frontier efficient on the *DEA*, *PPA* and *SFM* measures; Marina (M28, ESB) is frontier efficient on the *PPA*, *DSA* and *SFM* measures. Five other plants are 100% efficient on two of the measures of **K(u,x)**: Coleman (I91, Big Rivers Electric), Marshall (I126, Duke Power), Bay Shore (I156, Toledo Edison) and AM Williams (I172, South Carolina Generating) are efficient on the *DEA* and *SFM* measures; Dalhousie (M22, New Brunswick) is efficient on the *PPA* and *SFM* measures. Coleson Cove, Marina and

Table 6.13:   Summary of Tests of the Effect of Ownership on Efficiency: IOUs vs. MUNIs: MID60 (218 IOUs and 83 MUNIs).

Efficiency Measure	Analysis of Variance	Kruskal-Wallis	Median Scores (points above median)	Van der Waerden (1-way)	Savage (exponential)
	F ($Prob > F$)	χ^2 ($Prob > \chi^2$)	χ^2 ($Prob > \chi^2$)	χ^2 ($Prob > \chi^2$)	χ^2 ($Prob > \chi^2$)
K(u,x) DEA	2.948 (0.087)	2.6986 (0.1004)	2.6845 (0.1013)	2.4493 (0.1176)	0.741 (0.3893)
F(u,x) DEA	0.014 (0.9067)	0.0214 (0.8837)	0.1779 (0.6732)	0.0153 (0.9014)	0.9947 (0.3186)
C(u,x) DEA	14.333 (0.0002)	16.24 (0.0001)	7.1211 (0.0076)	17.333 (0.0001)	11.441 (0.0007)
S(u,x) DEA	0.7 (0.4034)	0.1753 (0.6754)	0.0783 (0.7796)	0.4065 (0.5238)	0.1581 (0.691)
K(u,x) PPA	2.953 (0.0867)	2.9068 (0.0882)	1.9069 (0.1673)	1.8538 (0.1733)	0.0033 (0.9545)
K(u,x) DSA	0.584 (0.4453)	0.2016 (0.6534)	0.027 (0.8695)	0.2887 (0.5911)	2.2218 (0.1361)
K(u,x) SFM	0.214 (0.6443)	0.0163 (0.8985)	0.3701 (0.543)	0.0059 (0.9387)	0.7471 (0.3874)

North Wall are both publicly owned and have high fuel efficiencies: Coleson Cove has a high load factor (57.03%); North Wall and Marina have the highest energy efficiencies in the sample. AM Williams and Dalhousie have high load factors and fuel efficiencies. Coleman and Bay Shore have load factors of very nearly 60%. Only two of the 37 frontier efficient plants under the *SFM* measure perform poorly on the other measures: Joslin 1 (I178, Central Power and Light) and New Ulm (M41, New Ulm Public Utility). The performance of UK plants is about average. The high load factor plants produce good efficiency scores: Agecroft [M78] (load factor = 57.4%) and Blyth B [M79] (load factor=58.61%) are on the frontier for the *SFM* measure.

6.6 Analysis of the BASE60 Dataset

The BASE60 dataset provides the best comparison of performance as it only contains base load plant and does not contain plant being operated at significantly below normal capacity due to planned or forced outages. The possibility exists of some of the plant in the previous three datasets used in this chapter being unfairly placed in lower load factor classes: this gives rise to the possibility that frontier efficient plant in the PEAK15 dataset may normally be run as baseload plant. We have no data on classifications of plant in order to detect this phenomenon and even if we had it is not clear why we would proceed differently.[13] The summary results for the 213 base load plants in BASE60 are given in Table 6.14. The summary results are much closer for public and private plants than for the previous three datasets analysed in this chapter. However MUNIs outperform IOUs on three out of the seven measures of *average* technical efficiency and on five out of seven measures of *median* efficiency.

The 11 co-operatively owned plants perform well. MUNIs average efficiency is within 1% on all four measures of $K(u,x)$. The standard deviation is higher for MUNIs than for IOUs indicating again the larger spread of efficiency scores for publicly owned plants: we can observe this in the previous analysis sections. The overall averages for the *DEA* and *PPA* measures of $K(u,x)$ are close (88.63% and 87.69%) and significantly lower than the average for *SFM* (95.27%). The median measure of *SFM* is very high (96.18%) which indicates very little variation in relative inefficiency.

The correlations in Table 6.15 indicate very high cross efficiency correlations: the lowest correlation coefficient is 79.16% (this compares with 74.99%, 60.69% and 57.24% for MID60, MID30 and PEAK15 respectively). Interestingly the *DEA* and *PPA* measures are relatively

Table 6.14: Summary Results for BASE60

	K(u,x) DEA	F(u,x) DEA	C(u,x) DEA	S(u,x) DEA	K(u,x) PPA	K(u,x) DSA	K(u,x) SFM
AV TOTAL	0.8863	0.9135	0.9905	0.9803	0.8769	0.8297	0.9527
AV COOP	0.8694	0.8827	0.9996	0.9854	0.8775	0.8263	0.9521
AV PRIVATE	0.8868	0.9135	0.9941	0.9771	0.8784	0.8299	0.9531
AV PUBLIC	0.8885	0.9191	0.9802	0.9870	0.8733	0.8299	0.9520
SD COOP	0.0368	0.0342	0.0009	0.0146	0.0390	0.0398	0.0309
SD PRIVATE	0.0628	0.0594	0.0210	0.0381	0.0661	0.0504	0.0360
SD PUBLIC	0.0781	0.0738	0.0431	0.0260	0.0838	0.0669	0.0526
MAX COOP	0.9262	0.9543	1.0000	0.9994	0.9588	0.8879	1.0000
MAX PRIVATE	1.0000	1.0000	1.0000	1.0000	1.0000	1.0000	1.0000
MAX PUBLIC	1.0000	1.0000	1.0000	1.0000	1.0000	0.9649	1.0000
MIN COOP	0.7969	0.8342	0.9972	0.9554	0.8162	0.7649	0.9056
MIN PRIVATE	0.6898	0.7659	0.8325	0.7536	0.6427	0.7213	0.8583
MIN PUBLIC	0.6797	0.7084	0.7508	0.8451	0.5937	0.6732	0.8063
MED COOP	0.8605	0.8837	1.0000	0.9930	0.8860	0.8202	0.9464
MED PRIVATE	0.8890	0.9132	1.0000	0.9902	0.8897	0.8302	0.9594
MED PUBLIC	0.9063	0.9335	0.9978	0.9963	0.8886	0.8348	0.9655

Table 6.15: Correlation Table: BASE60

	DEA	PPA	DSA	SFM
DEA	1.0000			
PPA	0.7916	1.0000		
DSA	0.8346	0.7924	1.0000	
SFM	0.8682	0.8478	0.9486	1.0000

Table 6.16: Fare Returns to Scale: BASE 60

	Likely DRS	Likely CRS	Likely IRS
Total	75	11	127
COOPs	4	0	7
IOUs	49	7	87
MUNIs	22	4	33

poorly correlated for this dataset compared with the correlations for the previous three datasets.

Table 6.16 indicates that 60% of plants in the BASE60 sample still exhibit increasing returns to scale. This suggests that returns to scale are not exhausted for the majority of base load plants. There is not a large difference in the returns to scale profile of IOUs (IRS=61%) and MUNIs (IRS=56%).

Table 6.17 lists the battery of one tailed tests on the efficiency of IOUs and MUNIs. The null hypothesis is that there is no difference in efficiency between the two ownership types: a figure of less than 0.05 indicates rejection of the null at the 5% level of significance. The results for **K(u,x)** indicate conclusive inability to reject the null hypothesis. Twenty out of 20 tests on **K(u,x)** indicate that public and private plants are equally efficient: only one of the tests yields a type 2 error probability of less than 28%. For the **K(u,x)** *DEA*, *DSA* and *SFM* measures the alternative hypothesis (on all but the ANOVA test for *SFM*) is that public plants are more efficient than private plants. The tests on the detailed *DEA* measures indicate conflicting results: the **C(u,x)** tests reject the null in favour of the alternative hypothesis that IOUs are more efficient than MUNIs; both **F(u,x)** and **S(u,x)** test the null against the alternative hypothesis that MUNIs are more efficient than IOUs, two of the tests on **S(u,x)** indicate rejection of the null in favour of this alternative hypothesis.

We now consider the unreported plant level results – the codes refer to the plant listings in Appendix 2.2.4. The *DEA* measure of **K(u,x)** indicates that five plants are frontier efficient. The *PPA* methodology estimates a Cobb-Douglas frontier[14] and four frontier efficient plants.

Table 6.17: Summary of Tests of the Effect of Ownership on Efficiency – IOUs vs. MUNIs: BASE60 (143 IOUs, 59 MUNIs).

Efficiency Measure	Analysis of Variance F $(Prob>F)$	Kruskal-Wallis χ^2 $(Prob>\chi^2)$	Median Scores (points above median) χ^2 $(Prob>\chi^2)$	Van der Waerden (1-way) χ^2 $(Prob>\chi^2)$	Savage (exponential) χ^2 $(Prob>\chi^2)$
K(u,x) DEA	0.027 (0.8687)	0.616 (0.4325)	1.1674 (0.2799)	0.2883 (0.5913)	0.9317 (0.3344)
F(u,x) DEA	0.322 (0.5713)	1.5153 (0.2183)	1.9297 (0.1648)	0.7023 (0.402)	1.857 (0.173)
C(u,x) DEA	9.518 (0.0023)	22.399 (0.0001)	19.239 (0.0001)	22.711 (0.0001)	21.547 (0.0001)
S(u,x) DEA	3.352 (0.0686)	4.6665 (0.0308)	2.8827 (0.0895)	4.3861 (0.0362)	2.5014 (0.1137)
K(u,x) PPA	0.21 (0.6473)	0.0051 (0.943)	0.0238 (0.8773)	0.0067 (0.9346)	0.1942 (0.6595)
K(u,x) DSA	0 (0.9933)	0.4309 (0.5115)	0.2144 (0.6433)	0.0677 (0.7948)	0.9223 (0.3369)
K(u,x) SFM	0.028 (0.867)	0.8667 (0.3519)	0.2144 (0.6433)	0.4088 (0.5226)	2.9472 (0.086)

The *SFM* measures estimate that 30 plants are 100% efficient. Mount Tom (I43, Hoylake Water and Power) is 100% efficient on all four measures. This privately owned US plant operates at a very high load factor (91.91%). Shinonda (I30, Chugoku) is efficient on three of the **K(u,x)** measures – *DEA*, *PPA* and *SFM*. Four other plants are efficient on two out of the four measures: Keephills (I9, TransAlta), Higashi Niigata (I35, Tohuku) and Somerset 1 (I82, New York State Electric) are efficient on the *DEA* and *SFM* measures; Beebee 12 (I86, Rochester Gas and Electric) and Rugeley B (M48, CEGB) are efficient on the *PPA* and *SFM* measures. Looking at the 30 plants which are on the frontier in the *SFM* approach, only one (I120, Oak Creek, West Texas Utilities), appears to perform poorly on all the single factor efficiency measures. The 14 UK plants perform very well compared with average efficiency, only High Marnham (M41, CEGB) and Methil (M53, Scottish Power) perform at below average efficiency: High Marnham has a low load factor and Methil has low labour and fuel efficiency.

6.7   Statistical Analysis of Efficiency Scores from BASE60

In this section we report the results of a statistical analysis of each of the **K(u,x)** measures for the BASE60 dataset. We attempt to model the efficiency scores as dependent variables that can be explained by data on the characteristics of the power stations. The explanatory variables consist of age of plant, load factor, capital size and three sets of dummy variables for ownership, technology and country. Two types of analysis are carried out: linear regression analysis and maximum likelihood Tobit analysis. Tobit analysis is more appropriate than OLS for the analysis of technical efficiency scores because the sample is censored at 1.0000: some observations on the dependent variable are bounded even though the independent variables are observed. OLS is inappropriate because the assumption of constant variance is invalid. The Tobit analysis estimates a maximum likelihood function censored at 1.0000.[15] The lower limit on efficiencies of zero is not binding (as it is usually 9+ standard deviations from the sample average efficiency measures).[16] Hence we model a situation where:

$$y_j = \alpha + \sum_{i=1}^{n} \beta_i x_{ij} + \varepsilon_j \quad if \quad \alpha + \sum_{i=1}^{n} \beta_i x_{ij} \leq 1.0000$$

$$y_j = 1.0000 \qquad if \quad \alpha + \sum_{i=1}^{n} \beta_i x_{ij} > 1.0000$$

where α, β_i are estimated by maximum likelihood techniques

Table 6.18: Tobit Analysis of BASE60 Efficiency Scores

Parameters	K(u,x) DEA	K(u,x) PPA	K(u,x) DSA	K(u,x) SFM
		Dependent Variables		
constant	1.380035 (0.283975)**	0.614282 (0.329694)*	1.046732 (0.216357)**	1.060534 (0.232105)**
COOP	-0.02185 (0.014115)	-0.013237 (0.018277)	-0.005771 (0.011997)	-0.003845 (0.011153)
MUNI	-0.025823 (0.010701)**	-0.02438 (0.013795)*	-0.010894 (0.009024)	-0.010244 (0.008597)
K	0.047255 (0.027066)*	0.201075 (0.034783)*	0.017216 (0.022819)	0.030832 (0.022009)
K2	-0.001296 (0.00223)	-0.015325 (0.002865)*	-0.001196 (0.001879)	-0.001924 (0.001816)
Load	-2.58168 (0.784359)*	-1.33747 (0.898536)	-1.27701 (0.589772)*	-1.01771 (0.644575)
Loadsq	2.15931 (0.539651)**	1.11009 (0.612868)*	1.22507 (0.402290)**	0.97932 (0.446876)**
Age	-0.000082 (0.001226)	0.001577 (0.001577)	0.000842 (0.001029)	0.000343 (0.00101)
Agesq	-0.000011 (0.00003)	-0.000048 (0.000039)	-0.000026 (0.000025)	-0.000012 (0.000025)
OIL	0.029996 (0.016251)	0.033843 (0.02098)	0.017655 (0.01377)	0.021423 (0.013346)
GOIL	0.029633 (0.017787)*	0.052719 (0.022853)**	0.041525 (0.014997)**	0.039133 (0.014237)**
COIL	0.006949 (0.018591)	0.008019 (0.022853)	0.006547 (0.015648)	0.004421 (0.015014)
CWOOD	0.040556 (0.043046)	0.040181 (0.055921)	0.037401 (0.036705)	0.038143 (0.033693)
LGGO	0.335111 (727.923)	0.081838 (0.061828)	0.061467 (0.040508)	0.233036 (569.14)
CGO	0.001979 (0.042672)	-0.00335 (0.055159)	0.000467 (0.036432)	0.001816 (0.03339)
CGAS	-0.014746 (0.016903)	-0.014688 (0.021958)	-0.0037229 (0.014412)	-0.00286 (0.013236)

Standard errors in parentheses. ** significant at 5%, * significant at 10%.

Table 6.18:   (Continued)

Parameters	K(u,x) DEA	Dependent Variables K(u,x) PPA	K(u,x) DSA	K(u,x) SFM
CSLURRY	0.000799 (0.04522)	-0.034272 (0.058759)	-0.062262 (0.03857)	-0.049644 (0.036015)
GAS	-0.016186 (0.032736)	0.018556 (0.042017)	0.004557 (0.027579)	0.005079 (0.025465)
GER	-0.074292 (0.022335)**	-0.055159 (0.028960)	-0.031171 (0.01901)	-0.0228 (0.018164)
HK	0.009196 (0.043799)	0.043799 (0.056921)	0.059349 (0.037357)	0.048765 (0.034359)
CAN	-0.036653 (0.018500)**	-0.117346 (0.023644)**	-0.046236 (0.015515)**	-0.04553 (0.014813)**
JAP	0.038519 (0.020287)*	0.052827 (0.026192)**	0.041702 (0.017014)**	0.047987 (0.018368)**
TAI	0.034547 (0.028109)	0.041427 (0.036473)	0.023183 (0.023853)	0.024904 (0.022376)
AUS	-0.021218 (0.023696)	-0.015584 (0.030793)	-0.01383 (0.020202)	-0.01543 (0.018693)
IRE	0.053337 (0.043417)	0.059556 (0.056468)	0.049442 (0.037063)	0.04212 (0.034043)
GREE	-0.028233 (0.02634)	-0.029264 (0.034262)	-0.016794 (0.022486)	-0.015881 (0.020689)
SA	0.002509 (0.024391)	0.020226 (0.031707)	0.031642 (0.020806)	0.025299 (0.01919)
THAI	0.009777 (0.024476)	-0.009839 (0.02933)	-0.03202 (0.019236)	-0.020826 (0.018703)
UK	0.031087 (0.016564)*	0.049297 (0.021333)**	0.0321 (0.013969)**	0.040867 (0.014396)**
Sigma	0.041868 (0.002086)**	0.054484 (0.002678)**	0.035766 (0.001739)**	0.032735 (0.001754)**
Tobit, LR	349.792	306.626	404.249	339.471
Regression, R^2	0.6161	0.413	0.5751	0.4673

Standard errors in parentheses. ** significant at 5%, * significant at 10%.

Table 6.19: Parameter Definitions for Tobit/Regression Analysis of BASE60 Efficiency Scores.

COOP = Dummy Variable
(COOP = 1, otherwise = 0)

GER = Country dummy variable
(Germany = 1, otherwise = 0)

MUNI = Dummy Variable
(MUNI = 1, otherwise = 0)

HK = Country dummy variable
(Hong Kong = 1, otherwise = 0)

K = Capital (MW).
K2 = Capital squared.

CAN = Country dummy variable
(Canada = 1, otherwise = 0)

Load = load factor.
Loadsq = Load squared.

JAP = Country dummy variable
(Japan = 1, otherwise = 0)

Age = average age of generating plant.
Agesq = Age squared.

TAI = Country dummy variable
(Thailand = 1, otherwise = 0)

OIL = Fuel dummy variable
(Oil = 1, otherwise = 0)

AUS = Country dummy variable
(Australia = 1, otherwise = 0)

GOIL = Fuel dummy variable
(Gas/oil = 1, otherwise = 0)

IRE = Country dummy variable
(Ireland = 1, otherwise = 0)

COIL = Fuel dummy variable
(Coal/oil = 1, otherwise = 0)

GREE = Country dummy variable
(Greece = 1, otherwise = 0)

CWOOD = Fuel dummy variable
(Coal/Wood = 1, otherwise = 0)

SA = Country dummy variable
(South Africa = 1, otherwise = 0)

LGGO = Fuel dummy variable
(Liquid gas/Gas/Oil = 1, otherwise = 0)

THAI = Country dummy variable
(Thailand = 1, otherwise = 0)

CGO = Fuel dummy variable
(Coal/Gas/Oil = 1, otherwise = 0)

UK = Country dummy variable
(United Kingdom = 1, otherwise = 0)

CSLURRY = Fuel dummy variable
(Coal Slurry = 1, otherwise = 0)

Sigma = Tobit parameter.

GAS = Fuel dummy variable
(Gas = 1, otherwise = 0)

In Table 6.18 we report the parameter estimates for the Tobit analysis and record the R^2 from the linear regression analysis of the dependent variable on same parameters. The parameter definitions are in Table 6.19. The dummy variables are defined such that a privately owned coal-fired US plant would have a zero entry on all of the ownership, technology and country dummy variables.

The regression results (parameter estimates are not reported to conserve space) indicate that the above variables can explain a relatively high percentage of the variation in each of the efficiency measures: the highest R^2 is 61% for the *DEA* measure of $K(u,x)$ and the lowest R^2 is 41% for the *PPA* measure.

The t-statistics on the MUNI dummy variable indicate some evidence for significantly lower technical efficiency in publicly owned plants compared to privately owned plants: the *DEA* regression indicates significance at 5% and *PPA* significance at 10%. These results are suspicious given the strong inability to reject the no difference null hypothesis in Table 6.17. Further investigation yields an explanation: all of the UK plants are publicly owned and have their own associated UK dummy variable; this implies that good relative performance of publicly owned plants in the UK is attributed to the UK dummy variable not the MUNI dummy variable. When we dropped the UK dummy variable in these two regressions the MUNI variable was no longer significant.

The Tobit analysis reported in Table 6.18 reveals the general importance of the load and capital variables. Load or Loadsq are significant in all four regressions. The Tobit parameter Sigma and the dummy variables on Canada, Japan, UK and gas/oil fuel type are significant across all four dependent variables. There is less conclusive support for the significance of the dummy variables on Germany and the oil fuel type. The COOPs dummy indicates no evidence for significantly different technical efficiency in COOPs compared with IOUs. The lack of significance of any of the age variables indicates no significant learning effect on power station efficiency. The result for the UK dummy variable suggests that the typical UK baseload plant has an efficiency score between 3.1 and 4.9% higher than a comparable US plant.[17]

The results in this section are encouraging when compared to previous work on regression analysis of efficiency scores. Rangan et al. (1988) and Aly et al. (1990), in their *DEA* analysis of productive efficiency in US banks, only use linear regression analysis and do not mention the possibility and desirability of using censored regressions in an efficiency score context. This is especially important for the *SFM* measure as 14.1% of plants are efficient. Aly et al. record an R^2 of 0.08 with technical efficiency as the dependent variable and Rangan et al. report a R^2 of 0.12 (admittedly on regressions with only four and three explanatory variables respectively and a constant).[18] It is possible that if we had had more data on each plant, e.g. on the number of generating sets at each plant and the average calorific value of fuel consumed, this may have improved the fit but there seems little reason to be optimistic about this given the large number of variables already used.

6.8 Conclusions

The results of this chapter indicate a clear inability to reject the null hypothesis that publicly owned and privately owned electric power plants exhibit no significant difference in technical efficiency. This hypothesis was tested by examination of a statistically very large sample of power plants operating in a recent year, 1989. The results were generated by the implementation of an advanced form of each of the four major methodologies for measuring productive efficiency identified in Lovell and Schmidt (1988). The analysis in this chapter represents a comprehensive test of the null hypothesis on a large sample of power plants and provides extensive 'cross-checking' of the results.

The results from the four methodologies reveal a relatively high correlation between the relative efficiency rankings produced by the different techniques. The two programming approaches, *DEA* and *PPA*, yield very similar results both in terms of absolute numbers and in terms of the correlation coefficient. There would seem to be little to distinguish between these two techniques except that the parametric frontier estimated under *PPA* represents what may be a poor approximation to the true frontier (in three out of the four datasets the estimated functional form was Cobb-Douglas with mildly increasing returns to scale). The two statistical approaches, *DSA* and *SFM*, produce very similar results with extremely high correlations. The *SFM* technique demonstrates very little average inefficiency and this is scarcely plausible. The *DSA* results produce greater measured inefficiency than under the other methodologies – this is due to the measuring of efficiency relative to a single 100% efficient outlier.

Examination of the firm level results reveals that some plants do appear to be 100% efficient on more than one methodology. This provides useful insights into the data and the methodologies. A plant which is efficient only on the *DEA* measure may contain suspect data, e.g. some frontier efficient plant appears to have suspiciously low labour data (one plant had just eight recorded employees). A plant which was efficient on just the *SFM* measure might have been so because of the false attribution to noise of inefficiency, simply because the data point was statistically unusual. A tentative conclusion on which method to use might be: the theoretical properties of *DEA* give its results a transparency which is not present under the other methods. In particular it is possible to link good *DEA* scores to single factor efficiency measures. The use of *DSA* or *SFM* techniques in conjunction with *DEA* provides a useful way of detecting whether high *DEA* scores are a reflection of suspicious data. The heavy reliance of *DEA* scores on individual plant data suggests the importance of accurate source data and careful data handling.

The regression results reveal the difficulties in detecting general reasons for good efficiency scores: many of the variables were not significant. The major explanatory factor would seem to be load factor which is a measure of the efficiency of capital utilization. There was limited evidence for the superior performance of IOUs over MUNIs but this evidence proved to be invalid on closer inspection. In general the country and fuel type dummies were insignificant explanators of variations in overall technical efficiency. The fuel type results may be due to selection bias in the BASE60 sample – only highly efficient plants of whatever type are operated at high load factors.

Scale inefficiency appears to be pervasive: when measured by the Fare RTS method increasing returns is pervasive in each of the four datasets. However the measured inefficiency due to suboptimal scale is very small. In contrast to the firm level scale results of Chapter 5 there is no evidence of a difference in the scale efficiency of public and private firms. This conclusion is also suggested by the regression results for base load plants which do not find capital to be a significant explanator of productive efficiency.

The results for UK plants are good with a large majority of the 48 plants analysed performing at or above the average for the sample. This suggests that there was no basis to the assertion that publicly owned UK plants were operated any less efficiently, in a technical sense, than privately owned plants overseas. The regression results suggest that, for base load plants at least, the performance of a typical UK plant is significantly better than the typical US privately owned plant.

Notes

1. The following types of thermal power station are included in the data sample: coal, oil, gas, wood and mixtures of the former.
2. London Economics are economic consultants based in London.
3. JEPIC is the non-profit association of the Japanese electric utility industry.
4. A 1000MW capacity power station can produce 1000MWh of electricity in an hour. There are 8760 hours in a year. Therefore this power station could produce 8,760,000MWh or 8,760 million kWh in a year.
5. This figure is recorded by the Mae Moh lignite power station operated by EGAT, the state owned electricity generator in Thailand.
6. An 'outage' is said to occur when a power station is forced to declare that all or part of its capacity is unavailable to supply electricity to the grid. Outages can be one of two types: *forced* outages which occur as a result of unexpected problems and *planned* outages which are anticipated in advance and are required for routine maintenance of equipment.
7. The correlation coefficients reported are the population correlation coefficient calculated in Microsoft Excel 4.0. The formula for this statistic is:

$$\rho_{X,Y} = \frac{COV(X,Y)}{\sigma_X \bullet \sigma_Y}$$

where X and Y are the two data series to be compared.

8. Lavrio has the highest fuel efficiency, 36.5% net, of any firm in the PEAK15 dataset.

9. The computer program PARAPROG.TL (written by the author) used to estimate these measures reports positive coefficients for 4 of a 10 variable (including constant), 3 input, 1 output translog functional form. The estimated frontier is:

$$\ln Y = -0.14313 + (3.4780E - 002) \times \ln K$$
$$+ (0.98519) \times \ln F + (1.0549E - 003) \times (\ln K)^2$$

$$Y = output\ (mkwh) \qquad K = capital\ (MW) \qquad F = fuel\ (TBTU)$$

As pointed out in Chapter 4, each of the coefficients corresponds to an efficient plant. This equation is not very plausible as labour has no effect on output: cost minimization involves the use of zero labour.

10. The computer program, PARAPROG.TL, estimates a four variable Cobb-Douglas frontier for the PPA measure:

$$\ln Y = 0.21028 + (0.26754) \times \ln K$$
$$+ (3.1738E - 002) \times \ln L + (0.71876) \times \ln F$$

$$L = labour\ (number\ of\ employees)$$

This yields four efficient plants: Shiriuchi (Hokkaido Electric Power), Akita (Tohuku Electric Power), Robinson 1 (Carolina Light and Power) and Peterhead (Hydro Electric).

11. Data supplied by SaskPower indicate a price of Can$0.47 per TBTU. This is around one quarter of the price paid by an average US utility.

12. The Cobb-Douglas functional form estimated by the PPA measure is:

$$\ln Y = 0.27037 + (0.18882) \times \ln K$$
$$+ (6.2747E - 003) \times \ln L + (0.81788) \times \ln F$$

13. Three choices present themselves: drop plants operating for abnormally short periods; reclassify plants to their normal operating class or continue to classify on the basis of actual load factor as we have done. Dropping plants is wasteful of data and reclassification to normal is arbitrary and relies on a company determined assessment of 'normal' class.

14. The estimated frontier is:

$$\ln Y = (-5.7684E - 002) + (8.2560E - 002) \times \ln K$$
$$+ (7.0618E - 003) \times \ln L + (0.94994) \times \ln F$$

15. For more information on the Tobit analysis see, for example, Maddala (1983), pp.151–62. The equations were estimated using the TOBIT command in the TSP program on the Oxford University Vax Network.

16. Table 6.14 indicates that average efficiencies vary from 82.97% to 95.27%

and the standard deviations vary from 8.64% to 2.09% (looking at the highest standard deviation within the ownership classes).

17. A comparable plant would be publicly owned. When UK plants are compared with 'comparable' US privately owned plants, they are more efficient by 0.5 to 2.2%.

18. The R-bar-squared crudely adjusts R-squared for the number of explanatory variables: the recorded R-bar-squareds for the results in Table 6.18 are 0.5577, 0.3237, 0.5105 and 0.4673. The formula for R-bar-squared is:

$$\overline{R^2} = 1 - (1 - R^2)\frac{n-1}{n-K}$$

n = *number of observations* K = *number of parameters*

CHAPTER 7

PRODUCTIVE EFFICIENCY IN BASE LOAD ELECTRIC POWER PLANTS

7.1 Introduction

This chapter seeks to complete the analysis of the previous chapter by presenting the results of an investigation into the overall and allocative productive efficiencies of a subsample of the baseload power plants in the BASE60 dataset. The chapter makes four original contributions in addition to those in Chapter 6. Firstly, we introduce an analysis based on additional new data on input prices collected from published and unpublished sources. Secondly, we calculate overall and allocative efficiency measures using the four major methodologies for measuring productive efficiency. This is the only published study to present comparable results on input price efficiency from these methodologies. This allows investigation of the comparative plausibility of the results of the methodologies and hence their relative merit in the empirical analysis of productive efficiency. Thirdly, we present overall and allocative efficiency measures calculated using both historic and current cost of capital (or capacity) measures. This is the first study of productive efficiency to compare the results obtained using different cost of capital assumptions. Fourthly, we present a regression analysis of the determinants of overall efficiency, using both historic and current cost overall efficiency measures as dependent variables, in order to further explain the plant level results.

The analysis is conducted using the 213 plants in the BASE60 dataset introduced in the previous chapter. We use data on the historic and current cost prices of capital, the price of labour and the price of fuel for 164 of these plants. The subsample of 164 plants includes 130 privately owned and 34 publicly owned plant operating in eight countries in 1989.

We noted in Chapter 4 that there are several ways of calculating overall and allocative efficiency scores using the *PPA*, *DSA* and *SFM* techniques. We suggested that more complex functional forms (e.g. translog) provide no difficulties for calculating technical efficiency scores but can be very difficult to handle when attempting to calculate separate overall and allocative efficiencies. In this chapter we calculate five measures of overall productive efficiency and three measures of allocative efficiency. The five measures of overall efficiency are calculated by the *DEA, PPA, SFM* and two *DSA* methodologies. The first *DSA* methodology [hence *DSA1*] assumes that the underlying production function has a Cobb-Douglas functional form. This allows the separate calculation of overall and allocative efficiencies by the cost minimization method. The second *DSA* methodology [hence *DSA2*] assumes a translog functional form for the cost function and allows direct calculation of overall efficiency scores only. The *SFM* scores are calculated relative to a translog cost function which only allows the calculation of overall efficiency measures. The *DEA, PPA* and *DSA1* methodologies use all 213 plants in BASE60 to model the production frontier. *DSA2* and *SFM* can only use the 164 plants for which we have input price data to estimate the cost frontier.

The results provide interesting further evidence on the relative efficiency of publicly owned and privately owned electric power plants. The allocative efficiencies scores indicate a general rejection of the null hypothesis of no difference in efficiency scores in favour of the alternative hypothesis that privately owned plants are more efficient than publicly owned plants. This suggests that the mix of factors in privately owned plants is better adjusted to the relative input prices faced by the plants than the mix of factors observed in publicly owned plants. The overall efficiency scores show similar but weaker evidence for the superior performance of privately owned plants. The results are robust with respect to the use of either historic or current cost of capital measures of the price of the capital input. The regression analysis confirms the significance of the higher average allocative and overall efficiency scores in privately owned plants. Analysis of the optimal input quantities for the *DEA, PPA* and *DSA1* measures reveals a general implausibility in the results obtained under the non-*DEA* methodologies and therefore strong support for the use of the *DEA* technique as the preferred methodology for generating productive efficiency scores.

The chapter is in seven sections. Section 7.2 introduces the dataset. Section 7.3 discusses the theoretical issues, following on from the discussion in Chapter 4. Sections 7.4 and 7.5 report the historic cost price of capital and current cost price of capital results respectively. Section 7.6 details the regression analysis of the overall efficiency scores from Sections 7.4 and 7.5. Section 7.7 is a conclusion.

7.2   The Dataset

This section describes the nature of the dataset used in the analysis in Sections 7.4 and 7.5. The dataset is based on the 213 plants in the

BASE60 dataset introduced in Chapter 6. BASE60 is drawn from baseload power plants (with load factors greater than 60%) operating in 12 countries in the accounting year ending in 1989. BASE60 contains data on output (mkWh) and three inputs – capital (MW), labour (number of employees) and fuel (TBTU) – as well as information on the age and the type of plant. In this chapter we use this technical data and additional data on input prices for 164 of the 213 sample plants. This input price dataset consists of the historic and current price of capital, the price of labour and the price of fuel. The technical data on output and the three inputs for the full 213 plant sample are used to estimate the production frontiers in the *DEA*, *PPA* and *DSA1* methodologies and hence technical efficiency measures for all 213 plants. The further input price data are then used to calculate historic and current cost of capital measures of $\mathbf{O(u,p,x)}$ and $\mathbf{A(u,p,x)}$ for *DEA*, *PPA* and *DSA1*. In the *DSA2* and *SFM* techniques a cost function is estimated on the data for the 164 plants for which we have input price data – this allows the calculation of historic and current cost capital measures of $\mathbf{O(u,p,x)}$. The age data are used in Section 7.6 in the estimation of regression equations for $\mathbf{O(u,p,x)}$. The sample plants for this chapter are listed in Appendix 2.3.

The sources for the data from BASE60 are listed in Appendix 1.2. The input price data are collected from information from a number of published and unpublished sources. US data are compiled from US Energy Information Agency source material. Data for Thailand were kindly supplied by London Economics, and Japanese data by the Japan Electric Power Information Centre (JEPIC) and from the electric power companies themselves. Other non-US data were collected from company accounts and communications with the companies. The current and historic prices of capital are measured in millions of local currency units per MW. The price of labour is measured in millions of local currency units per employee. The price of fuel is measured in millions of local currency units per TBTU. A more detailed account of the data is contained in Appendix 1.3.

We use data on the historic cost of capital and the age of plant to calculate current costs. Ideally we would like to know the replacement cost of a particular power plant in order to give a figure for the current cost of capital. Companies do often estimate such figures but they rarely publish these at the level of the power plant in their accounts or other published material. A second best approximation to current capital cost would be to use dates of installation and historic costs for each of the generating units at a plant site to estimate a current cost of capital figure:

$$C_{K.CURR} = \sum_i \frac{PI_{1989}}{PI_{1989-Age_i}} \cdot C_{K.HIST,i}$$

i = *generating unit i.*

$C_{K.CURR}$ = *current cost of capital at power plant.*   (7.2.1)

$C_{K.HIST,i}$ = *historic cost of capital of generating unit i.*

PI_{1989} = *price deflator index in 1989.*

PI_t = *price deflator index in year t.*

In practice we do not have information on the dates of installation and age of individual generating units, which leads us to calculate a very crude current cost of capital using the average age of the generating units:

$$C_{K.CURR} = \frac{PI_{1989}}{PI_{1989-Age}} \cdot C_{K.HIST}$$

$C_{K.CURR}$ = *current cost of capital at power plant.*

$C_{K.HIST}$ = *historic cost of capital at power plant.*   (7.2.2)

PI_{1989} = *price deflator index in 1989.*

$PI_{1989-Age}$ = *price deflator index in average first year*

of operation of plant.

Note that in the presence of rising prices in the period of operation current cost is strictly larger than historic cost and hence that the relative input prices are different. This makes it almost certain that the historic and current cost efficiency scores will be different under each of the four methodologies for measuring productive efficiency. The relatively higher price of capital using the current cost of capital measure implies that optimal mixes of the three inputs will involve using relatively less capital when capital is measured at current cost. Following Christensen and Jorgenson (1969)[1] the price of capital per MW (both historic and current cost) is then calculated using real interest rates and assuming a 3.33%[2] depreciation charge:

$$P_K = \frac{(r + 0.0333) \times C_K}{K}$$

$$(7.2.3)$$

r = real interest rate.

K = quantity of capital.

Details of the interest rates and price deflators used in calculating historic and current price of capital figures are given in Appendix 1.3.

7.3 Theoretical Issues

In Sections 7.4 and 7.5 we use the cost minimization solution method for calculating overall and allocative efficiencies from an estimated Cobb-Douglas production frontier in the *PPA* and *DSA1* techniques. This method for generating efficiency scores is conceptually straightforward and is relatively easy to implement. We detail the cost minimization solution method in this section.

Following Chapter 4, overall efficiency for a plant is calculated from the optimization problem:

$$Min \ \sum_i p_i X_i$$

$$(7.3.1)$$

$$s.t. \quad f(\underline{X}) \geq Y$$

p_i = price of input of i, X_i = quantity of input i, Y = output of plant.

The solution to this problem, C^*, is then used to calculate overall efficiency $O(u,p,x)$:

$$O(u,p,x) = C^*/C_A$$

$$(7.3.2)$$

where C_A is the actual cost of the plant.

We know that allocative efficiency, $A(u,p,x)$, is related to overall and technical efficiency, $K(u,x)$, by:

$$A(u,p,x) = O(u,p,x)/K(u,x)$$

$$(7.3.3)$$

We note that the solution to (7.3.1) is straightforward only if $f(\underline{X})$ is differentiable. We set and solve (7.3.1) where $f(X)$ is a three input Cobb-Douglas production function:

$$Min \ p_K K + p_L L + p_F F$$
$$s.t. \ A \cdot K^a \cdot L^b \cdot F^c \geq Y \qquad (7.3.4)$$

A = constant. K = quantity of capital.
L = quantity of labour. F = quantity of fuel.

We can rewrite (7.3.4) as a Lagrangian:

$$L = p_K K + p_L L + p_F F$$
$$+ \lambda (logY - logA - a \cdot logK - b \cdot logL - c \cdot logF) \qquad (7.3.5)$$

where λ = *Lagrange multiplier.*

Differentiating (7.3.5) we obtain the following formulae for the optimal values of capital, labour and fuel (K^*, L^*, F^*):

$$K^* = \exp \left[\frac{\left[logY - logA - b \cdot log\left(\frac{b \cdot p_K}{a \cdot p_L} \right) - c \cdot log\left(\frac{c \cdot p_K}{a \cdot p_F} \right) \right]}{a + b + c} \right] \qquad (7.3.6)$$

$$L^* = \frac{b \cdot p_K}{a \cdot p_L} \cdot K^* \qquad (7.3.7)$$

$$F^* = \frac{c \cdot p_K}{a \cdot p_F} \cdot K^* \qquad (7.3.8)$$

We can thus calculate C^* from (7.3.6), (7.3.7) and (7.3.8) as:
$$C^* = p_K K^* + p_L L^* + p_F F^* \qquad (7.3.9)$$

and hence $O(u,p,x)$ and $A(u,p,x)$ using (7.3.2) and (7.3.3). Note that there is no need for exchange rates to convert the input prices in different countries to a common currency in order to calculate overall and allocative efficiency scores. An exchange rate conversion only scales the maximand but does not affect the solution.

The *DEA* technique calculates overall and allocative efficiency with respect to a reference sample plant. This means that overall efficiency represents the percentage of actual costs that could be saved if the plant introduced the scaled factor proportions employed by another plant in the sample (constant returns to scale is assumed). This means that minimum cost production for each plant involves plausible capacity utilization, labour productivity and fuel efficiency.[3] It is an important and simple task to check whether the analytic solutions for K^*, L^* and F^* in the *PPA* and *DSA1* techniques are plausible.

Consider each of the cost minimizing values of the inputs in turn. K^* cannot be at a value so low that the theoretical load factor (LF) is greater than 100%.[4] We thus need to perform the following check:

$$\frac{\dot{Y}}{8.76 \times K} \leq 1.0 \tag{7.3.10}$$

If (7.3.10) is not satisfied then we must reject the efficiency score results as being implausible. We need also to check the theoretical labour and fuel productivity. If either of these figures is higher than the highest respective labour and fuel productivities in the sample we should consider rejecting the efficiency score results. *A priori* there is a high probability of implausible optimal values being generated under the *PPA* and *DSA1* efficiency scores. This points to a major strength of the *DEA* methodology against the non-*DEA* methodologies for measuring productive efficiency. Unfortunately it is not possible to straightforwardly check the plausibility of the *DSA2* and *SFM* overall efficiency scores.

7.4   Historic Cost Price of Capital Results

The summary results for overall and allocative efficiency using the historic cost price of capital are recorded in Table 7.1.

The results reveal that allocative efficiencies are highest under the *DEA* measures and that overall efficiencies are highest under the *SFM* measures. On average privately owned plants outperform publicly owned plants on all eight of the efficiency measures.

Comparing the allocative efficiencies for privately owned plants in Table 7.1 and the technical efficiencies in Table A in footnote 5[5] we observe that average allocative efficiency losses and average technical efficiency losses vary across the two ownership forms very much less than allocative efficiency losses – this implies that the observed

Table 7.1: Summary Results for Historic Cost Data

	O(u,p,x) DEA	O(u,p,x) PPA	O(u,p,x) DSA1	O(u,p,x) DSA2	O(u,p,x) SFM	A(u,p,x) DEA	A(u,p,x) PPA	A(u,p,x) DSA1
AV TOTAL	0.8403	0.6719	0.7183	0.7323	0.9998	0.9506	0.7643	0.8676
AV PRIVATE	0.8469	0.7031	0.7237	0.7411	0.9999	0.9544	0.7961	0.8703
AV PUBLIC	0.8148	0.5526	0.6975	0.6987	0.9996	0.9361	0.6427	0.8575
SD PRIVATE	0.0860	0.1130	0.0727	0.0589	0.0002	0.0577	0.1018	0.0728
SD PUBLIC	0.0863	0.1728	0.0954	0.0849	0.0006	0.0399	0.1771	0.0962
MAX PRIVATE	1.0000	0.8891	0.9155	1.0000	1.0000	1.0000	0.9385	0.9889
MAX PUBLIC	0.9582	0.9051	0.8777	0.9079	1.0000	0.9923	0.9247	0.9653
MIN PRIVATE	0.5932	0.3353	0.4872	0.6194	0.9990	0.7144	0.4102	0.6065
MIN PUBLIC	0.5967	0.1469	0.4135	0.5205	0.9980	0.8409	0.1870	0.5165
MED PRIVATE	0.8496	0.7244	0.7225	0.7403	1.0000	0.9756	0.8149	0.8763
MED PUBLIC	0.8305	0.5465	0.7136	0.6943	0.9998	0.9468	0.6394	0.8936

Table 7.2: Correlation Table: Historic Cost O(u,p,x) Results

	O(u,p,x) DEA	O(u,p,x) PPA	O(u,p,x) DSA1	O(u,p,x) DSA2	O(u,p,x) SFM
O(u,p,x) *DEA*	1.0000				
O(u,p,x) *PPA*	0.5519	1.0000			
O(u,p,x) *DSA1*	0.6074	0.2111	1.0000		
O(u,p,x) *DSA2*	0.3162	0.4065	0.3161	1.0000	
O(u,p,x) *SFM*	0.3182	0.3859	0.3252	0.7503	1.0000

Table 7.3: Correlation Table: Historic Cost A(u,p,x) Results

	A(u,p,x) DEA	A(u,p,x) PPA	A(u,p,x) DSA1
A(u,p,x) *DEA*	1.0000		
A(u,p,x) *PPA*	0.2905	1.0000	
A(u,p,x) *DSA1*	0.2923	-0.0854	1.0000

Table 7.4: Correlation Table: K(u,x) Results

	K(u,p,x) DEA	K(u,p,x) PPA	K(u,p,x) DSA1
K(u,x) *DEA*	1.0000		
K(u,x) *PPA*	0.7798	1.0000	
K(u,x) *DSA1*	0.8183	0.8548	1.0000

differences in overall efficiency come from allocative not technical inefficiency. A striking feature of Table 7.1 is the very low inefficiency shown in the *SFM* measures. Clearly the introduction of the possibility of stochastic errors in observed costs results in the variations in costs being almost wholly attributed to error rather than inefficiency. This measure suggests that maximum inefficiency is a mere 0.2% – this is scarcely credible. The standard deviations in Table 7.1 also suggest a larger spread of scores for publicly owned plants in addition to relatively poorer average and median scores. The minimum sample efficiency is exhibited by a public plant under each measure.

In the case of the *DEA*, *PPA* and *DSA1* methodologies the correlations for the $O(u,p,x)$ and $A(u,p,x)$ in Tables 7.2 and 7.3 should be compared with those for $K(u,x)$ in Table 7.4. The correlations in both tables reveal that the overall and allocative measures of price efficiency are less well correlated than those for technical efficiency. The reason for poorer correlations in the $O(u,p,x)$ measures appears to be due to the $A(u,p,x)$ measures rather than the $K(u,x)$ measures. The $A(u,p,x)$ measures are particularly poorly correlated across the *DEA*, *PPA* and *DSA1* methodologies. There is a small negative correlation between the *DSA1* measure of $A(u,p,x)$ and the *PPA* measure (-8.54%). The highest correlation is only 29.23%. There is however a reasonably high correlation between the *DSA2* and *SFM* measures (75.03% for $O(u,p,x)$). The surprisingly low correlation between *DSA1* and *DSA2* (31.61%) seems to indicate the importance of the choice of functional form in determining the efficiency score.

Table 7.5 records a battery of one-tailed statistical tests on overall and allocative efficiency in our sample of IOUs and MUNIs. The null hypothesis is that there is no difference in efficiency between the two ownership types: a figure of less than 0.05 indicates rejection of the null hypothesis at the 5% significance level. The results indicate strong evidence for the rejection of the null in favour of the alternative hypothesis that privately owned plants are more efficient than publicly owned plants on both the *PPA* and *DSA2* measures: 15 out of 15 tests reject the null. The *SFM* measure indicates rejection of the null in four out of five tests. The *DEA* evidence is only slightly less convincing with six rejections and four acceptances of the null. However the *DSA1* measure cannot reject the null on any test: 10 out of 10 tests accept the null. To summarize Table 7.5: 15 out of 25 tests on $O(u,p,x)$ and 9 out 15 tests on $A(u,p,x)$ reject the null. In general this indicates strong evidence for a significantly superior performance by privately owned firms. This would seem to be in line with our analysis of the summary results in Table 7.1.

We now consider the unreported detailed plant level scores – the

Table 7.5: Summary of Tests of the Effect of Ownership on Efficiency – Historic Cost Price of Capital Sample: 130 IOUs and 34 MUNIs.

Efficiency Measure	Analysis of Variance F (Prob>F)	Kruskal-Wallis χ^2 (Prob>χ^2)	Median Scores (points above median) χ^2 (Prob>χ^2)	Van der Waerden (1-way) χ^2 (Prob>χ^2)	Savage (exponential) χ^2 (Prob>χ^2)
O(u,p,x) *DEA*	3.7500 (0.0546)	4.7980 (0.0285)	3.6878 (0.0548)	4.2257 (0.0398)	3.3798 (0.0660)
O(u,p,x) *PPA*	37.555 (0.0001)	23.320 (0.0001)	14.751 (0.0001)	22.232 (0.0001)	5.3269 (0.0210)
O(u,p,x) *DSA*1	3.0500 (0.0827)	1.1774 (0.2779)	0.5901 (0.4424)	1.9340 (0.1643)	0.5338 (0.4650)
O(u,p,x) *DSA*2	11.495 (0.0009)	9.0225 (0.0027)	7.2281 (0.0072)	10.104 (0.0015)	2.5833 (0.1080)
O(u,p,x) *SFM*	19.554 (0.0001)	12.861 (0.0003)	0.0000 (0.9999)	15.409 (0.0001)	12.427 (0.0004)
A(u,p,x) *DEA*	3.0240 (0.0839)	13.566 (0.0002)	7.2281 (0.0072)	11.042 (0.0009)	11.210 (0.0008)
A(u,p,x) *PPA*	43.271 (0.0001)	22.409 (0.0001)	11.948 (0.0005)	24.477 (0.0001)	9.4472 (0.0021)
A(u,p,x) *DSA*1	0.7210 (0.3972)	0.1175 (0.7318)	0.1475 (0.7009)	0.6618 (0.4159)	0.6986 (0.4032)

codes refer to the plant listings in Appendix 2.3 (same as for Appendix 2.2.4) Only two firms are efficient on more than one measure of **O(u,p,x)**: Somerset 1 (I82, New York State Electric) is 100% efficient on both overall and allocative efficiencies on the *DEA* and *SFM* measures; and Williamsburg (I102, Pennsylvania Power and Light) is 100% efficient on the *DSA2* and *SFM* measures. Some of the results would seem to be implausibly low. Looking at the lowest efficiency score: Gibbons Creek (M39, Texas Municipal Power Agency) has a *PPA* **O(u,p,x)** score of just 14.69%. This suggests that moving to an efficient combination of inputs given input prices could reduce costs by 85.31%. This figure seems unlikely. Checking the unreported optimal input quantities of capital, labour and fuel, minimizing costs involves using 98.63% less capital, 95.95% less labour and 8.57% more fuel. This appears to be a function of the very high cost of capital at the plant. The suggested reduction in capital would give rise to a theoretical load factor of 56.40! The unreported optimal input quantities for the *PPA* measures in general suggest large reductions in capital and labour and moderate changes (positive and negative) in fuel. The reductions in capital would in general cause load factors of greater than 100%. The suggested number of employees falls to less than 20 for most plants.

The unreported optimal input quantities under the *DSA1* measures are also highly implausible. For example, Barry (I1, Alabama Power) has an efficiency score of 0.6632 for **O(u,p,x)** under the *DSA1* measure. This figure is achieved by increasing capital by 63.39%, reducing labour by 99.07% (from 449 to 4) and by reducing fuel by 48.91%. The optimal net fuel efficiency is 68.73%. This is impossible for a coal/gas plant not operating a CHP (combined heat and power) system. The results for the other plants are similar, in general very large rises in fuel efficiency are suggested. The *SFM* scores indicate that 100 out of 164 plants exhibit 100% efficiency. This inability to detect virtually any inefficiency leaves the usefulness of this technique (implemented as in Chapter 4) open to question. The *DEA* efficiency scores however do have a good theoretical basis, with plants being compared to referent plants within the sample. Barry (I1, Alabama Power) is compared to a high efficiency Japanese plant (I35, Higashi Niigata, Tohuku). However the *DEA* comparison assumes constant returns to scale. We therefore conclude that the *PPA* and *DSA1* measures are based on an implausible production frontier which gives rise to overall and allocative efficiency measures which, on investigation, cannot be justified.

The implausibility of the analytically derived results does not appear to be a consequence of using the Cobb-Douglas functional form for the production function. We did attempt to estimate overall efficiency scores for some of the plants analytically using a flexible translog functional form for the production function.[6] However the results were just as implausible as those produced under the Cobb-Douglas.[7] There were also additional problems in finding feasible starting values of the optimal inputs and in the dependency of the efficiency scores on the exact starting values used.[8] Both historic and current cost prices of capital gave rise to implausible optimal input values.

7.5 Current Cost Price of Capital Results

The summary results for overall and allocative efficiency using the current cost price of capital are recorded in Table 7.6. We note here that the current cost results are not that well correlated with their historic cost results.[9] This indicates that the cost of capital assumption does make a substantial difference to the relative performance of sample plants. The average efficiency results show that efficiency is highest on the *DEA* measures and lowest on the *PPA* measures. Privately-owned plants outperform publicly-owned plants on all eight of the measures of efficiency. The outperformance being large on the *PPA* and *DSA1* measures.

Table 7.6: Summary Results for Current Cost Data

	O(u,p,x) DEA	O(u,p,x) PPA	O(u,p,x) DSA1	O(u,p,x) DSA2	O(u,p,x) SFM	A(u,p,x) DEA	A(u,p,x) PPA	A(u,p,x) DSA1
AV TOTAL	0.8329	0.5065	0.7287	0.8260	0.9984	0.9428	0.5732	0.8785
AV PRIVATE	0.8399	0.5218	0.7472	0.8291	0.9984	0.9470	0.5876	0.8972
AV PUBLIC	0.8061	0.4481	0.6580	0.8145	0.9982	0.9269	0.5182	0.8069
SD PRIVATE	0.0714	0.1479	0.0913	0.0551	0.0007	0.0338	0.1469	0.0864
SD PUBLIC	0.0854	0.2069	0.1459	0.0711	0.0009	0.0513	0.2145	0.1587
MAX PRIVATE	1.0000	0.8275	0.9398	1.0000	1.0000	1.0000	0.8941	0.9934
MAX PUBLIC	0.9632	0.8855	0.9209	0.9645	1.0000	0.9907	0.9151	0.9773
MIN PRIVATE	0.6605	0.1500	0.4509	0.7089	0.9965	0.8438	0.1765	0.4950
MIN PUBLIC	0.6444	0.1261	0.3470	0.6719	0.9965	0.7825	0.1430	0.4419
MED PRIVATE	0.8376	0.5179	0.7623	0.8240	0.9984	0.9542	0.5944	0.9236
MED PUBLIC	0.8109	0.4527	0.6902	0.8142	0.9980	0.9369	0.5730	0.8622

The average allocative efficiency of the plants is very high on the *DEA* measure (94.28%) and very much lower on the *PPA* measure (57.32%). The large divergences between the averages and medians for publicly-owned and privately-owned plants on the *PPA* measure are not as large as under the historic cost price of capital results in Table 7.1. The standard deviations are larger than for the historic cost of capital results, especially under the *PPA* measure where IOUs have a standard deviation of 14.79% on $O(u,p,x)$ and 14.69% on $A(u,p,x)$ and MUNIs have a standard deviation of 20.69% on $O(u,p,x)$ and 21.45% on $A(u,p,x)$. The minimum efficiency scores are exhibited by publicly owned plants on seven out of eight measures (the *SFM* measure is the exception). The current cost price of capital results averages are similar to the averages for historic cost price of capital results except for the *PPA* measure where the average current cost results are substantially lower than those for historic cost of capital. The results for *PPA* suggest that allocative efficiency losses are substantially larger than the technical efficiency losses. The divergent *PPA* results suggest very large average allocative losses for both IOUs and MUNIs (41.24% and 48.18%).

The correlation tables for the $O(u,p,x)$ and $A(u,p,x)$ measures are contained in Tables 7.7 and 7.8. The results for both measures reveal a much higher degree of correlation for *DEA* with the other measures for $O(u,p,x)$ than was evident for the historic cost results in Tables 7.2 and 7.3. The $A(u,p,x)$ *DEA* scores again correlate poorly with the scores produced using the non-*DEA* measures. The *DSA2* and *SFM* measures of $O(u,p,x)$ correlate extremely well (91.94%).

Table 7.7: Correlation Table: Current Cost **O(u,p,x)** Results

	O(u,p,x) DEA	O(u,p,x) PPA	O(u,p,x) DSA1	O(u,p,x) DSA2	O(u,p,x) SFM
O(u,p,x) *DEA*	1.0000				
O(u,p,x) *PPA*	0.6253	1.0000			
O(u,p,x) *DSA1*	0.6957	0.8312	1.0000		
O(u,p,x) *DSA2*	0.7631	0.1942	0.4437	1.0000	
O(u,p,x) *SFM*	0.5258	-0.0350	0.2562	0.9194	1.0000

Comparing Table 7.8 and Table 7.3 the most marked improvement is the correlation between the *PPA* and *DSA1* measures for **A(u,p,x)** where the correlation improves from -8.54% to 79.85%. It appears that using the current cost price of capital data does produce more consistent results than using the historic cost price of capital data. Overall, out of 13 correlations in Tables 7.2 and 7.3, ten improve and only three get smaller as we move from the historic to current cost of capital analysis.

Table 7.8: Correlation Table: Current Cost **A(u,p,x)** Results

	A(u,p,x) DEA	A(u,p,x) PPA	A(u,p,x) DSA1
A(u,p,x) *DEA*	1.0000		
A(u,p,x) *PPA*	0.4436	1.0000	
A(u,p,x) *DSA1*	0.4154	0.7985	1.0000

Table 7.9 lists a battery of one-tailed statistical tests on the current cost overall and allocative efficiency score results. The null hypothesis is that there is no difference in efficiency between MUNIs and IOUs: a figure of less than 0.05 indicates rejection of the null hypothesis at the 5% significance level. The results indicate more evidence for the rejection of the null in favour of the alternative hypothesis that privately owned plants are more efficient than publicly owned plants: 11 out of 25 tests on **O(u,p,x)** reject the null at the 5% level. The tests on the *DEA* scores indicate rejection of the null on five out of ten measures. The tests on the *DSA2* and *SFM* measures provide the strongest support for the null: six out of ten tests support the null hypothesis. In summary out of 40 tests in Table 7.9: 19 tests reject the null at 5%. Table 7.9,

Table 7.9: Summary of Tests of the Effect of Ownership on Efficiency – Current Cost Price of Capital Sample: 130 IOUs and 34 MUNIs.

	Analysis of Variance	Kruskal-Wallis	Median Scores (points above median)	Van der Waerden (1-way)	Savage (exponential)
Efficiency Measure	F $(Prob>F)$	χ^2 $(Prob>\chi^2)$	χ^2 $(Prob>\chi^2)$	χ^2 $(Prob>\chi^2)$	χ^2 $(Prob>\chi^2)$
O(u,p,x) *DEA*	5.554 (0.0196)	4.3049 (0.038)	2.3602 (0.1245)	4.9548 (0.026)	2.0715 (0.1501)
O(u,p,x) *PPA*	5.597 (0.0192)	4.4321 (0.0353)	2.3602 (0.1245)	4.491 (0.0341)	0.1757 (0.6751)
O(u,p,x) *DSA1*	19.546 (0.0001)	12.029 (0.0005)	5.3104 (0.0212)	13.856 (0.0002)	6.4997 (0.0108)
O(u,p,x) *DSA2*	1.665 (0.1988)	2.0971 (0.1476)	1.1506 (0.2834)	2.3762 (0.1232)	0.2465 (0.6196)
O(u,p,x) *SFM*	2.174 (0.1423)	2.2692 (0.132)	1.8974 (0.1684)	2.5783 (0.1083)	0.0807 (0.7763)
A(u,p,x) *DEA*	7.513 (0.0068)	3.7126 (0.054)	2.3602 (0.1245)	4.4428 (0.035)	1.3871 (0.2389)
A(u,p,x) *PPA*	4.891 (0.0284)	2.7525 (0.0971)	1.3276 (0.2492)	3.465 (0.0627)	0.1608 (0.6884)
A(u,p,x) *DSA1*	19.864 (0.0001)	12.526 (0.0004)	5.3104 (0.0212)	15.19 (0.0001)	10.123 (0.0015)

therefore provides strong evidence for the significantly superior performance of privately owned plants on the overall and allocative measures of efficiency.

We now turn to the unreported detailed plant level scores – the codes refer to plant listings in Appendix 2.3. As in Section 7.4 only one firm is efficient on more than one measure of **O(u,p,x)**: Somerset 1 (I82, New York State Electric) is 100% efficient on the *DEA*, *DSA2* and *SFM* measures. There are several very low overall efficiency scores which would seem to be implausible. The lowest is the **O(u,p,x)** *PPA* score of 12.61% for Kingston (M36, Tennessee Valley Authority), this implies that Kingston could reduce costs by 87.39%. The optimal input quantities are achieved by reducing capital by 98.88%, reducing labour by 92.60% and increasing fuel by 24.23%. The suggested optimal theoretical load factor is 54.13. The unreported optimal input quantities for the other *PPA* results generally involve similar changes in actual quantities: large capital and labour reductions and increases in fuel consumption; in fact all of the optimal theoretical load factors are greater than 1.

The optimal input quantities associated with the *DSA1* measures are also generally implausible. For example, Barry (I1, Alabama Power) has an $O(u,p,x)$ *DSA1* score of 0.7658 which implies that costs can be reduced by 23.42%, this is achieved by a 35.47% reduction in capital, a 98.33% reduction in labour and a 7.76% reduction in fuel. At the optimal input levels Barry would have a theoretical load factor of 95.51% and a labour force of just eight: both of these figures imply single factor productivities for capital and labour which are not achieved by any plant in our dataset in Chapter 6. In general the achievement of overall efficiency according to the *DSA1* measure involves very large reductions in labour input – several plants would be left with less than 0.5 of an employee – and reductions in capital input which in many cases would give rise to load factors of greater than 1. The *SFM* results indicate far fewer frontier efficient firms under current cost of capital measures than under historic cost of capital measures (seven efficient plants compared with 100). However the amount of measured inefficiency is still implausibly low. Turning to the *DEA* measures, once again the optimal quantity changes suggested are plausible in so far as they reflect single factor productivities achieved by an actual plant in the sample. Barry (I1, Alabama Power), for example, is compared to Somerset 1 (I82, New York Electric and Gas). We conclude that, as with the historic cost results, the current cost of capital results suggest that out of the three sets of overall and allocative efficiency scores we report only the *DEA* scores can be justified.

7.6 Regression Analysis of $O(u,p,x)$ Efficiency Scores

This section presents the results of a regression analysis of the historic and current cost $O(u,p,x)$ efficiency scores.[10] The method of analysis is ordinary least squares (OLS). The analysis is similar to the regression analysis in Section 7 of Chapter 6. The variable definitions are contained in Table 6.19. The results of the regression analysis are presented in Tables 7.10 and 7.11.

We do not report an analysis of the *SFM* measures because of the very small amount of inefficiency to be explained (0.2% for historic cost of capital and 0.35% for current cost).[11] There is no need to conduct Tobit (censored) regression analysis in the case of the non-*SFM* overall efficiency measures due to the very small number of 100% efficient plants: out of the four sets of efficiency measures only two observations are 100% efficient (one on *DEA* and one on *DSA2*).

Looking at the results two things are striking when Tables 7.10 and 7.11 are compared with the regression analysis we conducted on $K(u,x)$ in Table 6.18. Firstly the ownership coefficient is significant in seven out of eight reported regressions: privately-owned firms have

Table 7.10:   Regression Results for Historic Cost Efficiency Scores

Parameters	$O(u,p,x),hist$ DEA	$O(u,p,x),hist$ PPA	$O(u,p,x),hist$ DSA 1	$O(u,p,x),hist$ DSA 2
		Dependent Variables		
constant	0.120238	-0.017015	0.509979	1.04776
	(0.333662)	(0.671434)	(0.421986)	(0.267102)**
MUNI	-0.037888	-0.165521	-0.049569	-0.055997
	(0.013471)**	(0.027108)**	(0.017037)**	(0.010784)**
K	0.230045	0.231659	0.118327	-0.094471
	(0.034654)**	(0.069736)	(0.043828)**	(0.027741)**
K2	-0.015147	-0.017428	-0.008833	0.005983
	(0.002891)**	(0.005817)**	(0.003656)**	(0.002314)**
Load	-0.812084	-0.760903	-0.611301	-0.385411
	(0.906634)	(1.82444)	(1.14663)	(0.725778)
Loadsq	0.900249	0.645178	0.674294	0.654511
	(0.617415)	(1.24244)	(0.780852)	(0.494252)
Age	0.003448	0.018102	-0.005509	0.000951
	(0.001577)**	(0.003173)**	(0.001994)**	(0.001262)
Agesq	-0.000108	-0.00037	0.000072	-0.000062
	(0.000038)**	(0.000077)**	(0.000048)**	(0.000031)**
OIL	0.04053	0.109403	-0.017407	0.012392
	(0.020163)**	(0.040573)**	(0.0255)	(0.01614)
GOIL	0.055278	0.14011	-0.050518	0.043171
	(0.022304)**	(0.044882)**	(0.028208)*	(0.017855)**
COIL	-0.007648	0.010344	-0.001167	-0.012375
	(0.022768)	(0.045816)	(0.028794)	(0.018226)
CWOOD	0.041581	0.023695	0.017257	0.04189
	(0.052243)	(0.105129)	(0.066072)	(0.041821)
CGO	0.013236	0.002531	0.032074	-0.011879
	(0.051786)	(0.10421)	(0.065494)	(0.041456)
CGAS	-0.005352	-0.004505	-0.006932	-0.001744
	(0.020592)	(0.041438)	(0.026043)	(0.016484)
GAS	0.026438	0.070445	-0.011776	0.006256
	(0.040174)	(0.080843)	(0.050808)	(0.03216)
CAN	-0.084245	-0.05114	-0.047429	0.06388
	(0.038323)**	(0.077118)	(0.048468)	(0.030678)**
JAP	0.013591	0.048529	0.023514	-0.000021
	(0.025424)	(0.051161)	(0.032154)	(0.020352)
AUS	-0.010588	0.042304	-0.022897	0.040028
	(0.028903)	(0.058162)	(0.036554)	(0.023138)*
IRE	0.010465	0.131881	0.048155	0.021988
	(0.052691)	(0.106031)	(0.066639)	(0.04218)
GREE	-0.012404	0.250846	-0.004891	0.004296
	(0.032135)	(0.064667)**	(0.040642)	(0.025725)
SA	-0.025451	0.206763	-0.066953	0.044397
	(0.053798)	(0.108260)*	(0.068039)	(0.043067)
THAI	-0.048748	0.207719	-0.043816	-0.036474
	(0.032202)	(0.064801)**	(0.040726)	(0.025778)
R^2	0.7029	0.5442	0.4172	0.6810
F	15.9954**	8.0745**	4.8401**	14.4333**

Standard errors in parentheses. **=significant at 5%, *=significant at 10%.

Table 7.11: Regression Results for Current Cost Efficiency Scores

Parameters	*O(u,p,x),curr* DEA	*O(u,p,x),curr* PPA	*O(u,p,x),curr* DSA 1	*O(u,p,x),curr* DSA 2
		Dependent Variables		
constant	0.351059	0.008236	-0.033952	0.590912
	(0.27268)	(0.75108)	(0.529536)	(0.208891)**
MUNI	-0.045824	-0.172529	-0.140174	-0.004992
	(0.011009)**	(0.030324)**	(0.021379)**	(0.008434)
K	0.106357	0.200859	0.203566	0.020759
	(0.028321)**	(0.078008)**	(0.054998)**)	(0.021696)
K2	-0.006435	-0.016026	-0.016602	-0.001641
	(0.002362)**	(0.006507)**	(0.004588)**	(0.000181)
Load	-0.411049	-0.315675	0.114667	-0.019712
	(0.740934)	(2.04086)	(1.43887)	(0.567604)
Loadsq	0.767541	0.306145	0.250061	0.615557
	(0.504574)	(1.38982)	(0.979865)	(0.386537)
Age	-0.000251	0.005669	0.003366	0.001099
	(0.001289)	(0.00355)	(0.002503)	(0.000987)
Agesq	-0.000026	-0.000287	-0.000186	-0.000038
	(0.000031)	(0.000086)**	(0.000061)**	(0.000024)
OIL	0.040979	0.1292	0.06352	0.01207
	(0.016478)**	(0.045386)**	(0.031999)**	(0.012623)
GOIL	0.062386	0.196173	0.07766	0.04154
	(0.018227)**	(0.050206)**	(0.035397)**	(0.013963)**
COIL	-0.009473	-0.005631	0.040459	-0.001816
	(0.018607)	(0.051250)*	(0.036133)	(0.014254)
CWOOD	0.021665	-0.033294	0.00701	0.027499
	(0.042695)	(0.117599)	(0.082911)	(0.032707)
CGO	0.006778	-0.012435	0.025557	-0.000813
	(0.042321)	(0.116571)	(0.082186)	(0.032421)
CGAS	-0.010719	-0.021426	0.004105	-0.000167
	(0.016829)	(0.046354)	(0.032681)	(0.012892)
GAS	0.032802	0.075195	0.002559	-0.02459
	(0.032832)	(0.090432)	(0.063758)	(0.025151)
CAN	-0.043573	-0.002312	-0.007513	-0.035516
	(0.031319)	(0.086266)	(0.060821)	(0.023992)
JAP	0.022091	0.163271	-0.03309	-0.023288
	(0.020777)	(0.057230)**	(0.040349)	(0.015917)
AUS	-0.000933	0.016038	0.039388	0.007581
	(0.023621)	(0.065062)	(0.045871)	(0.018095)
IRE	0.020041	0.123655	0.131036	0.011767
	(0.043061)	(0.118608)	(0.083622)	(0.032987)
GREE	-0.000041	0.167544	0.094712	0.001738
	(0.026262)	(0.072337)**	(0.051000)*	(0.020119)
SA	-0.007653	0.141951	0.111797	-0.046108
	(0.043966)	(0.121101)	(0.08538)	(0.033681)
THAI	-0.057285	0.244156	-0.008417	-0.079674
	(0.026317)**	(0.072488)**	(0.051106)	(0.020160)**
R^2	0.7378	0.5779	0.5382	0.7468
F	19.0285**	9.2572**	7.8797**	19.9393**

Standard errors in parentheses. **=significant at 5%, *=significant at 10%.

significantly higher overall efficiency scores.[12] This observation provides additional support for our conclusions from the analysis of the test statistics in Tables 7.5 and 7.9. Secondly, the goodness of fit (R^2) is substantially better for **O(u,p,x)** than for the regressions on **K(u,x)** in Chapter 6. The fit is particularly good for the current cost of measures of **O(u,p,x)**.

The historic cost results show that the gas/oil (dummy variable, GOIL) plants consistently have significantly lower overall efficiency scores. There is limited evidence that oil (dummy variable, OIL) plants have higher overall efficiency scores. The age variables (Age and Agesq) and the capital variables (K and K_2) also appear to be significant in determining the overall efficiency scores. The current cost results reveal the significantly lower costs in oil and gas/oil plants and that age has a significant effect on efficiency scores (via the Agesq variable). The current cost results indicate that ownership is significant in only three of the four reported regressions. Interestingly, load factor is only a significant explanatory variable in none of the eight regressions; this contrasts with the strong evidence we found in Chapter 6 for the significance of this variable in regressions involving the **K(u,x)** scores as dependent variable. In general, few of the variables in the regressions are significant and there is slight suggestion that ownership is more significant when the historic cost results are used rather than the current cost results.

7.7 Summary and Conclusions

The results reported in this chapter indicate strong evidence for the rejection of the null hypothesis that publicly-owned and privately-owned electric power plants exhibit no significant difference in overall and allocative productive efficiency. The null hypothesis is rejected in favour of the alternative hypothesis that privately-owned plants exhibit significantly higher overall and allocative efficiencies than publicly-owned plants. This means that we have found evidence that given input prices IOUs exhibit lower unit costs than MUNIs. This evidence came from the analysis of a sample of 164 base load power plants operating in eight countries in 1989. The allocative efficiency results were generated using *DEA* and cost minimization of Cobb-Douglas production functions for the *PPA* and *DSA1* methodologies. The overall efficiency results were calculated using five measures: *DEA*, Cobb-Douglas *PPA* and *DSA* (*DSA1*) and *DSA2* and *SFM*, from translog cost frontiers. Separate efficiency scores were produced for historic cost price of capital and current cost price of capital and gave rise to similar statistical conclusions on relative efficiency.

The results from the four methodologies revealed a much lower correlation between relative efficiency rankings for the overall and allocative efficiency measures compared with the correlations obtained for the technical efficiency measures in the previous chapter. The *DEA* results in particular were notably less well correlated with the other three efficiency measures. Investigation of the optimal input quantities underlying the overall efficiency scores revealed a general implausibility in the analytically derived efficiency scores. In particular the optimal load factor frequently exceeded 1 and the labour productivity was implausibly high. This problem may be a consequence of the Cobb-Douglas functional form of the production function or of the use of analytically derived rather than estimated efficiency scores. However attempts to analytically derive overall efficiency from a production frontier estimated using a translog functional form produced just as improbable results. There seems little reason to think that any attempt to estimate/derive overall efficiency scores from a sample can ensure the plausibility of all the plant level results. We were led to conclude that of the four methodologies only the *DEA* results were plausible in the weak sense of being based on theoretically feasible optimal input combinations. The strength of the *DEA* methodology in this chapter contrasts with the mixed evidence on the choice of methodology we reported in Chapter 6. The results from the *SFM* technique indicated an implausibly high level of efficiency: the lowest *SFM* efficiency score was 99.65%.

Both the regression results and the statistical tests confirm the rejection of the null. Publicly owned firms demonstrated significantly lower costs in seven out of eight reported regressions. The percentage of explained variation in overall efficiency scores was relatively high but the insignificance of most of the individual parameters meant that there was little information to be gained from the regressions on the determinants of the observed efficiency scores. Capital and age variables did however appear to have a significant explanatory effect. Unlike the regression analysis for the technical efficiency scores there was no evidence for the significant role of load factor in determining overall efficiency.

While there was considerable evidence from the differing methodologies in favour of rejecting the null hypothesis there were wide variations in the estimates of the *magnitude* of the average differences in efficiency between IOUs and MUNIs. The historic cost results in Table 7.1 indicate that IOUs have 15.05% higher average overall efficiency on the *PPA* measure and only 0.03% higher efficiency on the *SFM* measure, with an even bigger variation in median overall efficiencies. The current cost results in Table 7.6 show average overall efficiencies of IOUs being 8.92% higher than MUNIs on the *DSA1* measure and only 0.02% higher on the *SFM* measure. Taking a crude average of the five average overall efficiency scores we find that overall efficiency in IOUs is 5.11% higher than in MUNIs on the historic cost of capital measure and 4.23% higher on the current cost of capital measure. Combined with the evidence that the best public utilities in the sample are among the best private utilities, these figures indicate that the expected productivity gain due to ownership transfer, though significant, is small. Well-run publicly owned utilities can still operate at or above the average efficiencies of privately owned utilities.

The results of this chapter bring our analysis of relative efficiency in the international electricity generating industry to a close. We have shown that – in line with the common perception – publicly-owned plants do exhibit higher costs than privately owned plants but that this is a consequence of relative allocative inefficiency rather than relative technical inefficiency. This amounts to suggesting that MUNIs tend to be as close to the frontier as IOUs but further away from the optimal point on the frontier consistent with cost minimization given the actual input prices. This means that the input mix is less efficient for MUNIs. In the electricity industry input mix largely reflects the choice of technology and is a consequence of good (or providential) investment planning while technical efficiency is more a consequence of good managerial operation. Thus we seem to have provided strong support for the hypothesis that given the technology chosen public and private plants are equally well (or badly) operated and that the lower overall efficiency in publicly owned plants is a consequence of poor technology choice given the input prices faced by the plant. As in the case of the UK's CEGB which was forced to buy and use high price British coal, publicly-owned firms are more likely to be choosing technology within the framework of a wider national energy policy rather than on the basis of least cost planning. Such state interference in input procurement and investment planning, to the extent that it does exist internationally, would seem to have a significant effect on the unit costs of electricity generation.

Notes

1. See an explanation of the cost of capital used in productive efficiency studies in the appendix to Atkinson and Halvorsen (1980), p.87. We simplify their equation for the rental price of capital by assuming $q_t \approx q_{t-1}$ and $bs \approx bds$.
2. This is equivalent to assuming a straight-line depreciation of electricity generating plant over 30 years. This is in line with assumptions in company accounts. Atkinson and Halvorsen (1980) assume straight-line depreciation over 28 years. A more disaggregated approach might have assumed

different depreciation rates for different plant types. However the general lack of precision in the data makes the improved accuracy of such detailed calculations spurious.

3. Of course, this is not strictly true. The fuel type used by the two plants may not be the same. For example the achievement of 100% overall efficiency in a coal-fired plant may involve a fuel efficiency which is only obtainable in a CCGT plant. However this is only a problem *ex post, ex ante* inefficiency has arisen in the coal-fired plant because of the choice of an inappropriate technology.

4. No plant would be expected to be very close to 100%. In Chapter 6 the highest theoretical load factor was 92.2% (M30, Mae Moh, EGAT).

5. *Table A – Summary Statistics for the Subsample of 164* $K(u,x)$ *Measures.* These measures should be compared with the full sample results in Table 6.14.

	$K(u,x)$ DEA	$K(u,x)$ PPA	$K(u,x)$ DSA1
AV TOTAL	0.8832	0.8760	0.8284
AV PRIVATE	0.8865	0.8811	0.8320
AV PUBLIC	0.8707	0.8563	0.8149
SD PRIVATE	0.0621	0.0644	0.0517
SD PUBLIC	0.0875	0.0913	0.0799
MAX PRIVATE	1.0000	1.0000	1.0000
MAX PUBLIC	1.0000	1.0000	0.9632
MIN PRIVATE	0.6898	0.6427	0.7085
MIN PUBLIC	0.6797	0.5937	0.6250
MED PRIVATE	0.8884	0.8937	0.8288
MED PUBLIC	0.8836	0.8549	0.8029

6. The translog production function cannot be differentiated (unlike the Cobb-Douglas production function) but we used a NAG algorithm (routine E04VDF in NAG Version 14) on the Oxford University Vax System to solve the non-linear cost minimization problem. We attempted to calculate efficiency scores for I1, I43 and M17.

7. The I1 and I43 scores for overall efficiency were 100% on the *DSA* methodology (for both historic and current costs). This implies that the allocative efficiency score exceeds 100% for I1. The overall efficiency for M17 is less than 20% on the historic cost price of capital data and the optimal load factor exceeds 1.

8. In particular the attempts at calculating overall efficiency (historic cost basis) for M17 led to different efficiency scores depending on what starting values were used for capital, labour and fuel inputs.

9. The correlation coefficients for the historic and current cost $O(u,p,x)$ results (in the order *DEA-PPA-DSA1-DSA2-SFM*) are 0.8805-0.7498-

0.5477-0.7800-0.6303. The comparable correlations for historic and current cost **A(u,p,x)** results are 0.5477-0.6532-0.3376. This indicates that the historic and current cost *DSA1* results for **A(u,p,x)** are particularly poorly correlated.

10. OLS regression analysis was conducted for the **A(u,p,x)** measures. The results were very similar to those for **O(u,p,x)** and so in the interests of saving space and preserving the flow of the analysis we do not report these regression results.

11. We did however undertake OLS and Tobit analysis of the *SFM* scores: MUNIs had significantly lower efficiencies on the historic cost measure but insignificantly lower efficiencies in the case of the current cost measure.

12. The ownership coefficient was significant in each of the six unreported regressions for the **A(u,p,x)** measures.

CHAPTER 8

PRODUCTIVE EFFICIENCY IN ELECTRICITY TRANSMISSION AND DISTRIBUTION SYSTEMS

8.1 Introduction

This chapter seeks to widen our investigation into the relative performance of publicly-owned and privately-owned electric utilities by analysing the productive efficiency of a sample of utilities engaged in the transmission and distribution (T&D) of electricity. In the three previous chapters we concentrated our attention on the analysis of the generation function within electric utilities, now we proceed to present separate analysis of the transmission and distribution functions within electric utilities. The analysis reported in this chapter advances economic analysis of the ESI in four ways. Firstly, we analyse two new datasets collected from published and unpublished sources. The data are drawn from electric utilities operating in a different year to the two used in the previous chapters: 1990. Secondly, this chapter includes the first published *DEA* study on electricity transmission only. Previous *DEA* work has focused mainly on generation and only recently on distribution. Thirdly, the distribution study includes data from the UK and the USA and this constitutes the first international comparison of the efficiency of distribution systems using the *DEA* technique. Fourthly, both regression analysis and the *DEA* methodology are used to analyse the datasets to provide 'methodology cross-checking' of results.

The data used in this chapter is for 129 US electric utilities engaged in transmission and 145 US and UK utilities engaged in distribution in 1990. For the purposes of the *DEA* methodology the transmission dataset is divided into three subdatasets on the basis of numbers of employees (L): L>500, 500>L>150, and L<150. These subsets are referred to as Large, Medium, and Small and are of sizes 35, 57 and 37 utilities respectively. The distribution data are similarly divided: L>1000, 1000>L>300 and L<300. These subsets are referred to as Large, Medium and Small and are of sizes 65, 50 and 30 utilities respectively. The justification for these divisions is that it is unreasonable to compare widely differing utilities to assess relative performance and these splits divide the data into subsamples of roughly equal size.

Analysis of these datasets is conducted using multi-output multi-input *DEA* (ff. Weyman-Jones, 1992) and standard ordinary least squares (OLS) regression analysis (ff. Huettner and Landon, 1977). The *DEA* methodology is used to generate four technical efficiency measures: $K(u,x)$, $F(u,x)$, $C(u,x)$ and $S(u,x)$. Further analysis assumes some of the outputs and inputs may be thought of as environmental variables and thus not free to vary: this generates several additional measures of $K(u,x)$ which we label as $KENVx(u,x)$ where x is the number of environmental variables. The OLS analysis seeks to explain average costs in the T&D functions using data on physical inputs, environmental variables and wages.

The results indicate that the conclusions of the previous chapters on generation are confirmed for transmission and distribution. The null hypothesis of no difference in technical efficiency between private and public firms cannot be rejected at the 5% significance level for either transmission or distribution on the *DEA* scores. The regression results also indicate that there is no significant difference in average costs between publicly owned and privately owned firms in both transmission and distribution.

The chapter is in eight sections. Section 8.2 introduces the dataset. Section 8.3 discusses the difficulties involved in analysing the T&D functions in the ESI. Sections 8.4 and 8.5 examine previous studies of the T&D functions and propose feasible *DEA* and OLS regression functions to estimate for the transmission and distribution functions respectively. Sections 8.6 and 8.7 present the results for the transmission and distribution samples. Section 8.8 is a conclusion.

8.2 The Datasets

This section describes the two datasets used in the analysis of the transmission and distribution functions in Sections 8.6 and 8.7. The transmission dataset consists of 129 US firms transmitting electricity in the accounting year ending in 1990. This dataset includes 23 publicly owned firms and 106 privately owned utilities. The sample transmission networks are listed in Appendix 2.4.1. The dataset consists of nine variables: operation and maintenance costs (1000s of dollars), transformer capacity (MVA), peak output (MW), net energy transmitted (millions of kWh), average labour cost (1000s of dollars), circuit km*kV, overground circuit km, underground circuit km and labour employed. The distribution dataset consists of 145 firms from the USA (136) and the UK (9) distributing electricity in the accounting year ending in 1990. This dataset includes information on 119 privately owned firms and 26 publicly owned firms. The sample distribution systems are listed in Appendix 2.4.2. The dataset consists of 11 variables: residential sales (millions of kWh), total sales (millions of kWh), number of customers, circuit km, peak output (MW), service area (square km), labour cost (1000s of US dollars), operation and maintenance costs (1000s of US dollars), underground circuit km, labour employed and transformer capacity (MVA).

The data are collected from several sources. The US T&D data are mostly compiled from US Energy Information Agency source books and the Electric World *Directory of Electric Utilities*. Additional information was kindly supplied by the American Public Power Association (APPA). Data for the UK distribution companies were compiled from company accounts and annual statistical reviews. A detailed account of the data sources is contained in Appendix 1.4.

There is no published data on labour employed in the individual T&D functions for any of the firms in the samples. We therefore impute a labour employed figure for each firm by dividing operation and maintenance (O+M) cost in the function by the average salary in the utility. This figure is unsatisfactory particularly as the operation and maintenance cost series used includes rent and other non-labour costs. However such an approximation represents the best that can be obtained given the available data and should be thought of as a 'labour equivalent' figure.

For the purposes of *DEA* the datasets are subdivided into three subsamples on the basis of calculated labour employed. These divisions provide for a more meaningful analysis for three reasons. Firstly, analysis of the full dataset involves comparing very large utilities with very small utilities. These comparisons are invalid due to the diverse nature of production in such a case and the unlikely policy recommendations that might be generated. The smallest firm, by labour employed, in transmission has just 10 employees (19I) while the largest has 5066 (127M). A possible policy recommendation that the largest utility should split into 500+ separate companies is unlikely to be justifiable. Secondly, the variation in *DEA* efficiency scores is reduced if the sample size is lower. *DEA* scores should be plausible. This means that the majority of scores should be in the region of 0.6 to 1.0. It is unlikely that any utility can reduce all its inputs in T&D by more than 40% (i.e. have an efficiency score less than 0.6). Thirdly, it is easier to implement *DEA* techniques on smaller datasets. Reducing the intra subsample size variation of the utilities reduces scaling problems within the *DEA* calculations and hence makes it easier to generate *DEA* scores. The presence of smaller datasets for analysis also significantly reduces the time taken to run *DEA* scores.

The transmission dataset is divided into three datasets on the basis of labour employed (L): L>500, 500>L>150 and L<150 which we label Large, Medium and Small Transmission company data. Some of the companies in the Small dataset have very low numbers of people employed e.g. 10 at Newport (22I). The distribution dataset is also divided into three subsets on the basis of L: L>1000, 1000>L>300 and L<300 which we label as Large, Medium and Small Distribution company data. The larger cut-off points in distribution indicate the higher labour–output ratios in distribution relative to transmission. Listings of the T&D sample firms (divided by subsamples) are given in Appendix 2.4. The exact points of division into Large, Medium and Small are arbitrary, reflecting the arguments in the previous paragraph and the need to keep the subsets of roughly equal size (>30) in order to get a large enough subsample on which to perform a meaningful *DEA*.[1]

8.3   The Difficulties of Analysing the Transmission and Distribution Functions of the ESI

The analysis of the productive efficiency of generating firms or units is relatively straightforward. Production can be characterized as one output produced by the three classic textbook inputs: capital (or capacity), labour and fuel. However, this characterization has been challenged theoretically (e.g. Vickers and Yarrow, 1985) by those who point out that electricity at different voltages and different times constitutes a bundle of outputs. Data limitations and computational ease mean that the simple characterization is difficult to improve on in empirical work on productive efficiency. For the remaining functions of the ESI the key problem is the distinction between inputs, outputs and environmental variables which affect cost and output. In transmission the key capital inputs would seem to be the number of pylons, capacity of transformers and length of cables. Nevertheless, are these inputs not largely environmental i.e. fixed by the geography of the distribution and generation systems? And what does a transmission system produce? The length of cable might be a proxy for the amount of transporting such a system carries out? In principle it is easy to say what variables are important in each of these functions, the problem is one of assignment. In practice most of the variables have some of the characteristics of inputs, outputs and environmental variables.

Another key problem with functions other than generation is keeping the number of variables to a manageable size. In such complex multi-input multi-output production functions as those in the ESI it might be desirable to take every factor into account. Engineers will say that there are many different kinds of cables, transformers, customers, environmental factors etc. This makes each transmission and distribution system unique. However, given the reasonably small number of firms to be analysed (129 and 145) and the difficulties of collecting and standardizing data we need to keep the number of variables to minimum. The *DEA* technique has a declining ability to distinguish between units as the sum of the inputs and outputs increases.[2] It would therefore seem desirable to keep the number of variables in the *DEA* as low as possible and to test for the significance of some of the other variables using regression analysis.[3]

Turning to the functions themselves we need to clearly define the boundaries of the functions which we are comparing especially as they are often undertaken within a vertically integrated firm. This is potentially difficult. At what point along the line from the power station to the final consumer does transmission change into distribution? What exactly is the difference between distribution and supply? In general companies themselves distinguish between transmission and distribution cables, so it is possible to distinguish between these two functions. The distinction between distribution and supply is a new one brought about by the regulatory arrangements operating in the UK since the privatization of the ESI. The two functions are treated separately for accounting purposes and are supposed to distinguish the natural monopoly aspect of supplying electricity through a network from the potentially competitive market for metering, billing and other services with which the distribution function is bundled.[4] The distinctions are different for the USA and the best we can do in comparing US and UK firms is to accept the country standard definitions of distribution.[5]

8.4 Modelling the Transmission Function

We consider two ways to model the transmission function. The first is the *DEA* methodology and the second involves estimating a cost function for transmission. We examine each of these methods in turn.

8.4.1 *A DEA Model for Transmission*

A *DEA* run on transmission data is conceptually straightforward. For each firm we have various data on the characteristics of the transmission function. We need to decide what the outputs and inputs are in transmission in order to correctly assign data as output or input. Assignment of data to output or input occurs subject to the constraint that the number of outputs plus inputs must be small relative to the size of the dataset. In our study of electricity generating firms in Chapter 5 the number of outputs plus inputs was limited to just four with *DEA* runs being carried out on a sample containing 95 firms.[6] This ensured that the number of frontier firms was small in relation to the size of the dataset. In our transmission study the smallest available sample is just 35 firms but there are multiple inputs and outputs. It is therefore necessary to trade-off the desire to identify and include all relevant variables and the need to keep the number of frontier firms down in order to differentiate between the firms.

The production function in transmission transports electric current from the power station to nodes in the distribution network. This transportation involves the use of transmission capital, labour and energy. Transmission capital takes the form of pylons, transformers, substations and underground and overground cables. These capitals may take many different forms: cables may be high or low voltage, transformers have different capacity ratings etc. The energy used in transmission is equal to the resistance and transformation losses in electric energy incurred in transporting energy sent out from power stations (our measured output in generation) to the nodes in the distribution system. The output from the transmission system has several dimensions: the total amount of the electric energy transported, the load profile of the output, the voltage level of the output (a quality variable), and the dispersion of the distribution nodes and of the power stations from which the electricity is transported.

Taking into account the need to keep the number of outputs plus inputs small a simple *DEA* model of transmission might take the following form:

Inputs	*Outputs*
1. Number of Employees.	1. Electric Energy Delivered.
2. Circuit Km*Capacity (kV).	2. Maximum System Demand.
3. Electric Energy Losses.	3. Route Km.

(Model T1)

Looking first at the input side: the starting point for the above formulation is that the three inputs correspond to labour, capital and fuel inputs respectively. Inputs 1 and 3 are relatively uncontroversial. Input 2 is calculated by multiplying the length of the circuits in each voltage class by the average of the voltage class and summing over all the voltage classes. Modelling the capital input (2) as circuit km times capacity (kV) has the advantage of keeping the potentially large number of capital variables to a minimum while including information on the two capital inputs that are most important and consistently reported. Industry enquiries[7] suggest that this composite variable is a reasonably acceptable proxy for transmission system capacity. Alternative formulations of the capital input would inevitably involve the introduction of a greater number of inputs. A first extension might be to include total circuit km and transformer capacity (MVA) separately. Data on pylons and the number of substations do not exist for the US firms. Disaggregation to separate out the transmission circuit miles into subcategories by voltage level poses additional problems in that it is unclear where category boundaries should be drawn in order to draw fair comparisons. An attempt to include the UK's National Grid Company in the sample failed due to standardization problems.[8]

Turning to the output formulation the three outputs correspond to the size of the total output, the load profile of the output and the dispersion of the input and output nodes in the transmission system. No attempt to model the different voltages at which electricity is transported is made due to the difficulties of disaggregation noted in the discussion in the paragraph above. 1 is relatively uncontroversial but not without serious difficulties.[9] 2 is a highly unsatisfactory measure of load profile in the case of transmission. This is due to the characteristics of an electricity network in which there has to be continuous equilibrium between electricity supply and demand at every node in the system. For a system with many nodes 2 tells us very little about the profile of the load at individual nodes. In theory it must be possible to get information on the load profile at each node (system engineers must have this information to ensure continuity of supply) but in practice 2 represents the best simple approximation to system peak effects that is available. 3 attempts to measure the dispersion of the input and output nodes of the distribution system. Although this variable might be considered as an input and could enter as an input in a larger *DEA* model it has the characteristics of an environmentally determined output. Route km is a function of the dispersion of demand nodes and of environmental requirements/regulations concerning routing of underground or overground high voltage cables.

Unfortunately we cannot implement Model T1 due to problems of data availability. We have no data on electric energy losses in transmission only, route km or on the electric energy delivered via the transmission system to the entry nodes in the distribution system. This leads us to propose the theoretically inferior but practically feasible model:

Inputs	*Outputs*
1. Number of Employees.	1. Electric Energy Entered.
2. Circuit km*voltage Level (kV).	2. Maximum System Demand.
3. Transformer Capacity (MVA).	3. Circuit km.

(Model T2)

Circuit km and electric energy entered are the best available proxies that we have for route km and electric energy delivered. Transformer capacity is an available variable which provides additional information on the size of the capital stock and loosely proxies transformation losses.

Once we have estimated efficiencies using Model T2 we can then try holding some of the inputs and outputs constant and calculating the **KENVx(u,x)** measures of efficiency. In Section 8.6 we report three measures: **KENV2(u,x)** with circuit km*voltage level (kV) and circuit km as environmental variables; **KENV3(u,x)** with maximum system demand, circuit km and circuit km*voltage level as environmental variables; and **KENV4(u,x)** with circuit km*voltage level, transformer capacity, maximum system demand and circuit km as environmental variables.

8.4.2 *A Cost Function for Transmission*

We know of one published paper which attempts to estimate a cost function for transmission only. Huettner and Landon (1977) [hence H+L] divide costs in US electric utilities into the six cost categories listed in USEIA *Financial Statistics* and model each separately by OLS. The purpose of their paper is to identify economies and diseconomies of scale in the electricity industry. One of these six categories is transmission costs. Transmission costs per kWh (*TAC*) may be expressed as:

$$TAC = a + b_1 \log TCAP + b_2 (\log TCAP)^2 + b_3 \log UTCAP$$
$$+ b_4 (\log UTCAP)^2 + b_5 WC + b_6 UG$$
$$+ b_7 SM + b_8 Com + b_9 Ind + GDUMs + HDUMs$$

TCAP = Total capacity (MW).
UTCAP = Utilization of capacity.
WC = Wage cost per hour.
UG = Underground circuit miles/1000 customers.
SM = Structure miles/1000 customers.
Com = Commercial kWh (% of total).
Ind = Industrial kWh (% of total).
GDUMs = Geographical location dummies.
HDUMs = Holding company dummies.

(Model H+L 1)

H+L record an R^2 of 0.4347 for an estimating equation based on a sample of 74 firms. Two major criticisms can be levelled at this formulation. Firstly, H+L measure *TCAP* in terms of generating capacity and *UTCAP* as the utilization of the generating capacity linked to the transmission system (New Zealand Ministry of Energy (1989), p.7). It is clearly unsatisfactory to measure transmission capacity using generating capacity and these measures should be changed if possible. Secondly, the functional form of the cost function has only a loose theoretical foundation. The variables are those thought to be significant in explaining transmission costs and the general form is that for the textbook cost function:

$$C = g(\underline{Y}, \underline{P})$$

$\underline{Y} = output\ vector$

$\underline{P} = input\ price\ vector$

However the cost function has only one input price variable and an arbitrary formulation of the output variables. The theoretical basis for this functional form compares unfavourably with the translog cost functions estimated for the generation function (Atkinson and Halvorsen, 1984 and 1986) and for electricity distribution (New Zealand Ministry of Energy, 1989). The translog cost function represents a second order approximation to any arbitrary functional form. Estimation of a full translog cost function system requires information on the quantities of outputs and the price of each of the inputs.

The problem for transmission function estimation is the lack of available input price information. It is therefore unlikely that we can do any better than a rather arbitrary formulation of the cost function similar to the Huettner and Landon formulation. We therefore suggest the following formulation:

$$TAC = a + b_1 \log CAP + b_2 (\log CAP)^2 + b_3 Maxrat + b_4 (Maxrat)^2$$
$$+ b_5 UG + b_6 (UG)^2 + b_7 OG + b_8 Trans + b_9 WC + b_{10} ODUM$$

TAC = Transmission cost per million kWh.
CAP = Circuit km*voltage level.
Maxrat = Ratio of maximum to average demand.
Resid = Percentage of residential sales in total sales.
UG = Length of underground circuits (km).
OG = Length of overhead circuits (km).
Trans =Transmission transformer capacity (MVA).
WC = Wage cost per employee (1000s of $).
ODUM = Ownership dummy variable (MUNI=1, IOU=0).

(Model T3)

Note again that the dependent variable (*TAC*) is the average cost of transmitting a unit of electricity. This equation retains the form of Model H+L but reflects data availability constraints. *CAP* and *Maxrat* attempt to meet the data criticism which Model H+L has been subjected to.[10] We also drop the number of customers in *OG* and *UG* terms. It is not clear how the number of customers which the distribution network to which the transmission network is connected affects costs in transmission. We add a *(UG)²* term in order to pick up possible non-linearity in the underground circuit km costs.[11] This formulation has a major weakness over the *DEA* model T2 if used in an international context: the requirement to compare costs in different currencies. This implies the need for appropriate exchange rate conversions for the financial variables and introduces further scope for errors in measurement. Country dummy variables might be able to deal with some of these errors.

8.5   Modelling the Electricity Distribution Function

8.5.1   *Previous Studies of Electricity Distribution*

In this section we review seven previous studies of cost efficiency in electricity distribution. It is interesting to examine these studies to see what variables other authors have used in modelling electricity distribution. Three of the studies employ single equation regression analysis, two employ translog cost function systems and the two most recent a *DEA* approach.

The H+L paper in Section 8.4.2 estimates a cost function for distribution expenses in a sample of 74 US utilities using capacity, wage costs, number of transformers, sales per major customer class among the explanatory variables (see H+L 2 in Section 8.5.3). The dependent variable is distribution cost per kWh. The coefficients on the first three variables and on sales per residential customer were significant. The purpose of this study is to estimate economies of scale in the electric utility business units using US Energy Information Agency data for the year 1971. Minimum cost occurred for a firm size of 2600MW. This study like Model H+L in Section 8.4.2 uses generating capacity as a measure of distribution capacity.

Neuberg (1977) estimates a cost function for distribution using number of customers as the output explanatory variable as well as total sales, miles of overhead line, number of square miles of service territory, the price of labour, price of capital and an ownership dummy variable. The dependent variable is the sum of distribution, consumer accounts, sales and a proportion of administration and general activities costs. The purpose of the study is to estimate the effect of ownership on costs. Neuberg uses two data samples, the largest of these contains 374 firms operating in 1972. Neuberg finds that publicly owned firms exhibit significantly lower costs than privately owned firms.

Roberts (1986) examines the effects of economies of density and size on costs in the transmission and distribution of electric power. Roberts develops a translog cost function involving four inputs and four outputs. The inputs are kWh input, transmission capital, distribution capital and labour input. The outputs are low and high voltage deliveries, square miles of service area and the number of customers. Estimation was undertaken using a Zellner efficient estimation of a system of equations which included the cost function and three of the input share equations.[12] Roberts used US Energy Information Agency data on 65 firms operating in 1978. Roberts found significant reductions in average cost when energy deliveries increased to existing customers but not when increased deliveries were going to new customers.

Nelson and Primeaux (1988) [N+P] examine the effect of competition on costs in the transmission and distribution system. Total costs of T&D are apparently modelled by OLS. Total costs in distribution are modelled as a function of miles of transmission line, city size in square miles, total number of customers, output, price of a kWh, the wage rate, a time trend and a dummy variable for the nature of the competitive environment. The title of this study is misleading. It actually only models costs in distribution. Distribution costs are the sum of distribution, customer accounts, sales expenses and a proportion of administrative and general expenses and the cost of obtaining the power. The data are collected for 23 firms operating over the period 1961–76, which gives a total sample of 295 data points. N+P find evidence for a U-shaped average cost curve in distribution and a role for competition in reducing costs.

The New Zealand Ministry of Energy (1989) model costs in the 60 New Zealand Electricity Supply Authorities (ESAs) – distribution companies – using annual data from the 1986–87 accounting year. This study attempts to identify the optimal scale of operation for an ESA in New Zealand. The most sophisticated analysis involves estimating both a three input and a four input single output translog cost function.[13] The output is electricity distributed and the four inputs are labour, capital, electricity purchased and 'other'. The three input model drops the electricity purchased input on the grounds that the cost of purchased power was beyond the control of the individual ESA in 1986–87. Both of these translog equation systems are estimated by maximum likelihood. Minimum cost occurs at 1748MW and 2315MW respectively for the three input and four input cost function systems. The problem with these cost functions is the arbitrary nature of the calculation of the price of capital and the price of 'other'.

We now turn to the two *DEA* studies. Weyman-Jones (1992) [W-J] uses a *DEA* approach to measure productive efficiency within a sample of 12 UK Regional Electricity Companies (RECs) over the period 1970–1 to 1988–9 (240 observations in all). The purpose of this study is to examine whether comparative performance measures can be established for uncompetitive firms in order to facilitate yardstick competition.

W-J presents two *DEA* models. Firstly, Study A:

Inputs:

1. Number of Employees.
2. Network Size (Mains km).
3. Transformer Capacity (MVA).

Outputs:

1. Domestic Sales (kWh).
2. Commercial Sales (kWh).
3. Industrial Sales (kWh).
4. Maximum Demand (kW).

(Model W-J 1)

Secondly, Study B:

Inputs:

1. Number of Employees.

Outputs:

1. Number of Customers.

Environmental Variables:

1. Network Size (Mains km).
2. Transformer Capacity (MVA).
3. Total Sales (kWh).

4. Maximum Demand (kW).
5. Population Density.
6. Industrial Share in Sales (%).

(Model W-J 2)

W-J 2 attempts to allow for the different operating environments faced by the firms. This *DEA* is estimated by the linear programs which we outlined in Section 2.2 of Chapter 4. Study A reveals substantial inefficiency within the RECs and a correlation between cycles in regional GDP and efficiency. Efficiency rises as a regional GDP moves up the economic cycle. Study B is used to show that efficiency scores rose and the variance of the scores fell as the industry moved towards privatization.

The final paper we look at is by Hjalmarsson and Veiderpass (1992a) [H+V]. This paper examines productive efficiency and ownership in the Swedish electricity distribution industry. This study uses data on 285 Swedish retail electricity distributors operating in 1985.

The authors estimate the following *DEA*:

Inputs

1. Labour input (hours).
2. High voltage lines (km).
3. Low voltage lines (km).

4. Transformer Capacity (kVA).

Outputs

1. Low voltage output (MWh).
2. High voltage output (MWh).
3. Number of low voltage electricity customers.
4. Number of high voltage electricity customers.

(Model H+V)

H+V also estimate a second model with all four of the above inputs but just outputs 1 and 2, and a third model with the four inputs and outputs 3 and 4. The results show that average technical efficiency is low, rural distribution companies are relatively scale inefficient and that ownership, economic organization and service area do not appear to affect efficiency in any significant way.

We should note two points about the above studies. Firstly, the estimation of a translog cost function involves information on the price of all the inputs including capital. This information is difficult to obtain. It would seem that the best we can do with a parametric function is to estimate a naive single equation cost function. Secondly, there appear to be several different specifications we could use for a *DEA*. It would seem sensible to specify the largest feasible *DEA* and then to run additional *DEA*s designating some variables as environmental (fixed) variables.[14]

8.5.2 *A DEA Model for Distribution*

The production function for the distribution function can be characterized as using capital, labour and electricity supplied to the system at several different nodes to produce outputs differentiated by quantity of electric energy, location, voltage and load profile. Ideally we would want to include variables in our *DEA* to model these aspects of the production of electricity distribution services. A simple characterization might be:

Inputs:

1. Number of Employees.
2. Transformers (MVA).
3. Circuit km.

Outputs:

1. Number of Customers.
2. Residential Sales (mkWh).
3. Non-Residential Sales (mkWh).
4. Service Area (sq.km).
5. Maximum Demand (MW).

(Model D1)

The inputs are straightforward to rationalize: 2 and 3 represent the major capital inputs and 1 the labour input. Electric energy losses would be a desirable input variable but figures for this are unavailable at the distribution level only. The voltage data for a circuit km*voltage level measure of capital are also unavailable. On the output side 1 captures the number of nodes the utility must supply and together with 4 captures density effects (4 also captures the effects of franchise area requirements); 5 captures a load profile effect; 2 and 3 capture the quantity of output and distinguish voltage effects. It is interesting to note that the above characterization is consistent with the Hopkinson approach to costs used in electricity rate-making (see Crew and Kleindorfer, 1979). This approach splits costs into three categories (a) consumer related i.e. a function of the number of consumers (b) unit related i.e. a function of the volume of sales (c) demand related i.e. a function of load profile.

In Section 8.7 we generate four environmental measures of efficiency (**KENVx(u,x)**): **KENV2(u,x)** assumes that circuit km and service area are environmental variables; **KENV3(u,x)** assumes maximum demand is also an environmental variable; **KENV4(u,x)** further assumes that transformer capacity is an environmental variable; and **KENV6(u,x)** assumes that all the variables except the number of employees and the number of customers are environmental variables.

8.5.3   A Cost Function for Distribution

H+L (1977) estimate the following cost function for distribution:

$$DAC = a + b_1 \log TCAP + b_2 (\log TCAP)^2 + b_3 UTCAP + b_4 (UTCAP)^2$$
$$+ b_5 NTransC + b_6 ResidC + b_7 CommC + b_8 IndC + b_9 WC$$
$$+ GDUMs + HDUMs$$

DAC = Distribution cost per kWh.
TCAP = Total Capacity in MW.
UTCAP = Average demand as a ratio of maximum capacity.
NTransC = Number of line transformers per customer.
ResidC = Residential sales per customer (MWh).
CommC = Commercial sales per customer (MWh).
IndC = Industrial sales per customer (MWh).
WC = Company wage cost ($/hour).
GDUMs = Geographical dummy variables.
HDUMs = Holding company dummy variables.

[H+L 2]

The variable *TransC* is a measure of the density of the distribution network. The *ResidC, CommC* and *IndC* distinguish the effects of the nature of demand on cost while *TCAP* and *UTCAP* model economies of scale in distribution networks. Huettner and Landon report an R^2 of 60.45% for this function on a sample of 74 firms.

Following H+L 2 we propose the following single equation cost function for distribution:

$$DAC = a + b_1 \log SalesC + b_2 (\log SalesC)^2 + b_3 Maxrat + b_4 (Maxrat)^2$$
$$+ b_5 Cust + b_6 Resid + b_7 OGkmC + b_8 UGkmC + b_9 TransC$$
$$+ b_{10} WC + b_{11} AREA + b_{12} ODUM + b_{13} CDUM$$

DAC = Distribution cost in 1000s of US dollars per million kWh.
SalesC = Total sales per customer in million kWh.
Maxrat = Ratio of maximum to average demand.
Cust = Number of customers.
Resid = Share of residential sales in total sales (%).
OGkmC = Overground distribution circuit km per customer.
UGkmC = Underground distribution circuit km per customer.
TransC = Transformer capacity (MVA) per customer.
Area = Service area in square km.
WC = Wage cost in 1000s of US dollars per employee.
ODUM = Ownership dummy variable (MUNI = 1, IOU = 0).
CDUM = UK country dummy variable (UK = 1, US = 0).

(Model D2)

D2 involves using the available information. *Maxrat, SalesC* and *Cust* attempt to capture system scale effects. *CAP* and *UTCAP* are not used for the same reasons given in Section 8.5.2: it is clearly unsatisfactory to measure distribution system capacity using the generating capacity linked to it. In addition, measures of connected generating capacity are not available for the sample of distribution utilities that we analyse. *Area, TransC, OGkmC* and *UGkmC* capture density and environmental effects in a fuller way than just *NTransC* in H+L 2. The use of the percentage *Resid* rather than customer class sales *ResidC, CommC* and *IndC* avoids potential colinearity problems associated with these three series. In an international context the use of *Resid* also avoids problems of comparability of non-residential sales data.[15] Note that D2 directly or indirectly makes use of all of the variables which we proposed using in the *DEA* model of distribution D1.[16] We use a purchasing power parity exchange rate to convert operation and maintenance costs and wages in the UK RECs (Regional Electricity Companies) into US dollars. In the context of the present study an additional dummy variable is added for the UK to attempt to capture the effects of any remaining incompatibility in the data.

8.6   Results from the Analysis of the Transmission Sample

The average efficiencies for the transmission sample are recorded in Table 8.1. Average efficiencies increase as the size of the sample firms rises. The average environmental measures of efficiency, **KENVx(u,x)**, increase as the number of environmental variables increases from 2 to 4.

The averages for publicly owned and privately owned firms reveal mixed results. The **K(u,x)** measure shows that on average publicly owned firms are more efficient in the Small and Medium samples but not in the Large sample. The differences in the averages are in general less than 5%, except in the Large sample where the difference in the averages rises to 8.03% for **KENV2(u,x)**, though this is on a sample of only four public firms. The **KENVx(u,x)** measures for the Large sample show that all the large publicly owned firms are actually frontier efficient once their operating environment has been taken into account. Privately owned firms outperform publicly owned firms on all except one of the average **KENVx(u,x)** measures for the Small and Medium samples.

Table 8.2 indicates the nature of scale inefficiency in the transmission sample.

Table 8.1: Average Efficiencies for Transmission Sample

	K(u,x)	F(u,x)	C(u,x)	S(u,x)	KENV 2(u,x)	KENV 3(u,x)	KENV 4(u,x)
Av Total	0.7996	0.8954	0.9695	0.9215	0.8506	0.8785	0.8955
Av Total Private	0.8092	0.9061	0.9686	0.9219	0.8602	0.8848	0.9004
Av Total Public	0.7555	0.8462	0.9735	0.9195	0.8062	0.8496	0.8730
Av Small Total	0.6895	0.8024	0.9613	0.8988	0.7260	0.7933	0.8506
Av Small Private	0.6771	0.7812	0.9593	0.9078	0.7286	0.8013	0.8563
Av Small Public	0.7099	0.8373	0.9647	0.8840	0.7218	0.7802	0.8412
Av Medium Total	0.8196	0.9304	0.9638	0.9149	0.8833	0.8970	0.8962
Av Medium Private	0.8186	0.9383	0.9605	0.9089	0.8829	0.8944	0.8996
Av Medium Public	0.8297	0.8485	0.9980	0.9775	0.8874	0.9237	0.8605
Av Large Total	0.8833	0.9367	0.9874	0.9561	0.9289	0.9385	0.9418
Av Large Private	0.8912	0.9447	0.9891	0.9542	0.9197	0.9306	0.9343
Av Large Public	0.8224	0.8744	0.9738	0.9711	1.0000	1.0000	1.0000

Table 8.2: Fare Returns to Scale: Transmission Data

	Likely DRS	*Likely CRS*	*Likely IRS*
Total	36	37	56
Total Private	26	31	49
Total Public	10	6	7
Total Small	21	7	9
Small Private	12	4	7
Small Public	9	3	2
Total Medium	11	14	32
Medium Private	10	12	30
Medium Public	1	2	2
Total Large	4	16	15
Large Private	4	15	12
Large Public	0	1	3

Many firms (37 out of 129) do appear to be scale efficient, this is a function of the larger number of outputs plus inputs in the transmission *DEA* than for generation in Chapters 5, 6 and 7 and of the splitting of the dataset into three subsamples. Although the overall totals for DRS, CRS and IRS are roughly equal, the subsample results show that DRS is relatively more common in the Small sample (DRS = 57%) and IRS is relatively more common in the Medium and Large samples (IRS equals 56% and 43%).

Table 8.3 lists a battery of one-tailed statistical tests on the efficiency measures. The null hypothesis is that there is no difference in efficiency between publicly owned and privately owned electric utilities. The tests are as used in previous chapters. Note however that we collect the *DEA* scores calculated on different subsamples together – this is due to the need to have a sufficiently large sample of scores on which to conduct statistical testing. The results are conclusive, all 35 tests indicate that the null hypothesis of no difference in technical efficiency cannot be rejected at the 5% level of significance. Indeed all but four tests indicate that the null could not be rejected at the 20% level of significance and 25 of the tests indicate an inability to reject the null at even the 40% level. These results provide strong support from electricity transmission for the conclusions on relative technical efficiency of Chapters 5 and 6 on electricity generating firms and plants.

We now consider the unreported detailed firm level results – the codes refer to the transmission sample listings in Appendix 2.4.1. The arbitrary nature of the division of the dataset into three subsamples means that we should be wary of attaching too much significance to

Table 8.3: Summary of Tests of the Effect of Ownership on Efficiency – IOUs vs MUNIs: Transmission Sample: 106 IOUs and 23 MUNIs.

Efficiency Measure	Analysis of Variance F $(Prob>F)$	Kruskal-Wallis χ^2 $(Prob>\chi^2)$	Median Scores (points above median) χ^2 $(Prob>\chi^2)$	Van der Waerden (1-way) χ^2 $(Prob>\chi^2)$	Savage (exponential) χ^2 $(Prob>\chi^2)$
K(u,x)	1.559 (0.2141)	1.5511 (0.213)	1.2207 (0.2692)	1.3263 (0.2495)	0.6696 (0.4132)
F(u,x)	2.503 (0.1161)	3.3675 (0.0665)	0 (0.9999)	2.965 (0.0851)	3.1585 (0.0755)
C(u,x)	0.087 (0.7689)	0.0874 (0.7675)	0 (0.9999)	0.1002 (0.7516)	0.0738 (0.7859)
S(u,x)	0.011 (0.918)	0.0475 (0.8275)	0.5304 (0.4664)	0.0003 (0.9866)	0.0118 (0.9136)
KENV2(u,x)	1.256 (0.2646)	0.6873 (0.4071)	0 (0.9999)	0.9422 (0.3317)	0.5293 (0.4669)
KENV3(u,x)	0.608 (0.4371)	0.1098 (0.7403)	0 (0.9999)	0.2639 (0.6075)	0.0517 (0.8201)
KENV4(u,x)	0.367 (0.546)	0.0842 (0.7716)	0 (0.9999)	0.1797 (0.6717)	0.042 (0.8376)

any of the individual efficiency scores. The general trends in the firm level scores are of interest. The number of frontier efficient firms increases as the number of environmental variables is increased from 0 in **K(u,x)** to 4 in **KENV4(u,x)**. Looking at the Large transmission companies 29 out of 35 are frontier efficient on the **KENV4(u,x)** measure in which only the output, net energy transmitted, and the input of labour are free to vary. The limitations of using **K(u,x)** to measure efficiency in transmission are illustrated by some of the notable firm level results: eg. Bonneville Power Administration (128I) with the largest transmission network in the sample by circuit km*kV has a **K(u,x)** of just 0.4960 (the lowest in the subsample). This suggests that it could supply the same outputs using less than 50% of its current inputs – this seems unlikely. The **KENVx(u,x)** measures for the Bonneville Power Administration indicate that once operating environment is considered the company is actually frontier efficient. Some of the **KENVx(u,x)** measures are also unlikely to be of much practical use eg. **KENV4(u,x)** = 0.1862 for Naragansett (18I) – this indicates that given peak demand, circuit km, circuit km*kV and transformer capacity the company could theoretically supply its current output with 22 employees instead of the actual number of 120. Divergent results *may* be correct but in general extreme caution must be exercised in interpreting any of the individual firm level efficiency scores.

Table 8.4: Transmission OLS Variable Definitions

Cap = log (transmission circuit km*kV).
Capsq = *Cap* Squared.
Max = Ratio of Peak to Average Demand.
Maxsq = *Max* Squared.
Wage = Average Salary.
OGkm = Overground Transmission Circuit km.
UGkm = Underground Transmission Circuit km.
UGkmsq = *UGkm* squared.
Own = Ownership Dummy (1 = Public ,0 = Private).
Trans = Transmission Transformer Capacity (MVA).

Table 8.5: Estimated Transmission Cost Function

Parameters	*Dependent Variable* *O+M costs/mkWh*	
Constant	12.8309	(4.6949)**
Cap	-1.77766	(0.79844)**
Capsq	-0.07367	(0.03531)**
Max	-1.92864	(1.26120)
Maxsq	0.38623	(0.41158)
OGkm	-0.24210E-04	(0.26589E-04)
UGkm	0.00140	(0.00073)*
UGkmsq	-0.48822E-06	(0.28990E-06)*
Trans	-0.10692E-04	(0.74591E-05)
Wage	0.03030	(0.01560)*
Own	-0.34978	(0.23490)
R^2	0.2147	
F	3.2259**	

Standard Errors in parentheses.
* = significant at 10%, ** = significant at 5%.

The transmission cost function estimated by OLS is recorded in Table 8.5 (and the variable definitions are in Table 8.4). The F-test indicates that the regression is significant at 1% (i.e. there is a less than 1% chance that the regression equation explains none of the variation in transmission costs). The function indicates the significance of labour costs and terms in transmission circuit km*kV (a proxy for system capacity) in explaining the variation in average operation and mainten-ance costs in transmission. The regression explains only 21.47% of the variation in transmission sample costs. The negative coefficient on the ownership dummy indicates lower costs in public firms, however this coefficient is not significant. The insignificance of the ownership dummy indicates support from the regression analysis for the null hypothesis of no difference in cost efficiency between public and private firms.

8.7 Results from the Analysis of the Distribution Sample

The average efficiencies for the distribution sample are recorded in Table 8.6. This suggests mixed conclusions on the relative efficiency of publicly owned and privately owned distribution companies. Among large distribution companies publicly owned firms outperform privately owned firms on six out of the eight efficiency measures. The Small and Medium subsamples show that publicly owned firms exhibit superior performance on 9 out of 16 averages. The differences in the averages for public and private firms are usually of the order of 5% or less except for **KENV3(u,x)** and **KENV4(u,x)** for Large subsample firms (the difference is 6.11% for **KENV3(u,x)**). Comparing the average efficiencies in distribution with those for transmission (Table 8.1) we can observe that the average scores are higher in distribution than in transmission. This is unsurprising given the higher number of outputs plus inputs in the distribution analysis which should give rise to more frontier efficient firms.

Table 8.7 indicates the nature of returns to scale in the distribution sample. Roughly equal numbers of firms are classified as DRS, CRS,

Table 8.6: Average Efficiencies for Distribution Sample

	K(u,x)	F(u,x)	C(u,x)	S(u,x)	KENV 2(u,x)	KENV 3(u,x)	KENV 4(u,x)	KENV 6(u,x)
Av Total	0.8517	0.9274	0.9684	0.9491	0.9348	0.9611	0.9644	0.9822
Av Total Private	0.8455	0.9264	0.9668	0.9448	0.9337	0.9560	0.9613	0.9797
Av Total Public	0.8798	0.9319	0.9759	0.9687	0.9399	0.9845	0.9788	0.9939
Av Small Total	0.8944	0.9492	0.9608	0.9788	0.9641	0.9777	0.9727	0.9872
Av Small Private	0.8792	0.9481	0.9564	0.9677	0.9608	0.9821	0.9738	0.9797
Av Small Public	0.9206	0.9509	0.9683	0.9981	0.9699	0.9702	0.9708	1.0000
Av Medium Total	0.8791	0.9589	0.9628	0.9539	0.9649	0.9679	0.9544	0.9766
Av Medium Private	0.8807	0.9610	0.9595	0.9564	0.9626	0.9660	0.9545	0.9775
Av Medium Public	0.8650	0.9397	0.9924	0.9306	0.9853	0.9853	0.9540	0.9682
Av Large Total	0.8108	0.8932	0.9763	0.9317	0.8981	0.9483	0.9683	0.9842
Av Large Private	0.8051	0.8907	0.9764	0.9274	0.9006	0.9389	0.9625	0.9814
Av Large Public	0.8424	0.9071	0.9760	0.9553	0.8842	1.0000	1.0000	1.0000

Table 8.7: Fare Returns to Scale: Distribution Data

	Likely DRS	*Likely CRS*	*Likely IRS*
Total	43	46	61
Total Private	35	36	53
Total Public	8	10	8
Total Small	9	15	6
Small Private	8	8	3
Small Public	1	7	3
Total Medium	20	15	15
Medium Private	18	14	13
Medium Public	2	1	2
Total Large	14	16	35
Large Private	9	14	32
Large Public	5	2	3

and IRS. 54% of Large distribution companies exhibit increasing returns to scale – this provides weak evidence in favour of the textbook suggestion that there are likely to be increasing returns even in large electricity distribution systems.

Table 8.8 lists a battery of one-tailed statistical tests on the efficiency measures. The null hypothesis is that there is no difference in efficiency between publicly-owned and privately-owned electric utilities. The tests are as used in previous chapters and in Section 8.5. As in the previous section for transmission the results are conclusive, all 35 tests indicate that the null hypothesis of no difference in productive efficiency cannot be rejected at the 5% level of significance. Only six of the tests indicate that the null could not be rejected at the 20% level of significance. We have now established a consistent picture of no statistically significant difference in the relative technical efficiency of publicly-owned and privately-owned electric utilities in generation, transmission and distribution.

We now consider the unreported detailed firm level results – the codes refer to the sample listings in Appendix 2.4.2. The environmental measures of efficiency reveal that the number of frontier efficient firms increases steadily as the number of environmental variables is increased. The **KENV6(u,x)** measure, which only allows for one output variable (number of customers) and one variable input (labour), has only one (out of 30) non-frontier efficient firm in the Small subsample, five in the Medium subsample (of 50) and seven in the Large subsample (of 65). This suggests that once allowance has been made for the diversity

Table 8.8: Summary of Tests of the Effect of Ownership on Efficiency – IOUs vs MUNIs: Distribution Sample: 119 IOUs and 26 MUNIs.

Efficiency Measure	Analysis of Variance F $(Prob>F)$	Kruskal-Wallis χ^2 $(Prob>\chi^2)$	Median Scores (points above median) χ^2 $(Prob>\chi^2)$	Van der Waerden (1-way) χ^2 $(Prob>\chi^2)$	Savage (exponential) χ^2 $(Prob>\chi^2)$
K(u,x)	1.116 (0.2925)	0.6635 (0.4153)	0.1543 (0.6945)	1.0949 (0.2954)	0.5897 (0.4425)
F(u,x)	0.044 (0.835)	0.1321 (0.7163)	0 (0.9999)	0.027 (0.8695)	0.2002 (0.6545)
C(u,x)	0.293 (0.5889)	0.5591 (0.4546)	0 (0.9999)	0.5714 (0.4497)	0.6752 (0.4112)
S(u,x)	1.724 (0.1913)	1.6404 (0.2003)	0.813 (0.3672)	1.689 (0.1937)	1.218 (0.2698)
KENV2(u,x)	0.072 (0.7894)	0.0028 (0.9578)	0 (0.9999)	0.0386 (0.8443)	0.0007 (0.9785)
KENV3(u,x)	2.352 (0.1273)	2.7956 (0.0945)	0 (0.9999)	2.9423 (0.0863)	2.769 (0.0961)
KENV4(u,x)	0.779 (0.3789)	0.79 (0.3741)	0 (0.9999)	0.9702 (0.3246)	0.7521 (0.3858)
KENV6(u,x)	1.016 (0.3152)	0.8807 (0.348)	0 (0.9999)	1.0085 (0.3153)	0.8473 (0.3573)

of operating environments most distribution utilities are *relatively* efficient. The UK firms are around the average for the firms in the Large subsample with LE (London Electricity, 139M) exhibiting 100% efficiency on all eight measures. Some of the results are implausible e.g. **KENV2(u,x)** for 104I and 140M. Kansas City Power and Light (104I) has a **KENV2(u,x)** of just 4.67%. **KENV2(u,x)** assumes that circuit km and service area are environmental variables and hence a figure of 4.67% implies a possible reduction in transformer capacity and labour employed of 95.33%, however by **KENV6(u,x)** Kansas City is 100% efficient. The **KENV2(u,x)** for MANWEB (140M) is 31.89% implying a possible 68.11% reduction in transformer capacity and labour given the service area and circuit km (MANWEB is 100% efficient on **KENV3(u,x)**). As we suggested for the transmission results the distribution results suggest individual firm level measures need to be treated with a lot of caution.

The distribution cost function estimated by OLS is recorded in Table 8.10 (and the variable definitions are in Table 8.9). The F-test reveals that the estimated equation is significant at 0.1%. The estimated function indicates the significance of sales per customer, sales per customer squared, number of customers, overground circuit km per

Table 8.9: Distribution OLS Variable Definitions

SalesC = log(Total final sales per customer (mkWh)).
SalesCsq = *SalesC* squared.
Max = Ratio of Peak to Average Demand.
Maxsq = *Max* Squared.
Resid = Ratio of Residential Sales in Total Sales.
Cust = Number of Customers.
OGkmC = Total Overground Distribution Circuit km per Customer.
UGkmC = Total Underground Distribution Circuit km per Customer.
TransC = Distribution Transformer Capacity per Customer (MVA).
Wage = Average Salary.
Area = Service Area in square km.
Own = Ownership Dummy
(1 = Public, 0 = Private).
UK = Country Dummy (1 = UK, 0 = US).

Table 8.10: Estimated Distribution Cost Function

Parameters	Dependent Variable O+M costs/mkWh	
Constant	9.70338	(4.67211)**
SalesC	7.36637	(2.58802)**
SalesCsq	1.38415	(0.35484)**
Max	0.18299	(0.23970)
Maxsq	-0.00713	(0.00993)
Resid	-0.29575	(1.25080)
Cust	-0.23254E-06	(0.13578E-06)*
OGkmC	4.66158	(2.39363)*
UGkmC	2.31798	(9.61318)
TransC	-9.99060	(6.58952)
Wage	0.04131	(0.01633)**
Area	-0.18010E-05	(0.14818E-05)
Own	-0.26968	(0.31201)
UK	0.34114	(0.59941)
R^2	0.6247	
F	16.7730**	

Standard Errors in parentheses.
* = significant at 10%, ** = significant at 5%.

customer and labour costs in explaining the variation in average operation and maintenance costs in distribution. The percentage of the variation in electricity distribution costs that is explained by the regression is very good: 62.47% is explained. The negative coefficient on the ownership dummy indicates lower costs in public firms. The coefficients on ownership and the UK country dummy variables are not significant. The regression results therefore indicate that there is no significant difference in costs between publicly owned and privately owned electricity distribution costs.

8.8 Conclusions

The results of this chapter indicate that it is not possible to reject the null hypothesis that publicly-owned and privately-owned electricity transmission and distribution systems exhibit no significant difference in technical or cost efficiency. The null hypothesis was tested using new data for a recent year: 1990. The *DEA* methodology was used to generate the four measures of technical efficiency used in Chapters 5 and 6 and also to generate several efficiency measures which assigned some variables as environmental (or fixed) variables. OLS cost functions were also estimated for transmission and distribution and these provided further cross-checking of the *DEA* results.

Estimation of efficiency scores was not as straightforward as for generation. The *DEA*s undertaken in Chapters 5, 6 and 7 for generation involved four outputs plus inputs; the transmission *DEA* involved six outputs plus inputs and the distribution *DEA* eight outputs plus inputs. The larger number of variables and the smaller sample sizes meant that a much larger percentage of firms were shown to be 100% efficient. It is not surprising that the multi-dimensional nature of production in transmission and distribution functions should give this result but it means that the analysis is not as capable of differentiating between the performance of individual production units in the context of electricity T&D as it is for electricity generation. We note again that an efficiency score of 100% does not imply that there is no scope for higher efficiency but that the firm is *relatively* efficient. 100% *DEA* scores provide no information for frontier efficient firms on how they can reduce inputs per unit of output.

The **KENVx(u,x)** measures were particularly important in the context of T&D. These measures revealed that some of the more implausible unrestricted *DEA* scores were only the result of comparing very different utilities with totally different characteristics. The **KENVx(u,x)** measures showed that a large number of utilities could be shown to be efficient if enough of the so-called outputs and inputs were considered fixed. The Fare RTS measures revealed little of interest: roughly equal numbers of firms were DRS, CRS and IRS within both the transmission and distribution subsamples.

The *DEA* measures used in this chapter looked at technical efficiency. The regression analysis looked at cost efficiency. The goodness of fit was surprisingly high for the distribution cost function at over 60%. In both functions wages were a significant explanator of costs. The theoretical basis for the estimated functions was necessarily weak but the results were in line with those for *DEA* with the coefficient on the ownership dummy not being significant at less than 10% in either the transmission or distribution functions. The regression results suggest that once environmental variables are incorporated into the cost function there appears to be no role for ownership in determining costs. This implies that, in contrast to the conclusions for electricity generation in Chapter 7, private sector investment decision making does not result in lower costs for IOUs relative to MUNIs. Perhaps this is because the level of external interference in investment decision making is equally high in IOUs and MUNIs as a result of the environmental impact of so many (even incremental) investment decisions in transmission and distribution.

The transmission study just looked at a sample of US firms. However the distribution study looked at both US and UK distribution companies. The UK utilities did not exhibit a notably different performance on the *DEA* scores from their US counterparts and by **KENV3(u,x)** the UK utilities are all 100% efficient. The UK firms did have higher operation and maintenance costs but the OLS regression analysis suggested system characteristics rather than a UK dummy variable can explain this. Together the *DEA* and OLS results suggest that there is no evidence that the UK RECs were performing poorly relatively to US distribution utilities prior to privatization.

Notes

1. As mentioned in Section 8.3.1 the number of firms in a sample to be analysed by *DEA* must be significantly greater than the number of outputs plus the number of inputs in order to avoid getting a large number of frontier efficient firms.
2. This is especially true as whole systems have different types, rather than mixes, of inputs when defined narrowly.
3. We do not proceed any further with this due to the lack of good information on such things as the amount of electricity supplied at each voltage level.
4. Weyman-Jones (1992), p.2.
5. The USEIA *Financial Statistics* distinguishes six operation and maintenance cost categories: production, transmission, distribution, customer accounts, customer service and information expenses, sales expenses and

administrative and general expenses. The UK distribution companies also distinguish six operating cost categories in their statistical reviews: purchases of electricity, distribution, customer service, meter reading, billing and collection, administrative and general expenses and training and welfare. The UK figures include depreciation while US figures do not. It would therefore seem that the distribution costs adjusted for depreciation are roughly comparable.

6. In generation plant level study in Chapter 6 we had utility subsamples of 108, 129, 318 and 213.

7. Thanks are due to Clive Harris at London Economics for suggesting the use of this variable to measure the capacity of a transmission system.

8. In the UK the National Grid mostly operates 132kV or above lines while in the US 69kV or above is considered to be a transmission voltage. The UK situation is further complicated by the ownership of substantial quantities of 132kV line by the distribution companies.

9. US transmission systems receive a lot of purchased power at various entry points to the system. One cannot imagine power as being transmitted from one end of the system to the other. A lot of power may be transmitted along small sections of the system.

10. The use of *CAP* ensures a comparability in the variables used in the *DEA* and regression analysis.

11. We wish to thank an anonymous industry source for suggesting the use of this additional variable.

12. This is a similar cost function system to that of Atkinson and Halvorsen (1984, 86) employed in Chapter 5 of this book.

13. The three input cost function has the same form as the cost function employed in Chapter 5.

14. We could experiment with dropping variables but this gives rise to greater variation in efficiency scores and more unlikely policy recommendations. Therefore we do not attempt to do this in what follows.

15. US EIA data (in *Financial Statistics*) on sales are divided into seven categories: residential, commercial, industrial, public street and highway lighting, other public authorities, railroads and railways and interdepartmental. UK company accounts data on sales are typically given in five categories: domestic, farms, commercial, industrial and public lighting.

16. This note explains how the variables used in D1 can be derived from the variables used in D2. The input variables of D1 are number of employees, transformer capacity, circuit km. Number of employees is derived from *(DAC*SalesC*Cust)/WC*, transformer capacity is equal to *TransC*Cust* and circuit km is equal to *(OGkmC+UGkmC)*Cust*. The output variables are number of customers, residential sales, non-residential sales, service area and maximum demand. Residential sales can be derived from *(SalesC*Cust*Resid)*, non-residential sales equals *(SalesC*Cust*(1-Resid))* and maximum demand equals *(Maxrat*SalesC*Cust)/8.76*.

CHAPTER 9

SUMMARY AND CONCLUSIONS

This book set out to conduct an empirical investigation, using the latest efficiency measurement techniques, into the claim that privately-owned electric utilities exhibit higher productive efficiency than publicly-owned electric utilities. The investigation was conducted using new data on electricity generation, transmission and distribution from an international sample of utilities. The use of differing methodologies allowed the measurement techniques to be compared and evaluated. The motivation for the study was the growing move towards restructuring and privatization of large sections of state owned electricity industries across the world. In this chapter we briefly review the findings of the earlier chapters and offer an overall conclusion.

In Chapter 2 we reviewed the theoretical evidence on the likely links between ownership and productive efficiency. We outlined property rights, bureaucracy and regulation theories. While the theoretical evidence, in general, suggested the superior efficiency of privately-owned utilities, this was subject to substantial qualification. The key theoretical issues were the relative efficiency of monitoring in large managerial utilities and the degree of political interference in the investment decisions of public utilities. We noted that any empirical comparison of public and private firms in electricity actually implied the comparison of the combination of ownership and (often explicit) regulation under private ownership with the combination of ownership and (often implicit) regulation under public ownership. We concluded that the theoretical evidence suggested that large electric utilities were unlikely to exhibit significant differences in efficiency across ownership types. This left the question of relative efficiency open to empirical analysis.

Previous empirical studies of relevance to the ownership–productive efficiency question were reviewed in Chapter 3. We began by examining the related empirical evidence on the effects of competition, economies of scale, vertical structure and regulation of various types on efficiency in the ESI. The evidence suggested that all these factors did affect costs, independently of ownership. This implied that ownership is not the only or even the most important issue in determining the relative productive efficiency of a given utility. We noted the difficulty this implied for conducting comparisons of efficiency between ownership types given the diverse characteristics of the utilities being compared.

Next we reviewed the previous work on ownership and efficiency. The evidence from the US studies was extremely mixed. Many of the early studies were subjected to serious methodological criticism. The later studies, using sophisticated parametric and non-parametric techniques, indicated no significant difference in productive efficiency between ownership types in electricity generation. The few non-US studies, if they addressed the issue at all, indicated no evidence for the superior performance of one ownership form over the other. The conclusion we drew from the previous empirical literature was that there was little evidence that ownership transfer *per se* could be expected to reduce costs.

Chapter 4 introduced the four methodologies for measuring the efficiency of decision making units. We followed Lovell and Schmidt (1988) in identifying the *DEA*, *PPA*, *DSA* and *SFM* techniques as being representative of the current state of the technology for measuring productive efficiency. We outlined each of these techniques in turn, noting their strengths and weaknesses and briefly reviewing the theoretical and empirical literature associated with them. Our presentation of *DEA* followed Fare et al. (1985a) and produced six measures of productive efficiency including a decomposition of overall technical efficiency into three mutually exclusive and exhaustive components. The *PPA* method followed Aigner and Chu (1968) in outlining the computation of a translog type production frontier for the analysis of productive efficiency and a differentiable Cobb-Douglas production frontier for analysis of overall and allocative efficiency. The *DSA* method followed Afriat (1972) in presenting the estimation of a statistical translog production frontier in order to calculate technical efficiency scores. A Cobb-Douglas production frontier and a translog cost frontier were developed in order to enable estimation of overall and allocative efficiency scores. The *SFM* technique followed Aigner, Lovell and Schmidt (1977) and Jondrow et al. (1982) in presenting the procedure for estimating overall productive efficiency scores from a stochastic translog cost frontier. The *DEA* and *PPA* scores are computed while the *DSA* and *SFM* scores are estimated. The *SFM* technique takes explicit account of errors while the *DEA* method makes no a priori assumptions about functional form of the production frontier. Together we expected these four techniques to provide for extensive 'methodology cross-checking' of results.

The empirical analysis began in Chapter 5. This chapter presented a comparison of the relative efficiency of a sample of 95 thermal electricity generating functions operating in eight countries in 1986. The analysis was conducted using the parametric approach of Atkinson and Halvorsen (1986) and the *DEA* method of Fare et al. (1985a). The results from the *DEA* methodology showed that there was limited evidence of significantly higher efficiency in IOUs compared with MUNIs. The A+H methodology detected no significant difference in efficiency between the two ownership types. Both of these techniques were adjusted to make allowance for differences in technology between the two ownership forms and there was a suggestion that this was driving the weakness of the result. There was strong evidence from both methodologies that many small MUNIs were operating at a point of significant increasing returns to scale. Scale analysis further suggested that optimal scale for a generating function in an IOU was 20,000 to 30,000mkWh and hence that a privatized CEGB could have been split into five to ten firms in order to exploit minimum efficient scale. However the estimate of the size of the potential scale economies in the CEGB varied markedly between the two methodologies.

Chapter 6 introduced the main dataset used in the book and reported the results of the analysis of technical efficiency for this dataset using the *DEA, PPA, DSA* and *SFM* techniques. The dataset consisted of 768 thermal power plants operating in 14 countries in 1989 and was subdivided into four smaller datasets: PEAK15, MID30, MID60 and BASE60. These subsets consisted of plants grouped by load factor in order to facilitate more meaningful comparison of plants producing similar 'goods'. For each of the four datasets efficiency analysis was conducted. The results showed a clear inability to reject the null hypothesis of no difference in technical efficiency between IOUs and MUNIs. Further regression/Tobit analysis of the technical efficiency scores from BASE60 again showed no significant role for ownership once allowance was made for load factor, age of plant, technology and country. Overall the results of this chapter constituted strong empirical support for the view that given the technology employed (i.e. the factor mix) IOUs and MUNIs were being operated equally efficiently.

In Chapter 7 we examined the overall and allocative efficiency of a sample of 164 plants from the BASE60 dataset. The analysis was conducted using the *DEA, PPA, DSA* and *SFM* techniques and both historic and current cost data. The results indicated a strong rejection of the null hypothesis in favour of the alternative hypothesis that IOUs have lower costs than MUNIs. Regression analysis of the overall efficiency scores also indicated the significance of ownership on cost efficiency. Given the results of Chapter 6, this implied that while MUNIs may be operating equally close to the production frontier, their factor mix is further away from being optimal. This suggests that the investment decisions which decide the factor mix are less efficient in MUNIs than in IOUs. We were led to conclude that government interference in the investment decisions of publicly owned electricity generators does significantly increase costs. However the different methodologies gave rise to divergent estimates of the size of the average cost differences (0.02% to 15.05%) and the best MUNIs were still among the best IOUs.

Chapter 8 extended the empirical analysis to look at the technical and cost efficiency of electricity transmission and distribution functions. The results were presented from the analysis of 129 US transmission utilities and 145 US and UK distribution utilities operating in 1990. *DEA* multiple input – multiple output measures of technical efficiency were calculated and further measures were computed which designated some of the outputs and inputs as environmental variables. OLS analysis of average costs in transmission and distribution was also conducted following Huettner and Landon (1977). The *DEA* results showed a complete inability to reject the null hypothesis of no significant difference in technical efficiency between the two ownership types. This was true whether or not allowance was made for the presence of environmental variables. These results were consistent with the results for the generation function in Chapter 6. The OLS analysis however also revealed the insignificance of ownership effects on average costs once environmental factors such as scale, service area, local wage rates are allowed for. The evidence of Chapters 7 and 8 together suggests that while privatization of electricity generation might be expected to lower costs, there is no evidence from our study that the same can be said about the electricity transmission and distribution functions. Perhaps this is because the level of government interference in investment in transmission and distribution functions is equally high independent of ownership. This may be due to the environmental nature of many investment decisions, particularily over routing the system. Such environmental regulation reduces the scope for IOUs to lower costs relative to MUNIs via better investment planning.

Before drawing a final conclusion on the question of ownership and efficiency in the ESI we note some caveats in the interpretation of our results. Firstly, given the many variables involved, our comparison of IOUs and MUNIs involves testing joint hypotheses concerning regulation, industry structure and ownership. Secondly, we have only examined efficiency in the static sense by taking a snapshot of the industry in particular years. We examine only the levels of efficiency in firms, not the growth rates. It may be that private firms starting from a lower base exhibit better productivity growth rates and hence that privatization could be expected to improve the dynamic performance of an electric utility. Thirdly, our significance tests compare the relative performance of ownership classes and do not constitute estimates of the expected efficiency gain for an individual firm. A given MUNI may therefore benefit substantially from privatization, even if on average the performance of IOUs and MUNIs is the same. Fourthly, our assumption that input prices are given biases the efficiency scores upwards because we are ignoring the potential cost savings resulting from utilizing cheaper inputs. For example, the UK electricity industry has derived substantial benefits from lower coal prices since its privatization. Fifthly, as with all empirical studies the results are only as good as the data. Thus this study cannot be definitive but constitutes a contribution to the existing empirical literature.

In conclusion, can privatization be expected to reduce production costs in the ESI? Our evidence suggests that the answer to this question is yes, for electricity generation in the long run, as better investment planning leads to lower operating costs. However in the short run, given existing technology, we cannot expect privatization to lower costs. We find no evidence for expecting lower costs in the transmission and distribution functions in the short or the long run. In the ESI as a whole it is likely that the biggest gains are from restructuring and better government management of state owned electricity assets.

APPENDIX 1

DATA SOURCES AND APPROXIMATIONS

Appendix 1.1: Chapter 5 Data: Firm level data for 1986

The US data is constructed from plant level data aggregated by firm, the plants being those listed in the US EIA publication *Historical Plant Cost and Annual Production Expenses for Selected Electric Utilities 1986* (hence HPC, 1986). The non-US data is constructed from firm level data on thermal power production available from company accounts for the accounting year ending in 1986. It is not clear what biases this distinction introduces: it seems to imply that the US data is closer to the economic variables we are trying to measure than the accounting data reported in non-US company accounts. In some cases the non-US data under-records the actual resources employed in production as the legal structure of the company leads to discrepancies between accounting and economic measures.

Output – measured in millions of kilowatt hours. The measure used is net output generated by power stations, i.e. gross power station output minus electricity consumed at power stations. For US firms this is available in HPC, 1986. Japanese data was taken from information supplied by the Japan Electric Power Information Centre (JEPIC). For non-US firms this is estimated from company accounts.

Capital – measured as nameplate rating in MW. This represents the gross physical capacity of the power station generators. Data for the USA is in HPC, 1986 and non-US data is published in company accounts.

Labour – number of employees employed at power stations (or in generation). Ideally this should be an average full-time equivalent figure, but these figures are not generally available. Part-time working in power companies is not very significant (<5%) while the year end figures usually quoted introduce a small bias of uncertain direction. More significant is the non-reporting of subcontracted labour. This is especially common in Japan, where the number of subcontracted employees at a power station may be equal to the number of power company employees. There is no attempt to correct the biases this introduces into the analysis. For US firms labour figures are available in HPC, 1986. For the non-US firms the source is generally the accounts. Labour employed in Japanese firms has been collected in communication with the JEPIC or estimated from the total number of employees multiplied by the proportion of total labour costs in generation (e.g. CEGB). A major problem with this data is the definition of 'employees in generation' in company accounts, this may sometimes include off-site managers or construction staff which are not included in the US figures. This may introduce potentially large discrepancies e.g. EdF accounts report that one-third of 'generation' staff are classified as working off-site.

Fuel – measured in TBTU (BTU*10^{12}).[1] These are calculated from heat efficiencies recorded in HPC, 1986 for US firms and in company accounts and technical reports for non-US firms. For the Japanese firms these are calculated from JEPIC data.

Price of Capital – measured in millions of dollars per MW. This is calculated via Christensen and Jorgenson (1969): using the historic cost of capital services, the price of capital per MW is equal to historic cost of a MW multiplied by the sum of the real interest rate and the depreciation rate (for more details see Appendix 1.3). The depreciation rate is assumed to be 3.33%. The inflation rates and nominal interest rates used are five year averages ending in 1986. The historic capital cost is taken from HPC for US firms and from historic cost data in company accounts for non-US firms. For MUNIs the interest rate used is the national government bond rate and for IOUs the interest rate used is the national lending rate both as reported in *International Financial Statistics* (various issues). The inflation rate is a PPI taken from various *OECD Main Economic Indicators*. While these measures do not represent the actual capital costs facing individual firms they do estimate the economic cost of capital used in the firm and are easily obtained. The choice of five year averaging and a 3.33% depreciation charge is arbitrary and a more detailed analysis using different interest rate assumptions might lead to slightly different results.

Price of Labour – measured in millions of dollars per employee. For US IOUs and non-US utilities these figures are calculated as the result of total labour costs in the utility divided by the total number of employees. The US IOU figures are reported in USEIA *Financial Statistics of Selected Electric Utilities 1986* and the non-US figures are reported in company accounts. For US MUNIs labour costs are estimated as the average labour cost of IOUs registered in the state where the MUNI is operating – this is unsatisfactory but the inaccuracy is likely to be small given a reasonably competitive labour market for skilled power workers. It is not possible to separate the average cost of labour in the thermal and nuclear generation departments of the utilities from the average labour costs in the whole utility due to the lack of available data. It may be that this approximation does not accurately reflect true labour costs in the separate generation departments, but again the effect of this inaccuracy is likely to be small.

Price of Fuel – measured in millions of US dollars per TBTU. This is calculated as firm fuel costs divided by firm fuel input. The fuel cost figures are available for US firms in HPC, 1986 and for non-US firms in company accounts.

Appendix 1.2: Chapter 6 Data: Plant level data for 1989

The major data sources for each country are given in Table A.1.2.1 below. In what follows, unless otherwise mentioned, particular data for an individual country comes from the major source. The data is for the accounting year ending in 1989[2] (1991 for Thailand).[3]

Table A.1.2.1: Major Sources of Chapter 6 Data

Country	Major Source
USA	*US EIA/REA* *
Canada	*Company Accounts* **
Denmark	*Communication*
Germany	*London Economics*
Hong Kong	*Communication*
Japan	*JEPIC*
Taiwan	*London Economics*
Australia	*Company Accounts*
Greece	*Communication*
Ireland	*ESB Annual Report*
New Zealand	*ECNZ Annual Report*
South Africa	*Eskom Statistical Review*
Thailand	*London Economics*
UK	*London Economics*

*   US data is available on database from Utility Data Institute,[4] Washington, DC.
**   TransAlta and Ontario Hydro data is supplied by London Economics.

Output – measured in millions of kilowatt hours. The measure used is net output generated by power station, i.e. gross station output minus electricity consumed in the station. All data is from the major sources.

Capital – measured as nameplate rating in MW. This represents the gross physical capacity of the power station generators. All data is collected from the major sources above.

Labour – number of employees employed at power stations (including subcontracted staff). Ideally this should be an average full-time equivalent figure but for many stations it is unclear what the basis of estimation was. Much of the data is collected from the major sources, but the data for Canada, Japan, Australia, Ireland, New Zealand and South Africa were collected via communication with the companies operating the power stations. All of the Japanese Electric Power Companies responded to requests for labour data but most of the Japanese power plants had to be dropped from the sample due to a lack of information on the number of subcontracted employees at each site.

Fuel – measured in TBTU (BTU*10^{12}).[5] Most of the data is collected from the major sources. Data for Canada (except Ontario Hydro), Australia (ETSA and SECWA), Ireland and New Zealand are collected from communication with the companies concerned.

For BASE60 power plants only:

Age – measured in years. This is calculated as 1989 (1991 for Thailand) minus the average year of commissioning of generating units at the plant. The years of commissioning of individual units are weighted by the size of the generating units. The US database only gave data for the year of commissioning of the first and last unit: simple averages were taken.[6] The Danish and South African data is based on the age of the first unit to be commissioned. The data is mainly collected from the major sources, however data for SaskPower (Canada) and Ireland are obtained via communication with the company.

Appendix 1.3: Chapter 7 Data: Plant level data for 1989

The output, capital, labour, fuel and age data used in Chapter 7 are the same as for BASE60 in Chapter 6 and the sources of this data are listed in Appendix 1.2. In this appendix we detail the sources of the input price data used in Chapter 7. All the input price data are measured in millions of local currency unit. The data is for the accounting year ending in 1989, except for Thailand where 1991 data are used. The major data sources for each country are given in Table A.1.3.1 below.

Table A.1.3.1: Major Sources of Chapter 7 Data

Country	*Major Source*
USA	*US EIA/REA**
Canada	*Communication*
Japan	*JEPIC*
Australia	*Company Accounts*
Greece	*Communication*
Ireland	*ESB Annual Report*
South Africa	*Eskom Statistical Review*
Thailand	*London Economics*

* US data is available on database from Utility Data Institute, Washington DC.

In what follows historic cost price of capital at each power station is calculated from the historic cost of the power plant by the following formula:

$$P_{K.HIST} = \frac{(r+0.0333) \times C_{K.HIST}}{K}$$

$C_{K.HIST}$ = *historic cost of capital at power plant.*   (A.1.3.1)

r = *real interest rate.*

K = *quantity of capital.*

This formula is a simplified version of the Christensen and Jorgenson (1969) formula reported in Atkinson and Halvorsen (1980). (A.1.3.1) is taken to represent the rental price of capital. The *0.0333* term being the depreciation charge, which implicitly reflects an assumption that a thermal power station has an expected life of 30 years. The real interest rate is a 5 year average for the years ending in 1989 (1991 for Thailand) of the nominal interest rate minus the retail price index. The nominal interest rates are taken from *International Financial Statistics* (various): for IOUs the lending rate is used and for MUNIs the government bond rate is used; the use of these rates reflects the different terms on which finance for investment is available to privately owned and publicly owned firms. The inflation rates are mainly taken from various issues of *OECD Main Economic Indicators.*[7] The cost of capital is taken from the major sources except for South Africa where the data collection was by communication.

Current cost price of capital per MW – This is calculated in two stages. Firstly, we need to convert the historic cost of capital into the current cost using the following formula:

$$C_{K.CURR} = \frac{PI_{1989}}{PI_{1989-Age}} \cdot C_{K.HIST}$$

$C_{K.CURR}$ = *current cost of capital at the power plant.*

$C_{K.HIST}$ = *historic cost of capital at the power plant.*   (A.1.3.2)

PI_{1989} = *price deflator index in 1989 (1991 for Thailand).*

$PI_{1989-Age}$ = *price deflator index in average first year*

of operation of the plant.

The US price deflators are calculated from the total steam production plant cost index in Handy-Whitman's *Cost Trends of Electric Utility Construction*[7] (see Whitman et al., 1992). The price deflators used are generally machinery and equipment deflators from *OECD Main Economic Indicators* (various).[9] The *Age* (see Appendix 1.2) is the number of years between the average first year of operation of the plant and 1989 (1991 in the case of Thailand).

Secondly, we calculate the current cost of capital using the result from (A.1.3.2) using a formula similar to (A.1.3.1):

$$P_{K.CURR} = \frac{(r+0.0333) \times C_{K.CURR}}{K}$$

(A.1.3.3)

r = *real interest rate.*

K = *quantity of capital.*

where the real interest rate is the same as for the historic cost price of capital calculations.

Price of labour per employee – This is the average labour cost per employee. For the US IOUs data is taken from US EIA *Financial Statistics of Selected Privately-Owned Electric Utilities 1989*. Total wages and salaries are divided by the sum of full-time employees plus half the part-time employees. For US MUNIs the state average labour cost for the IOUs in the sample is used. Other country data come from the major sources except for *Eskom* where data were collected through communication.

Price of fuel per TBTU – All these data come from the major sources in Table A.1.3.1.

Appendix 1.4: Chapter 8 Data: Transmission and Distribution System level data for 1990

Appendix 1.4.1 Transmission Data

All data were taken from the relevant US Energy Information Agency *Financial Statistics* (FSTAT) 1990 unless otherwise stated. The source for publicly owned firms is *Financial Statistics of Selected Publicly-Owned Electric Utilities* and that for privately owned firms is *Financial Statistics of Selected Investor-Owned Electric Utilities*. In every case data is for the accounting year ending in 1990.

Operation and Maintenance Costs – Operation and maintenance costs in transmission in 1000s of dollars. This figure includes rent but not depreciation.

Transformer Capacity – The maximum capacity of transformers in the transmission system in MVA. This is in FSTAT for IOUs and was collected from the American Public Power Association (APPA) for MUNIs.

Peak Output – Maximum demand on the system in MW. These data were mainly supplied by APPA from USEIA form EIA-861 with some additional data from the UDI *Pocket to US Electric Utilities*. It is not clear at what point in the system this is measured.

Net Energy Transmitted – Net energy entered and received in millions of kWh. This figure may include purchases and so both peak output and circuit km*kV may underestimate the peakedness and scale of the transmission system required to transmit the measured amount of electricity from the power station to the distribution system entry nodes. Some of the ratios of maximum to average demand are therefore less than 1.

Labour Cost – Average salary in 1000s of dollars in the utility. This is total wages and salaries divided by the number of full-time employees plus half the number of part-time employees. The source for IOUs is FSTAT. Data for MUNIs were supplied by APPA from their *Performance Indicators Survey, 1990*.

Circ km*kV – Circuit km times voltage (kV) of transmission cable. This figure measures the main capital input to transmission: each length of circuit is multiplied by the voltage it is operated at. The source for IOUs is Electric World *Directory of Electric Utilities* 1992 (hence *Directory*). The source for MUNIs is a combination of the *Directory* and a survey conducted by APPA.

OG circ km – Overhead circuit km. The sources are the same as for Circ km*kV.

UG circ km – Underground circuit km. The sources are the same as for Circ km*kV.

Labour – Number of employees in the transmission function. This figure is derived by dividing operation and maintenance costs in transmission by the labour cost. This gives a labour equivalent operation and maintenance cost.

Appendix 1.4.2 Distribution Data

As for transmission all the US data were taken from the relevant US Energy Information Agency *Financial Statistics* (FSTAT) 1990 unless otherwise stated. All the UK data were taken from Annual Statistical Reviews of the RECs unless otherwise stated. In every case data are for the accounting year ending in 1990.

Resid sales – Sales to residential consumers in millions of kWh.

Total sales – Total sales to ultimate consumers in millions of kWh.

Customers – Total number of customers in all classes.

Circ km – Total primary circuit km in distribution system. Data for

US IOUs were taken from the *Directory*. Data for US MUNIs were supplied by APPA from *Performance Indicators Survey, 1990*. UK data do not include 132 and 66kV lines owned by the RECs – this to improve the comparability of US and UK distribution systems.

Peak Output – Maximum demand on the system in MW. This information is mainly supplied by APPA from USEIA form EIA-861 with some additional data from the UDI *Pocket Guide to US Electric Utilities*. This is the same as for transmission where a utility is engaged in both transmission and distribution. Hence this figure is unsatisfactory as it is not clear at what point in the T&D system it is measured.

Service Area – Service Area in square km. The US figures are largely taken from the UDI *Pocket Guide to US Electric Utilities*, some additional information on US publicly owned utilities is supplied by APPA. The UK data were supplied by London Economics.

Labour Cost – Average salary in 1000s of US dollars in the utility. This is total wages and salaries divided by the number of full-time employees plus half the number of part-time employees. The source for IOUs is FSTAT. Data for MUNIs were supplied by APPA from their *Performance Indicators Survey, 1990*. The UK data were similarly derived from the *Annual Reports* of the RECs. UK data has been converted to US dollars using a Purchasing Power Parity exchange rate of 0.609 £/$ (taken from IEA (1993b) *Energy Taxes and Prices Quarter 4, 1992*).

Operation and Maintenance Costs – Operation and maintenance costs in distribution in 1000s of US dollars. This figure includes rent but not depreciation. UK data is converted to US dollars using a Purchasing Power Parity exchange rate of 0.609 £/$ (taken from IEA *Energy Taxes and Prices Quarter 4, 1992*). UK data include operation and maintenance costs of 132 and 66kV lines which are not counted as part of the distribution system. This implies UK labour and average cost data are biased upwards when compared to US data. This refers to the whole of the distribution system but only primary circuit km is measured to keep the data series as comparable as possible. Differing amounts of secondary and tertiary circuits will affect the relative costs among the utilities introducing biases of uncertain direction.

UG Circ km – Underground Primary Circuit km. The data are largely from the main sources except for US MUNIs where the data were supplied by APPA. UK data do not include 132 and 66kV lines.

Labour – Number of employees in the distribution function. This figure is derived by dividing operation and maintenance costs in distribution by the labour cost. This gives a labour equivalent operation and maintenance cost.

Transformer Capacity – The maximum capacity of transformers in the distribution system in MVA. The US data were taken from FSTAT for IOUs and was supplied by the American Public Power Association (APPA) for MUNIs.

Notes
1. BTU = British Thermal Unit; 1 kWh = 3412.08 BTU.
2. Year ends vary. UK and Japan have year ends on 31 March, while Ireland, Canada, South Africa and Greece have year ends on 31 December. Output and fuel are annual totals. Capital and labour are usually figures for the last day of the accounting year.
3. This was the only available data on Thai electric utilities. The source reported that the data had changed little from 1989.
4. UDI Utility Data Base Production Cost (O+M) Data Files are derived from Federal Energy Regulatory Commission (FERC) Form 1, from the Energy Information Administration (EIA) Form 412, and from the Rural Electrification Administration (REA) Form 12.
5. BTU = British Thermal Unit; 1 kwh = 3412.08 BTU.
6. We could have used the US EIA *Inventory of Electric Power Plants in the US* to obtain data on the commissioning dates of all the US generating units. However it was considered that the considerable extra time involved in constructing new average plant ages did not justify the marginal degree of improvement in the quality of the data, especially in view of the poor quality of the data for most of the other countries.
7. We use consumer prices for Ireland and Greece and we use the implicit price level for USA, Canada, Japan and Australia. The data for Thailand were taken from the consumer price indices in the *Statistical Yearbook* of the National Statistical Office of Thailand. The data for South Africa were taken from the consumer prices in *International Financial Statistics*.
8. Following Handy-Whitman 6 different regional indices are used: North Atlantic, South Atlantic, North Central, South Central, Plateau and Pacific. Each state of the USA is in one of these 6 regions. The information on power station location in Appendix 2 is used to allocate the relevant regional cost index to each individual plant.
9. The OECD *Main Economic Indicators* price indices used for each country are as follows: Canada: 1971–89 Electrical Machinery Producer Prices, 1955– 71 Wholesale prices: manufactured goods; Japan: 1967–89 Producer prices: machinery and equipment, 1955–67 Wholesale prices: manufactured goods, investment; Australia: 1969–89 Producer prices: machinery and equipment; Greece: 1964–89 Wholesale prices: industrial goods; Ireland: 1975–89 Wholesale prices: investment goods, 1964–75 Wholesale prices:

manufactured goods. The data for South Africa is taken from the Central Statistical Service Republic of South Africa's *Bulletin of Statistics*. The data used for Thailand is as follows: *UN Statistical Yearbook for Asia and the Pacific* 1976–79 wholesale price of machinery and equipment index, 1979–89 Producer price index for machinery and equipment; the 1989–91 data is taken from the Capital Equipment Index in the *Statistical Yearbook* of Thailand.

APPENDIX 2

LISTINGS OF SAMPLE FIRMS, PLANTS AND TRANSMISSION AND DISTRIBUTION SYSTEMS

Appendix 2.1: Chapter 5 Sample Firms

Code	Company	Country
I1	ELSAM	Denmark
I2	TEPCO	Japan
I3	HOKKAIDO	Japan
I4	TOHOKU	Japan
I5	KYUSHU	Japan
I6	HOKURIKU	Japan
I7	SHIKOKU	Japan
I8	KANSAI	Japan
I9	CHUBU	Japan
I10	CHUGOKU	Japan
I11	NORTHERN STATES	USA
I12	GEORGIA POWER	USA
I13	DUQUESNE LIGHT	USA
I14	DETROIT EDISON	USA
I15	DUKE POWER	USA
I16	INDIANA AND MICHIGAN POWER	USA
I17	OKLAHOMA GAS AND ElECTRIC	USA
I18	OHIO POWER	USA
I19	CAROLINA POWER AND LIGHT	USA
I20	OHIO EDISON	USA
I21	FLORIDA POWER AND LIGHT	USA
I22	COLUMBUS AND SOUTHERN	USA
I23	BOSTON EDISON	USA
I24	ALABAMA POWER	USA
I25	PACIFIC GAS AND ELECTRIC	USA
I26	ARIZONA PUBLIC SERVICE CO.	USA
I27	ARKANSAS POWER AND LIGHT	USA
I28	SOUTHERN CALIFORNIA EDISON	USA
I29	FLORIDA POWER CO.	USA
I30	COMMONWEALTH EDISON	USA
I31	KANSAS GAS AND ELECTRIC	USA
I32	CONSUMERS POWER	USA
I33	MISSISSIPI POWER AND LIGHT	USA
I34	SOUTHERN CAROLINA GAS AND ELECTRIC	USA
I35	VIRGINIA ELECTRIC	USA
I36	SAN DIEGO GAS AND ELECTRIC	USA
I37	GULF POWER CO.	USA
I38	CENTRAL ILLINOIS LIGHT CO.	USA
I39	CENTRAL PUBLIC SERVICE OF ILLINOIS	USA
I40	NORTHERN INDIANA PUBLIC SERVICE	USA
I41	PUBLIC SERVICE CO. OF INDIANA	USA

Code	Company	Country
I42	KANSAS POWER AND LIGHT	USA
I43	LOUSIANA POWER AND LIGHT	USA
I44	BALTIMORE GAS AND ELECTRIC	USA
I45	MINNISOTA POWER AND LIGHT	USA
I46	DAYTON POWER AND LIGHT	USA
I47	METROPOLITAN EDISON	USA
I48	TAMPA ELECTRIC	USA
I49	INDIANAPOLIS POWER AND LIGHT	USA
I50	CENTRAL LOUISIANA ELECTRIC	USA
I51	PUBLIC SERVICE OF OKLAHOMA	USA
I52	PENNSYLVANNA ELECTRIC	USA
I53	PENNSYLVANIA POWER AND LIGHT	USA
I54	HOUSTON LIGHT AND POWER	USA
I55	TEXAS UTILITIES ELECTRIC	USA
I56	WEST TEXAS UTILITIES CO.	USA
I57	SOUTH WESTERN PUBLIC SERVICE CO.	USA
I58	UTAH POWER AND LIGHT	USA
I59	APPALACHIAN POWER CO.	USA
I60	MONONGAHELA POWER CO.	USA
M1	ECNSW	Australia
M2	SECV	Australia
M3	QEC	Australia
M4	SECWA	Australia
M5	ETSA	Australia
M6	ESB	Ireland
M7	CEGB	UK
M8	SSEB	UK
M9	NIES	UK
M10	ENEL	Italy
M11	EdF	France
M12	SASKPOWER	Canada
M13	RICHMOND,CITY OF	USA
M14	BURBANK,CITY OF	USA
M15	CEDAR FALLS, CITY OF	USA
M16	HENDERSON,CITY OF	USA
M17	OWENSBORO,CITY OF	USA
M18	LANSING,CITY OF	USA
M19	MARQUETTE,CITY OF	USA
M20	AUSTIN,CITY OF	USA
M21	ROCHESTER,CITY OF	USA
M22	COLUMBIA,CITY OF	USA
M23	INDEPENDENCE,CITY OF	USA
M24	VINELAND,CITY OF	USA
M25	FARMINGTON,CITY OF	USA
M26	JAMESTOWN,CITY OF	USA
M27	ORVILLE,CITY OF	USA
M28	GREENVILLE,CITY OF	USA
M29	SAN ANTONIO,CITY OF	USA
M30	BURLINGTON,CITY OF	USA
M31	SOUTH CAROLINA PUBLIC SERVIC AUTH	USA
M32	POWER AUTHORITY OF NEW YORK	USA
M33	GREENWOOD	USA
M34	NEW ULM PUBLIC UTILITIES COMMISSION	USA
M35	MARSHFIELD	USA

Appendix 2.2: Chapter 6 Sample Plants (2 letter State codes refer to US state except UK)

Appendix 2.2.1 The PEAK15 Plants

Code	Operator	Unit	State	Type
C1	WESTERN FARMERS ELEC COOP	MOORELAND	OK	GAS
C2	BRAZOS ELEC POWER COOP	NORTH TEXAS	TX	GAS/OIL
C3	DAIRYLAND POWER COOP	EJ STONEMAN	WI	COAL
I1	ALABAMA POWER CO	GADSDEN	AL	COAL
I2	ARKANSAS POWER & LIGHT CO	ROBERT RITCHIE	AR	GAS/OIL
I3	ARIZONA PUBLIC SERVICE CO	WEST PHOENIX	AZ	GAS/OIL
I4	ARIZONA PUBLIC SERVICE CO	SAGUARO	AZ	GAS
I5	SOUTHERN CALIF EDISON CO	SAN BERNARDINO	CA	GAS/OIL
I6	PUBLIC SERVICE COLORADO	ZUNI	CO	GAS/OIL
I7	UNITED ILLUMINATING CO	ENGLISH	CT	OIL
I8	POTOMAC ELECTRIC POWER CO	BENNING	DC	OIL
I9	SEAS	Masnedovaerket	Denmark	Coal
I10	FLORIDA POWER & LIGHT CO	SANFORD	FL	OIL/GAS
I11	IOWA ELEC LIGHT & POWER	SUTHERLAND	IA	COAL
I12	COMMONWEALTH EDISON CO	CRAWFORD	IL	COAL/GAS
I13	COMMONWEALTH EDISON CO	FISK 19	IL	COAL
I14	COMMONWEALTH EDISON CO	WILL COUNTY	IL	COAL
I15	COMMONWEALTH EDISON CO	STATE LINE	IN	COAL
I16	PUBLIC SERVICE INDIANA	NOBLESVILLE	IN	COAL
I17	PUBLIC SERVICE INDIANA	EDWARDSPORT	IN	COAL
I18	Chugoku	Kudamatsu	Japan	Oil
I19	Hokuriku	Toyama Shinko	Japan	Oil
I20	CENTEL CORP KANSAS DIV	JUDSON LARGE 4	KS	GAS
I21	KANSAS GAS & ELECTRIC CO	MURRAY GILL	KS	GAS/OIL
I22	KANSAS GAS & ELECTRIC CO	GORDON EVANS	KS	GAS/OIL
I23	KANSAS POWER & LIGHT CO	HUTCHINSON	KS	GAS/OIL
I24	KENTUCKY UTILITIES CO	TYRONE (KY)	KY	COAL
I25	KENTUCKY UTILITIES CO	PINEVILLE 3	KY	COAL
I26	GULF STATES UTILITIES CO	WILLOW GLEN	LA	GAS/OIL
I27	LOUISIANA POWER & LIGHT	STERLINGTON	LA	GAS/OIL
I28	SOUTHWESTERN ELEC PWR CO	ARSENAL HILL 5	LA	GAS
I29	SOUTHWESTERN ELEC PWR CO	LIEBERMAN	LA	GAS
I30	CAMBRIDGE ELEC LIGHT CO	BLACKSTONE ST	MA	OIL/GAS
I31	BANGOR HYDRO-ELECTRIC CO	EM GRAHAM	ME	OIL
I32	CENTRAL MAINE POWER CO	MASON	ME	OIL
I33	CONSUMERS POWER CO	DE KARN 3&4	MI	OIL
I34	DETROIT EDISON CO	GREENWOOD 1	MI	OIL
I35	MINNESOTA POWER & LIGHT	SYL LASKIN	MN	COAL
I36	NORTHERN STATES POWER CO	MINNESOTA V'Y 3	MN	COAL/GAS
I37	ST JOSEPH LIGHT & POWER	LAKE ROAD	MO	COAL/OIL/GAS
I38	UNION ELECTRIC CO	MERAMEC	MO	COAL
I39	MISSISSIPPI POWER & LIGHT	BAXTER WILSON	MS	OIL/GAS
I40	MISSISSIPPI POWER & LIGHT	DELTA	MS	GAS
I41	DUKE POWER CO	DAN RIVER	NC	COAL/OIL
I42	PUBLIC SERVICE ELEC & GAS	KEARNY	NJ	OIL
I43	CONSOLIDATED EDISON CO	59TH STREET	NY	OIL
I44	DAYTON POWER & LIGHT CO	HUTCHINGS	OH	COAL/GAS
I45	TOLEDO EDISON CO	ACME	OH	COAL

Code	Operator	Unit	State	Type
I46	OKLAHOMA GAS & ELEC CO	MUSTANG	OK	GAS
I47	PORTLAND GENERAL ELEC CO	BOARDMAN 1	OR	COAL
I48	PHILADELPHIA ELECTRIC CO	SCHUYLKILL 1	PA	OIL
I49	CENTRAL POWER & LIGHT CO	VICTORIA	TX	GAS/OIL
I50	HOUSTON LIGHTING & POWER	SAM BERTRON	TX	GAS/OIL
I51	HOUSTON LIGHTING & POWER	DEEPWATER (TX) 9	TX	GAS
I52	HOUSTON LIGHTING & POWER	WEBSTER 3	TX	GAS
I53	SOUTHWESTERN ELEC PWR CO	KNOX LEE	TX	GAS
I54	SOUTHWESTERN ELEC PWR CO	WILKES	TX	GAS
I55	SOUTHWESTERN PUB SERV CO	PLANT X	TX	GAS/OIL
I56	TEXAS UTILITIES ELEC CO	RIVER CREST 1	TX	GAS/OIL
I57	TEXAS UTILITIES ELEC CO	DALLAS	TX	GAS/OIL
I58	TEXAS UTILITIES ELEC CO	NORTH MAIN 4	TX	GAS/OIL
I59	TEXAS UTILITIES ELEC CO	PARKDALE	TX	GAS/OIL
I60	TEXAS UTILITIES ELEC CO	EAGLE MOUNTAIN	TX	GAS/OIL
I61	PUGET SOUND POWER & LT	SHUFFLETON	WA	OIL
I62	WISCONSIN ELEC POWER CO	PORT WASHINGTON	WI	COAL
M1	SALT RIVER PROJECT	KYRENE	AZ	GAS/OIL
M2	LOS ANGELES DEPT WTR PWR	HARBOR	CA	GAS/OIL
M3	Manitoba H	Selkirk	Canada	Coal
M4	Ontario Hydro	Lennox	Canada	Oil
M5	ESB	Tarbert	Eire	Oil
M6	GAINESVILLE REGIONAL UTIL	JR KELLY	FL	GAS
M7	JACKSONVILLE ELEC AUTH	JD KENNEDY	FL	GAS/OIL
M8	PPC of Greece	Lavrio	Greece	Oil
M9	CEDAR FALLS MUNI UTIL	STREETER	IA	COAL
M10	PERU UTILITIES	PERU (IN)	IN	COAL
M11	COFFEYVILLE MUNI LT DEPT	COFFEYVILLE	KS	GAS
M12	KANSAS CITY BD PUB UTIL	KAW	KS	COAL/GAS
M13	WINFIELD MUN LT & POWER	WINFIELD	KS	GAS
M14	HENDERSON MUN POWER & LT	HENDERSON ONE	KY	COAL
M15	LAFAYETTE UTIL SYSTEM	BONIN	LA	GAS
M16	DETROIT PUBLIC LIGHTING	MISTERSKY	MI	OIL
M17	LANSING BOARD WTR & LT	OTTAWA STREET	MI	COAL
M18	COLUMBIA WTR & LIGHT DEPT	COLUMBIA (MO)	MO	COAL
M19	INDEPENDENCE POWER & LT	BLUE VALLEY	MO	COAL/GAS
M20	CEN NEBRASKA PUB PWR&IRR	CANADAY 1	NE	GAS/OIL
M21	FARMINGTON ELEC UTIL	ANIMAS	NM	GAS
M22	ECNZ	Stratford	N.Zealand	Gas
M23	Eskom	Ingagene	S.Africa	Coal
M24	BRYAN MUNICIPAL ELEC SYS	BRYAN (TX)	TX	GAS/OIL
M25	DENTON MUN UTILITIES	DENTON	TX	GAS/OIL
M26	GARLAND POWER & LT SYSTEM	CE NEWMAN	TX	GAS/OIL
M27	LOWER COLORADO RIVER AUTH	TC FERGUSON 1	TX	GAS
M28	LUBBOCK POWER & LIGHT	PLANT TWO (TX)	TX	GAS
M29	SAN ANTONIO PUB SERV BD	LEON CREEK	TX	GAS
M30	SAN ANTONIO PUB SERV BD	WB TUTTLE	TX	GAS/OIL
M31	CEGB	Wakefield	UK	Coal
M32	CEGB	Elland	UK	Coal
M33	CEGB	Carrington	UK	Coal
M34	CEGB	Bold	UK	Coal
M35	CEGB	Pembroke	UK	Oil
M36	CEGB	Ince	UK	Oil
M37	CEGB	Stella North	UK	Coal
M38	CEGB	Stella South	UK	Coal
M39	CEGB	Littlebrook	UK	Oil

Code	Operator	Unit	State	Type
M40	CEGB	Grain	UK	Oil
M41	CEGB	Hams Hall	UK	Coal
M42	Scot Power	Cockenzie	UK	Coal
M43	MENASHA ELECTRIC & WATER	RIVER STREET	WI	COAL

Appendix 2.2.2 The MID30 Plants

Code	Operator	Unit	State	Type
C1	CAJUN ELECTRIC POWER COOP	BIG CAJUN ONE	LA	GAS/OIL
C2	UNITED POWER ASSOCIATION	ELK RIVER	MN	RDF/GAS/OIL
I1	ARKANSAS POWER & LIGHT CO	LAKE CATHERINE	AR	GAS/OIL
I2	ARKANSAS POWER & LIGHT CO	HARVEY COUCH	AR	GAS/OIL
I3	ARIZONA PUBLIC SERVICE CO	OCOTILLO	AZ	GAS
I4	TUCSON ELECTRIC POWER CO	IRVINGTON	AZ	COAL/GAS
I5	PACIFIC GAS & ELEC CO	HUMBOLDT BAY 1&2	CA	GAS/OIL
I6	PACIFIC GAS & ELEC CO	CONTRA COSTA	CA	GAS/OIL
I7	SOUTHERN CALIF EDISON CO	HUNTINGTON BEACH	CA	GAS/OIL
I8	SOUTHERN CALIF EDISON CO	ETIWANDA	CA	GAS/OIL
I9	SOUTHERN CALIF EDISON CO	EL SEGUNDO	CA	GAS/OIL
I10	SOUTHERN CALIF EDISON CO	REDONDO BEACH	CA	GAS/OIL
I11	SOUTHERN CALIF EDISON CO	ALAMITOS	CA	GAS/OIL
I12	SOUTHERN CALIF EDISON CO	ORMOND BEACH	CA	GAS/OIL
I13	FLORIDA POWER & LIGHT CO	LAUDERDALE	FL	GAS/OIL
I14	FLORIDA POWER & LIGHT CO	CUTLER	FL	GAS
I15	FLORIDA POWER & LIGHT CO	MARTIN COUNTY	FL	GAS/OIL
I16	FLORIDA POWER CORP	TURNER	FL	OIL/GAS
I17	GEORGIA POWER CO	SCHERER	GA	COAL
I18	GEORGIA POWER CO	ARKWRIGHT	GA	COAL/GAS
I19	IOWA ELEC LIGHT & POWER	SIXTH STREET	IA	COAL/RDF/GAS
I20	IOWA ELEC LIGHT & POWER	PRAIRIE CREEK	IA	COAL
I21	IOWA-ILLINOIS GAS & ELEC	RIVERSIDE (IA)	IA	COAL/GAS
I22	CENT ILLINOIS PUBLIC SERV	GRAND TOWER	IL	COAL
I23	CENT ILLINOIS PUBLIC SERV	MEREDOSIA	IL	COAL
I24	CENT ILLINOIS PUBLIC SERV	HUTSONVILLE	IL	COAL
I25	COMMONWEALTH EDISON CO	WAUKEGAN	IL	COAL
I26	COMMONWEALTH EDISON CO	JOLIET	IL	COAL
I27	COMMONWEALTH EDISON CO	POWERTON	IL	COAL
I28	ILLINOIS POWER CO	HAVANA	IL	COAL/OIL
I29	ILLINOIS POWER CO	WOOD RIVER	IL	COAL/GAS
I30	INDIANAPOLIS POWER & LT	HT PRITCHARD	IN	COAL
I31	PUBLIC SERVICE INDIANA	WABASH RIVER	IN	COAL
I32	Chugoku	Mizushima	Japan	C/O
I33	Hokkaido	Shiriuchi	Japan	Oil
I34	Hokkaido	Date	Japan	Coal
I35	Shikoku	Anan	Japan	Oil
I36	Tohuku	Shin Sendai	Japan	Oil
I37	Tohuku	Akita	Japan	Oil
I38	CENTRAL LOUISIANA ELEC CO	COUGHLIN	LA	GAS/OIL
I39	LOUISIANA POWER & LIGHT	LITTLE GYPSY	LA	GAS/OIL
I40	LOUISIANA POWER & LIGHT	WATERFORD 1&2	LA	GAS/OIL
I41	NEW ORLEANS PUBLIC SERV	MICHOUD	LA	GAS/OIL
I42	COMMONWEALTH ELECTRIC CO	CANNON STREET	MA	OIL/GAS
I43	WESTERN MASS ELEC CO	WEST SPRINGFIELD	MA	OIL/GAS

Code	Operator	Unit	State	Type
I44	BALTIMORE GAS & ELEC CO	WESTPORT	MD	OIL
I45	BALTIMORE GAS & ELEC CO	RIVERSIDE (MD)	MD	OIL/GAS
I46	DETROIT EDISON CO	HARBOR BEACH 1	MI	COAL
I47	INTERSTATE POWER CO	FOX LAKE	MN	COAL/GAS
I48	NORTHERN STATES POWER CO	BLACK DOG	MN	COAL/GAS
I49	NORTHERN STATES POWER CO	WILMARTH	MN	RDF/GAS
I50	NORTHERN STATES POWER CO	HIGH BRIDGE	MN	COAL/GAS
I51	MISSISSIPPI POWER & LIGHT	ANDRUS 1	MS	GAS/OIL
I52	MISSISSIPPI POWER & LIGHT	REX BROWN	MS	GAS/OIL
I53	MISSISSIPPI POWER CO	VJ DANIEL	MS	COAL
I54	CAROLINA POWER & LIGHT CO	WEATHERSPOON	NC	COAL
I55	CAROLINA POWER & LIGHT CO	LEE (NC)	NC	COAL
I56	DUKE POWER CO	BUCK 6	NC	COAL
I57	DUKE POWER CO	RIVERBEND (NC) 5	NC	COAL
I58	DUKE POWER CO	ALLEN	NC	COAL
I59	JERSEY CENT POWER & LIGHT	WERNER 4	NJ	OIL
I60	JERSEY CENT POWER & LIGHT	GILBERT	NJ	OIL/GAS
I61	JERSEY CENT POWER & LIGHT	SAYREVILLE	NJ	GAS/OIL
I62	PUBLIC SERVICE ELEC & GAS	SEWAREN	NJ	GAS/OIL
I63	PUBLIC SERVICE ELEC & GAS	BURLINGTON (NJ)	NJ	OIL
I64	PUBLIC SERVICE ELEC & GAS	LINDEN	NJ	OIL
I65	PUBLIC SERVICE ELEC & GAS	BERGEN	NJ	GAS/OIL
I66	NEVADA POWER CO	CLARK	NV	GAS/OIL
I67	NEVADA POWER CO	SUNRISE 1	NV	GAS/OIL
I68	SIERRA PACIFIC POWER CO	TRACY	NV	GAS/OIL
I69	CONSOLIDATED EDISON CO	WATERSIDE	NY	GAS/OIL
I70	CONSOLIDATED EDISON CO	EAST RIVER	NY	OIL/GAS
I71	NIAGARA MOHAWK POWER CORP	OSWEGO	NY	OIL/GAS
I72	OHIO EDISON CO	EDGEWATER	OH	COAL
I73	OKLAHOMA GAS & ELEC CO	SEMINOLE (OK)	OK	GAS/OIL
I74	PUBLIC SERVICE OKLAHOMA	SOUTHWESTERN	OK	GAS
I75	PUBLIC SERVICE OKLAHOMA	NORTHEASTERN 1&2	OK	GAS
I76	PHILADELPHIA ELECTRIC CO	DELAWARE	PA	OIL
I77	PHILADELPHIA ELECTRIC CO	EDDYSTONE	PA	COAL/OIL/GAS
I78	CAROLINA POWER & LIGHT CO	ROBINSON 1	SC	COAL
I79	DUKE POWER CO	LEE (SC)	SC	COAL/GAS
I80	CENTRAL POWER & LIGHT CO	LON HILL	TX	GAS/OIL
I81	HOUSTON LIGHTING & POWER	TH WHARTON 2	TX	GAS/OIL
I82	SOUTHWESTERN PUB SERV CO	NICHOLS	TX	GAS
I83	SOUTHWESTERN PUB SERV CO	JONES	TX	GAS/OIL
I84	TEXAS UTILITIES ELEC CO	HANDLEY	TX	GAS/OIL
I85	TEXAS UTILITIES ELEC CO	TRINIDAD	TX	GAS/OIL
I86	TEXAS UTILITIES ELEC CO	LAKE CREEK	TX	GAS/OIL
I87	TEXAS UTILITIES ELEC CO	COLLIN 1	TX	GAS/OIL
I88	TEXAS UTILITIES ELEC CO	NORTH LAKE	TX	GAS/OIL
I89	WEST TEXAS UTILITIES CO	PAINT CREEK	TX	GAS/OIL
I90	MADISON GAS & ELECTRIC CO	BLOUNT STREET	WI	COAL/G/RDF
I91	NORTHERN STATES POWER CO	BAY FRONT	WI	WOOD/COAL/G
I92	WISCONSIN ELEC POWER CO	VALLEY (WI)	WI	COAL
M1	QEC	Swanbank	Australia	Coal
M2	SECWA	Bunbury	Australia	Coal
M3	SALT RIVER PROJECT	AGUA FRIA	AZ	GAS/OIL
M4	GLENDALE PUB SERVICE DEPT	GRAYSON	CA	GAS
M5	Manitoba H	Brandon	Canada	Coal
M6	Ontario Hydro	Lakeview	Canada	Coal
M7	Quebec Hydro	Tracy	Canada	Oil

Code	Operator	Unit	State	Type
M8	SaskPower	Queen Elizabeth	Canada	Gas/Coal
M9	SaskPower	Estevan	Canada	Lignite
M10	ESB	Poolbeg	Eire	Gas/Oil
M11	FORT PIERCE UTIL AUTH	KING	FL	GAS/OIL
M12	JACKSONVILLE ELEC AUTH	NORTHSIDE	FL	OIL
M13	TAUNTON MUNICIPAL LT COMM	BF CLEARY 8	MA	OIL
M14	TRAVERSE CITY LT & POWER	BAYSIDE	MI	COAL/WOOD
M15	ROCHESTER PUB UTILITIES	SILVER LAKE	MN	COAL/GAS
M16	WILLMAR MUN UTIL COMM	WILLMAR	MN	COAL
M17	GREENWOOD UTILITIES	HENDERSON (MS)	MS	GAS/COAL
M18	FREMONT DEPT UTILITIES	LD WRIGHT	NE	COAL/GAS
M19	VINELAND ELECTRIC UTIL	DOWN	NJ	COAL/OIL
M20	ECNZ	New Plymouth	N.Zealand	Gas
M21	PIQUA MUN POWER SYSTEM	PIQUA	OH	COAL
M22	Eskom	Camden	S.Africa	Coal
M23	Eskom	Grootvlei	S.Africa	Coal
M24	GARLAND POWER & LT SYSTEM	RAY OLINGER	TX	GAS
M25	GREENVILLE MUN POWER & LT	GREENVILLE	TX	GAS/OIL
M26	LOWER COLORADO RIVER AUTH	SIM GIDEON	TX	GAS/OIL
M27	SAN ANTONIO PUB SERV BD	VH BRAUNIG	TX	GAS
M28	SAN ANTONIO PUB SERV BD	OW SOMMERS	TX	GAS/OIL
M29	CEGB	Fawley	UK	Oil
M30	CEGB	Meaford	UK	Coal
M31	CEGB	Ferrybridge B	UK	Coal
M32	CEGB	Tilbury	UK	Coal
M33	Hydro Electric	Peterhead	UK	Oil/Gas
M34	MANITOWOC PUBLIC UTIL	MANITOWOC	WI	COAL
M35	MARSHFIELD ELEC & WATER	WILDWOOD	WI	COAL

Appendix 2.2.3 The MID60 Plants

Code	Operator	Unit	State	Type
C1	ALABAMA ELECTRIC COOP	CR LOWMAN	AL	COAL
C2	ARIZONA ELEC POWER COOP	APACHE	AZ	COAL/GAS
C3	SOUTH ILLINOIS POWER COOP	MARION	IL	COAL
C4	SOYLAND POWER COOP	PEARL 1	IL	COAL
C5	HOOSIER ENERGY REC	MEROM	IN	COAL
C6	EAST KENTUCKY POWER COOP	DALE	KY	COAL
C7	EAST KENTUCKY POWER COOP	HL SPURLOCK	KY	COAL
C8	EAST KENTUCKY POWER COOP	JS COOPER	KY	COAL
C9	CAJUN ELECTRIC POWER COOP	BIG CAJUN TWO	LA	COAL
C10	WOLVERINE ELEC PWR SUPP	ADVANCE	MI	COAL
C11	ASSOCIATED ELECTRIC COOP	THOMAS HILL	MO	COAL
C12	CENTRAL ELEC PWR COOP MO	CHAMOIS	MO	COAL
C13	BASIN ELECTRIC POWER COOP	LELAND OLDS	ND	COAL
C14	BRAZOS ELEC POWER COOP	RW MILLER	TX	GAS/OIL
C15	DAIRYLAND POWER COOP	ALMA	WI	COAL
C16	DAIRYLAND POWER COOP	GENOA 3	WI	COAL
C17	DAIRYLAND POWER COOP	MADGETT 1	WI	COAL
I1	ALABAMA POWER CO	GORGAS TWO	AL	COAL
I2	ALABAMA POWER CO	GASTON	AL	COAL
I3	ALABAMA POWER CO	GREENE COUNTY	AL	COAL
I4	ARKANSAS POWER & LIGHT CO	INDEPENDENCE	AR	COAL

Code	Operator	Unit	State	Type
I5	SOUTHWESTERN ELEC PWR CO	FLINT CREEK 1	AR	COAL
I6	PACIFIC GAS & ELEC CO	HUNTERS POINT	CA	GAS/OIL
I7	PACIFIC GAS & ELEC CO	MOSS LANDING	CA	GAS/OIL
I8	PACIFIC GAS & ELEC CO	PITTSBURG	CA	GAS/OIL
I9	PACIFIC GAS & ELEC CO	MORRO BAY	CA	GAS/OIL
I10	SAN DIEGO GAS & ELEC CO	ENCINA	CA	GAS/OIL
I11	SAN DIEGO GAS & ELEC CO	SOUTH BAY	CA	GAS/OIL
I12	SOUTHERN CALIF EDISON CO	MANDALAY	CA	GAS/OIL
I13	CENTEL CORP COLORADO DIV	PUEBLO NEW	CO	GAS
I14	CENTEL CORP COLORADO DIV	WN CLARK	CO	COAL/GAS
I15	PUBLIC SERVICE COLORADO	CAMEO	CO	COAL/GAS
I16	PUBLIC SERVICE COLORADO	ARAPAHOE	CO	COAL
I17	PUBLIC SERVICE COLORADO	CHEROKEE	CO	COAL/GAS
I18	PUBLIC SERVICE COLORADO	COMANCHE (CO)	CO	COAL
I19	PUBLIC SERVICE COLORADO	PAWNEE 1	CO	COAL
I20	CONNECTICUT LIGHT & POWER	MONTVILLE	CT	OIL/GAS
I21	CONNECTICUT LIGHT & POWER	MIDDLETOWN	CT	OIL
I22	CONNECTICUT LIGHT & POWER	DEVON	CT	OIL
I23	DELMARVA POWER & LIGHT CO	INDIAN RIVER (DE)	DE	COAL
I24	DELMARVA POWER & LIGHT CO	EDGE MOOR	DE	OIL/COAL/GAS
I25	SEAS	Stigsnaesvaerket	Denmark	Coal
I26	FLORIDA POWER & LIGHT CO	MANATEE	FL	OIL
I27	FLORIDA POWER & LIGHT CO	RIVIERA	FL	OIL/GAS
I28	FLORIDA POWER & LIGHT CO	CAPE CANAVERAL	FL	GAS/OIL
I29	FLORIDA POWER & LIGHT CO	PORT EVERGLADES	FL	OIL/GAS
I30	FLORIDA POWER & LIGHT CO	FORT MYERS	FL	OIL
I31	FLORIDA POWER & LIGHT CO	TURKEY POINT 1&2	FL	GAS/OIL
I32	FLORIDA POWER CORP	HIGGINS	FL	OIL/GAS
I33	FLORIDA POWER CORP	SUWANNEE RIVER	FL	GAS/OIL
I34	FLORIDA POWER CORP	ANCLOTE	FL	OIL
I35	FLORIDA POWER CORP	BARTOW	FL	OIL/GAS
I36	FLORIDA POWER CORP	CRYSTAL RIVER 1&2	FL	COAL
I37	GULF POWER CO	CRIST	FL	COAL
I38	GULF POWER CO	LANSING SMITH	FL	COAL
I39	TAMPA ELECTRIC CO	GANNON	FL	COAL
I40	GEORGIA POWER CO	MITCHELL (GA)	GA	COAL
I41	GEORGIA POWER CO	YATES	GA	COAL
I42	GEORGIA POWER CO	MCDONOUGH	GA	COAL
I43	GEORGIA POWER CO	HAMMOND	GA	COAL
I44	SAVANNAH ELEC & POWER CO	PORT WENTWORTH	GA	COAL/OIL/GAS
I45	CENTRAL IOWA POWER COOP	FE FAIR	IA	COAL
I46	INTERSTATE POWER CO	LANSING	IA	COAL
I47	INTERSTATE POWER CO	DUBUQUE	IA	COAL/GAS
I48	INTERSTATE POWER CO	ML KAPP	IA	COAL/GAS
I49	IOWA POWER & LIGHT CO	COUNCIL BLUFFS	IA	COAL
I50	IOWA PUBLIC SERVICE CO	GEORGE NEAL	IA	COAL/GAS
I51	IOWA SOUTHERN UTILITIES	BURLINGTON (IA) 1	IA	COAL
I52	IOWA SOUTHERN UTILITIES	OTTUMWA 1	IA	COAL
I53	IOWA-ILLINOIS GAS & ELEC	LOUISA 1	IA	COAL
I54	CENT ILLINOIS PUBLIC SERV	NEWTON	IL	COAL
I55	CENT ILLINOIS PUBLIC SERV	COFFEEN	IL	COAL
I56	CENTRAL ILLINOIS LIGHT CO	ED EDWARDS	IL	COAL
I57	CENTRAL ILLINOIS LIGHT CO	DUCK CREEK 1	IL	COAL
I58	COMMONWEALTH EDISON CO	KINCAID	IL	COAL
I59	ILLINOIS POWER CO	VERMILION	IL	COAL
I60	ILLINOIS POWER CO	BALDWIN	IL	COAL

Code	Operator	Unit	State	Type
I61	ILLINOIS POWER CO	HENNEPIN	IL	COAL
I62	INDIANA MICHIGAN POWER CO	ROCKPORT	IN	COAL
I63	INDIANA MICHIGAN POWER CO	BREED 1	IN	COAL
I64	INDIANA MICHIGAN POWER CO	TANNERS CREEK	IN	COAL
I65	INDIANAPOLIS POWER & LT	EW STOUT	IN	COAL
I66	INDIANAPOLIS POWER & LT	PETERSBURG	IN	COAL
I67	NO INDIANA PUBLIC SERVICE	MICHIGAN CITY	IN	COAL/GAS
I68	NO INDIANA PUBLIC SERVICE	RM SCHAHFER	IN	COAL/GAS
I69	NO INDIANA PUBLIC SERVICE	DH MITCHELL	IN	COAL/GAS
I70	NO INDIANA PUBLIC SERVICE	BAILLY	IN	COAL
I71	PUBLIC SERVICE INDIANA	GALLAGHER	IN	COAL
I72	PUBLIC SERVICE INDIANA	GIBSON	IN	COAL
I73	PUBLIC SERVICE INDIANA	CAYUGA	IN	COAL
I74	SOUTHERN INDIANA GAS ELEC	AB BROWN	IN	COAL
I75	SOUTHERN INDIANA GAS ELEC	CULLEY	IN	COAL
I76	Chugoku	Iwakuni	Japan	O/G
I77	Chugoku	Tamashima	Japan	Oil
I78	Chugoku	Shimonoseki	Japan	C/O
I79	Hokkaido	Sunakawa	Japan	Coal
I80	Hokuriku	Toyama	Japan	Oil
I81	Hokuriku	Fukui	Japan	Oil
I82	Shikoku	Sakaide	Japan	O/G
I83	Tohuku	Niigata	Japan	LG/G/O
I84	Tohuku	Hachinohe	Japan	Oil
I85	EMPIRE DISTRICT ELEC CO	RIVERTON (KS)	KS	COAL
I86	KANSAS CITY POWER & LIGHT	LA CYGNE	KS	COAL
I87	KANSAS POWER & LIGHT CO	LAWRENCE	KS	COAL/GAS
I88	KANSAS POWER & LIGHT CO	TECUMSEH	KS	COAL/GAS
I89	KANSAS POWER & LIGHT CO	JEFFREY	KS	COAL
I90	BIG RIVERS ELECTRIC CORP	HENDERSON TWO	KY	COAL
I91	BIG RIVERS ELECTRIC CORP	COLEMAN	KY	COAL
I92	CINCINNATI GAS & ELEC CO	EAST BEND 2	KY	COAL
I93	KENTUCKY UTILITIES CO	GHENT	KY	COAL
I94	KENTUCKY UTILITIES CO	GREEN RIVER	KY	COAL
I95	KENTUCKY UTILITIES CO	EW BROWN	KY	COAL
I96	LOUISVILLE GAS & ELEC CO	CANE RUN	KY	COAL
I97	LOUISVILLE GAS & ELEC CO	MILL CREEK	KY	COAL
I98	CENTRAL LOUISIANA ELEC CO	RODEMACHER	LA	COAL/GAS
I99	CENTRAL LOUISIANA ELEC CO	TECHE	LA	GAS
I100	LOUISIANA POWER & LIGHT	NINEMILE POINT	LA	GAS/OIL
I101	BOSTON EDISON CO	MYSTIC	MA	OIL/GAS
I102	CAMBRIDGE ELEC LIGHT CO	KENDALL SQUARE	MA	GAS/OIL
I103	BALTIMORE GAS & ELEC CO	GOULD STREET 3	MD	OIL
I104	BALTIMORE GAS & ELEC CO	CP CRANE	MD	COAL/RDF
I105	BALTIMORE GAS & ELEC CO	HA WAGNER	MD	COAL/OIL/GAS
I106	DELMARVA POWER & LIGHT CO	VIENNA 8	MD	OIL
I107	POTOMAC EDISON CO	RP SMITH	MD	COAL
I108	POTOMAC ELECTRIC POWER CO	CHALK POINT	MD	COAL/OIL/GAS
I109	CENTRAL MAINE POWER CO	WF WYMAN	ME	OIL
I110	CONSUMERS POWER CO	BC COBB	MI	COAL
I111	CONSUMERS POWER CO	DE KARN 1&2	MI	COAL
I112	DETROIT EDISON CO	RIVER ROUGE	MI	COAL/GAS
I113	DETROIT EDISON CO	TRENTON CHANNEL	MI	COAL
I114	DETROIT EDISON CO	ST CLAIR	MI	COAL
I115	NORTHERN STATES POWER CO	RIVERSIDE (MN)	MN	COAL/GAS
I116	OTTER TAIL POWER CO	HOOT LAKE	MN	COAL

Code	Operator	Unit	State	Type
I117	KANSAS CITY POWER & LIGHT	MONTROSE	MO	COAL
I118	KANSAS CITY POWER & LIGHT	HAWTHORN 5	MO	COAL
I119	UNION ELECTRIC CO	SIOUX	MO	COAL
I120	UNION ELECTRIC CO	RUSH ISLAND	MO	COAL
I121	UNION ELECTRIC CO	LABADIE	MO	COAL
I122	UTILICORP UNITED	SIBLEY	MO	COAL
I123	CAROLINA POWER & LIGHT CO	SUTTON	NC	COAL
I124	CAROLINA POWER & LIGHT CO	CAPE FEAR	NC	COAL
I125	DUKE POWER CO	CLIFFSIDE 5	NC	COAL
I126	DUKE POWER CO	MARSHALL (NC)	NC	COAL
I127	MONTANA-DAKOTA UTILITIES	COYOTE 1	ND	COAL
I128	PUBLIC SER NEW HAMPSHIRE	SCHILLER	NH	OIL/COAL
I129	ATLANTIC CITY ELECTRIC CO	BL ENGLAND	NJ	COAL/OIL
I130	DEEPWATER OPERATING CO	DEEPWATER (NJ)	NJ	COAL/OIL/GAS
I131	PUBLIC SERVICE ELEC & GAS	HUDSON	NJ	COAL/OIL/GAS
I132	EL PASO ELECTRIC CO	RIO GRANDE	NM	GAS/OIL
I133	SOUTHWESTERN PUB SERV CO	CUNNINGHAM	NM	GAS
I134	SOUTHWESTERN PUB SERV CO	MADDOX 1	NM	GAS
I135	SIERRA PACIFIC POWER CO	FORT CHURCHILL	NV	GAS/OIL
I136	SOUTHERN CALIF EDISON CO	MOHAVE	NV	COAL/GAS
I137	CONSOLIDATED EDISON CO	ARTHUR KILL	NY	OIL
I138	CONSOLIDATED EDISON CO	RAVENSWOOD	NY	GAS/OIL
I139	CONSOLIDATED EDISON CO	ASTORIA	NY	OIL/GAS
I140	LONG ISLAND LIGHTING CO	EF BARRETT	NY	GAS/OIL
I141	LONG ISLAND LIGHTING CO	GLENWOOD	NY	GAS/OIL
I142	LONG ISLAND LIGHTING CO	PORT JEFFERSON	NY	OIL
I143	LONG ISLAND LIGHTING CO	FAR ROCKAWAY 4	NY	GAS/OIL
I144	LONG ISLAND LIGHTING CO	NORTHPORT	NY	OIL
I145	NEW YORK STATE ELEC & GAS	JENNISON	NY	COAL
I146	ORANGE & ROCKLAND UTIL	LOVETT	NY	COAL/GAS
I147	ORANGE & ROCKLAND UTIL	BOWLINE POINT	NY	OIL/GAS
I148	CINCINNATI GAS & ELEC CO	WC BECKJORD	OH	COAL
I149	CINCINNATI GAS & ELEC CO	MIAMI FORT	OH	COAL
I150	COLUMBUS SOUTHERN POWER	CONESVILLE	OH	COAL
I151	COLUMBUS SOUTHERN POWER	PICWAY 5	OH	COAL
I152	OHIO EDISON CO	GORGE	OH	COAL
I153	OHIO EDISON CO	TORONTO	OH	COAL
I154	OHIO EDISON CO	RE BURGER	OH	COAL
I155	OHIO POWER CO	GAVIN	OH	COAL
I156	TOLEDO EDISON CO	BAY SHORE	OH	COAL
I157	OKLAHOMA GAS & ELEC CO	MUSKOGEE	OK	COAL/GAS
I158	OKLAHOMA GAS & ELEC CO	HORSESHOE LAKE	OK	GAS/OIL
I159	OKLAHOMA GAS & ELEC CO	SOONER	OK	COAL
I160	PUBLIC SERVICE OKLAHOMA	RIVERSIDE (OK)	OK	GAS
I161	PUBLIC SERVICE OKLAHOMA	NORTHEASTERN 3&4	OK	COAL/GAS
I162	DUQUESNE LIGHT CO	ELRAMA	PA	COAL
I163	METROPOLITAN EDISON CO	PORTLAND	PA	COAL
I164	PENNSYLVANIA ELECTRIC CO	FRONT STREET	PA	COAL
I165	PENNSYLVANIA POWER CO	NEW CASTLE	PA	COAL
I166	PENNSYLVANIA POWER CO	BRUCE MANSFIELD	PA	COAL
I167	PHILADELPHIA ELECTRIC CO	CROMBY	PA	COAL/OIL
I168	WEST PENN POWER CO	MITCHELL (PA) 3	PA	COAL
I169	SOUTH CAROLINA ELEC & GAS	CANADYS	SC	COAL/GAS
I170	SOUTH CAROLINA ELEC & GAS	WATEREE	SC	COAL
I171	SOUTH CAROLINA ELEC & GAS	MCMEEKIN	SC	COAL/GAS
I172	SOUTH CAROLINA GEN CO	AM WILLIAMS 1	SC	COAL

Code	Operator	Unit	State	Type
I173	SOUTH CAROLINA PUB SERV	GRAINGER	SC	COAL
I174	SOUTH CAROLINA PUB SERV	JEFFERIES	SC	COAL
I175	SOUTH CAROLINA PUB SERV	WINYAH	SC	COAL
I176	BLACK HILLS POWER & LIGHT	KIRK	SD	COAL
I177	OTTER TAIL POWER CO	BIG STONE 1	SD	COAL
I178	CENTRAL POWER & LIGHT CO	JOSLIN 1	TX	GAS/OIL
I179	CENTRAL POWER & LIGHT CO	BATES	TX	GAS/OIL
I180	CENTRAL POWER & LIGHT CO	NUECES BAY	TX	GAS/OIL
I181	CENTRAL POWER & LIGHT CO	LAREDO	TX	GAS/OIL
I182	CENTRAL POWER & LIGHT CO	LA PALMA	TX	GAS
I183	CENTRAL POWER & LIGHT CO	BARNEY DAVIS	TX	GAS/OIL
I184	EL PASO ELECTRIC CO	NEWMAN	TX	GAS/OIL
I185	GULF STATES UTILITIES CO	SABINE	TX	GAS/OIL
I186	GULF STATES UTILITIES CO	LEWIS CREEK	TX	GAS
I187	HOUSTON LIGHTING & POWER	GREENS BAYOU 5	TX	GAS/OIL
I188	HOUSTON LIGHTING & POWER	PH ROBINSON	TX	GAS/OIL
I189	HOUSTON LIGHTING & POWER	CEDAR BAYOU	TX	GAS/OIL
I190	HOUSTON LIGHTING & POWER	WA PARISH	TX	COAL/GAS
I191	SOUTHWESTERN ELEC PWR CO	PIRKEY 1	TX	COAL
I192	SOUTHWESTERN ELEC PWR CO	WELSH	TX	COAL
I193	TEXAS UTILITIES ELEC CO	VALLEY (TX)	TX	GAS/OIL
I194	TEXAS UTILITIES ELEC CO	MOUNTAIN CREEK (TX)	TX	GAS/OIL
I195	TEXAS UTILITIES ELEC CO	LAKE HUBBARD	TX	GAS/OIL
I196	TEXAS UTILITIES ELEC CO	MORGAN CREEK	TX	GAS/OIL
I197	TEXAS UTILITIES ELEC CO	PERMIAN BASIN	TX	GAS/OIL
I198	TEXAS UTILITIES ELEC CO	STRYKER CREEK	TX	GAS/OIL
I199	TEXAS UTILITIES ELEC CO	GRAHAM	TX	GAS/OIL
I200	TEXAS UTILITIES ELEC CO	TRADINGHOUSE CREEK	TX	GAS/OIL
I201	TEXAS UTILITIES ELEC CO	DECORDOVA 1	TX	GAS/OIL
I202	WEST TEXAS UTILITIES CO	FORT PHANTOM	TX	GAS/OIL
I203	WEST TEXAS UTILITIES CO	RIO PECOS	TX	GAS/OIL
I204	APPALACHIAN POWER CO	GLEN LYN	VA	COAL
I205	POTOMAC ELECTRIC POWER CO	POTOMAC RIVER	VA	COAL
I206	VIRGINIA ELEC & POWER CO	POSSUM POINT	VA	OIL/COAL
I207	VIRGINIA ELEC & POWER CO	YORKTOWN	VA	COAL/OIL/GAS
I208	VIRGINIA ELEC & POWER CO	BREMO BLUFF	VA	COAL
I209	WISCONSIN ELEC POWER CO	SOUTH OAK CREEK	WI	COAL
I210	WISCONSIN POWER & LIGHT	ROCK RIVER	WI	COAL
I211	WISCONSIN POWER & LIGHT	EDGEWATER (WI)	WI	COAL
I212	WISCONSIN POWER & LIGHT	COLUMBIA (WI)	WI	COAL
I213	WISCONSIN POWER & LIGHT	NELSON DEWEY	WI	COAL
I214	WISCONSIN PUBLIC SERVICE	JP PULLIAM	WI	COAL/GAS
I215	APPALACHIAN POWER CO	KANAWHA RIVER	WV	COAL
I216	APPALACHIAN POWER CO	AMOS	WV	COAL
I217	CENTRAL OPERATING CO	PHILIP SPORN	WV	COAL
I218	OHIO POWER CO	MITCHELL (WV)	WV	COAL
M1	TENNESSEE VALLEY AUTH	WIDOWS CREEK	AL	COAL
M2	TENNESSEE VALLEY AUTH	COLBERT	AL	COAL
M3	ECNSW	Munmorah	Australia	Coal
M4	ECNSW	Liddell	Australia	Coal
M5	ECNSW	Vales Point,B	Australia	Coal
M6	ECNSW	Wallerawang,C	Australia	Coal
M7	ECNSW	Eraring	Australia	Coal
M8	ECNSW	Bayswater	Australia	Coal
M9	ETSA	Torrens Island	Australia	Gas
M10	ETSA	Port Augusta	Australia	Coal

Code Operator	Unit	State	Type
M11 QEC	Gladstone	Australia	Coal
M12 SECV	Newport D	Australia	Coal
M13 SECV	Morwell	Australia	Gas
M14 SECV	Hazelwood	Australia	Coal
M15 SECWA	Kwinana	Australia	Gas/Coal/Oil
M16 SECWA	Muja	Australia	Coal
M17 SALT RIVER PROJECT	CORONADO	AZ	COAL
M18 PASADENA WTR & POWER DEPT	BROADWAY	CA	GAS/OIL
M19 New Brunswick	Courtenay Bay	Canada	Oil
M20 New Brunswick	Grand Lake	Canada	Coal
M21 New Brunswick	Coleson Cove	Canada	Oil
M22 New Brunswick	Dalhousie 1/2	Canada	Oil/Coal
M23 NFL+Lab H	Hollyrood	Canada	Oil
M24 Ontario Hydro	Lambton	Canada	Coal
M25 Ontario Hydro	Nanticoke	Canada	Coal
M26 ESB	Aghada	Eire	Gas/Oil
M27 ESB	North Wall	Eire	Gas/Oil
M28 ESB	Marina	Eire	Gas
M29 GAINESVILLE REGIONAL UTIL	DEERHAVEN	FL	COAL/GAS
M30 ORLANDO UTILITIES COMM	INDIAN RIVER (FL)	FL	GAS/OIL
M31 PPC of Greece	Liptol	Greece	Lignite
M32 PPC of Greece	Aliveri	Greece	Oil/Lignite
M33 PPC of Greece	Megalopolis	Greece	Lignite
M34 PPC of Greece	Ptolemaida	Greece	Lignite
M35 MUSCATINE POWER & WATER	MUSCATINE	IA	COAL
M36 KANSAS CITY BD PUB UTIL	QUINDARO THREE	KS	COAL/GAS
M37 TENNESSEE VALLEY AUTH	SHAWNEE	KY	COAL
M38 GRAND HAVEN BD LT & PWR	JB SIMS	MI	COAL/GAS
M39 LANSING BOARD WTR & LT	ECKERT	MI	COAL
M40 MARQUETTE BD LT & POWER	SHIRAS	MI	COAL
M41 NEW ULM PUBLIC UTIL COMM	NEW ULM	MN	GAS/COAL
M42 SPRINGFIELD CITY UTIL	SOUTHWEST 1	MO	COAL
M43 SPRINGFIELD CITY UTIL	JAMES RIVER	MO	COAL/GAS
M44 GRAND ISLAND UTILITIES	PLATTE 1	NE	COAL
M45 HASTINGS UTILITIES DEPT	HASTINGS 1	NE	COAL
M46 NEBRASKA PUBLIC POWER DIS	SHELDON	NE	COAL
M47 NEBRASKA PUBLIC POWER DIS	GERALD GENTLEMAN	NE	COAL
M48 OMAHA PUBLIC POWER DIST	NEBRASKA CITY 1	NE	COAL
M49 OMAHA PUBLIC POWER DIST	NORTH OMAHA	NE	COAL/GAS
M50 JAMESTOWN BD PUBLIC UTIL	CARLSON	NY	COAL
M51 NEW YORK POWER AUTHORITY	CHARLES POLETTI 1	NY	GAS/OIL
M52 ECNZ	Huntly	N.Zealand	Gas/Coal
M53 Eskom	Komati	S.Africa	Coal
M54 Eskom	Kendal	S.Africa	Coal
M55 Eskom	Matimba	S.Africa	Coal
M56 Eskom	Lethabo	S.Africa	Coal
M57 Eskom	Tukuka	S.Africa	Coal
M58 Eskom	Hendrina	S.Africa	Coal
M59 TENNESSEE VALLEY AUTH	JOHNSONVILLE	TN	COAL
M60 TENNESSEE VALLEY AUTH	TH ALLEN	TN	COAL
M61 TENNESSEE VALLEY AUTH	GALLATIN	TN	COAL
M62 BRYAN MUNICIPAL ELEC SYS	RC DANSBY 1	TX	GAS/OIL
M63 LOWER COLORADO RIVER AUTH	FAYETTE	TX	COAL
M64 CEGB	Castle Donnington	UK	Coal
M65 CEGB	West Thurrock	UK	Coal
M66 CEGB	Willington A	UK	Coal

Code	Operator	Unit	State	Type
M67	CEGB	Uskmouth	UK	Coal
M68	CEGB	Didcot	UK	Coal
M69	CEGB	Padiham	UK	Coal
M70	CEGB	Skelton Grange	UK	Coal
M71	CEGB	Willington B	UK	Coal
M72	CEGB	Aberthaw A	UK	Coal
M73	CEGB	Drakelow B	UK	Coal
M74	CEGB	Ironbridge	UK	Coal
M75	CEGB	Drakelow C	UK	Coal
M76	CEGB	Kingsnorth	UK	Coal
M77	CEGB	Rugeley A	UK	Coal
M78	CEGB	Agecroft	UK	Coal
M79	CEGB	Blyth B	UK	Coal
M80	Scot Power	Longannet	UK	Coal
M81	BURLINGTON ELEC LT DEPT	JC MCNEIL	VT	WOOD/OIL/GAS
M82	Taipower	Taichung	Taiwan	G/Distillate
M83	Taipower	Talin	Taiwan	Oil/Gas

Appendix 2.2.4 *The BASE60 Plants*

Code	Operator	Unit	State	Type
C1	COLORADO-UTE ELEC ASSN	CRAIG	CO	COAL
C2	COLORADO-UTE ELEC ASSN	HAYDEN	CO	COAL
C3	HOOSIER ENERGY REC	RATTS	IN	COAL
C4	SUNFLOWER ELEC POWER COOP	HOLCOMB 1	KS	COAL
C5	ASSOCIATED ELECTRIC COOP	NEW MADRID	MO	COAL
C6	BASIN ELECTRIC POWER COOP	ANTELOPE VALLEY	ND	COAL
C7	UNITED POWER ASSOCIATION	STANTON	ND	COAL
C8	PLAINS ELEC G&T COOP	PLAINS 1	NM	COAL
C9	WESTERN FARMERS ELEC COOP	HUGO 1	OK	COAL
C10	DESERET GEN & TRANS COOP	BONANZA 1	UT	COAL
C11	BASIN ELECTRIC POWER COOP	LARAMIE RIVER	WY	COAL
I1	ALABAMA POWER CO	BARRY	AL	COAL/GAS
I2	ALABAMA POWER CO	MILLER	AL	COAL
I3	ARKANSAS POWER & LIGHT CO	WHITE BLUFF	AR	COAL
I4	ARIZONA PUBLIC SERVICE CO	CHOLLA	AZ	COAL
I5	CENTURY POWER CORP	SPRINGERVILLE 1	AZ	COAL
I6	PACIFIC GAS & ELEC CO	POTRERO 3	CA	GAS/OIL
I7	TransAlta	Keephills	Canada	Coal
I8	TransAlta	Sundance	Canada	Coal
I9	TransAlta	Wabanum	Canada	Coal
I10	PUBLIC SERVICE COLORADO	VALMONT 5	CO	COAL
I11	CONNECTICUT LIGHT & POWER	NORWALK HARBOR	CT	OIL
I12	UNITED ILLUMINATING CO	BRIDGEPORT HARBOR	CT	COAL/OIL
I13	UNITED ILLUMINATING CO	NEW HAVEN HARBOR 1	CT	OIL/GAS
I14	FLORIDA POWER CORP	CRYSTAL RIVER 4&5	FL	COAL
I15	GULF POWER CO	SCHOLZ	FL	COAL
I16	GEORGIA POWER CO	BOWEN	GA	COAL
I17	GEORGIA POWER CO	HARLLEE BRANCH	GA	COAL
I18	GEORGIA POWER CO	WANSLEY	GA	COAL
I19	SAVANNAH ELEC & POWER CO	MCINTOSH (GA) 1	GA	COAL
I20	RWE	Frimmersdorf	Germany	Coal
I21	RWE	Niederaubem	Germany	Coal

Code	Operator	Unit	State	Type
I22	RWE	Nuerath	Germany	Coal
I23	RWE	Welsweller	Germany	Coal
I24	HAWAII ELEC LIGHT CO	WH HILL	HI	OIL
I25	MAUI ELECTRIC CO	KAHULUI	HI	OIL
I26	China P+L	Castle Peak	HK	Coal
I27	ELECTRIC ENERGY INC	JOPPA	IL	COAL
I28	ALCOA GENERATING CORP	WARRICK	IN	COAL
I29	INDIANA-KENTUCKY ELEC COR	CLIFTY CREEK	IN	COAL
I30	Chugoku	Shinonoda	Japan	C/O
I31	Hokkaido	Ebetsu	Japan	Coal
I32	Hokkaido	Naie	Japan	Coal
I33	Hokkaido	TomatoAtsuma	Japan	Oil
I34	Shikoku	Saijo	Japan	C/O
I35	Tohuku	Higashi Niigata	Japan	LG/G/O
I36	Tohuku	Sendai	Japan	C/O
I37	BIG RIVERS ELECTRIC CORP	DB WILSON 1	KY	COAL
I38	BIG RIVERS ELECTRIC CORP	GREEN	KY	COAL
I39	KENTUCKY POWER CO	BIG SANDY	KY	COAL
I40	CENTRAL LOUISIANA ELEC CO	DOLET HILLS 1	LA	COAL
I41	BOSTON EDISON CO	NEW BOSTON	MA	OIL/GAS
I42	CANAL ELECTRIC CO	CANAL	MA	OIL
I43	HOLYOKE WATER POWER CO	MOUNT TOM 1	MA	COAL
I44	MONTAUP ELECTRIC CO	SOMERSET (MA)	MA	COAL/OIL
I45	NEW ENGLAND POWER CO	BRAYTON POINT	MA	COAL/OIL
I46	NEW ENGLAND POWER CO	SALEM HARBOR	MA	OIL/COAL
I47	BALTIMORE GAS & ELEC CO	BRANDON SHORES 1	MD	COAL
I48	POTOMAC ELECTRIC POWER CO	DICKERSON	MD	COAL
I49	POTOMAC ELECTRIC POWER CO	MORGANTOWN	MD	COAL
I50	CONSUMERS POWER CO	JC WEADOCK	MI	COAL
I51	CONSUMERS POWER CO	JH CAMPBELL	MI	COAL
I52	CONSUMERS POWER CO	JR WHITING	MI	COAL
I53	DETROIT EDISON CO	BELLE RIVER	MI	COAL
I54	DETROIT EDISON CO	MONROE (MI)	MI	COAL
I55	MINNESOTA POWER & LIGHT	CLAY BOSWELL	MN	COAL
I56	NORTHERN STATES POWER CO	AS KING 1	MN	COAL/WOOD
I57	NORTHERN STATES POWER CO	SHERBURNE COUNTY	MN	COAL
I58	EMPIRE DISTRICT ELEC CO	ASBURY 1	MO	COAL
I59	KANSAS CITY POWER & LIGHT	IATAN 1	MO	COAL
I60	MONTANA POWER CO	COLSTRIP	MT	COAL
I61	MONTANA POWER CO	JE CORETTE 1	MT	COAL/GAS
I62	MONTANA-DAKOTA UTILITIES	LEWIS & CLARK 1	MT	COAL
I63	CAROLINA POWER & LIGHT CO	ASHEVILLE	NC	COAL
I64	CAROLINA POWER & LIGHT CO	MAYO 1	NC	COAL
I65	CAROLINA POWER & LIGHT CO	ROXBORO	NC	COAL
I66	DUKE POWER CO	BELEWS CREEK	NC	COAL
I67	MINNKOTA POWER COOP	MR YOUNG	ND	COAL
I68	MONTANA-DAKOTA UTILITIES	HESKETT	ND	COAL
I69	PUBLIC SER NEW HAMPSHIRE	MERRIMACK	NH	COAL
I70	PUBLIC SER NEW HAMPSHIRE	NEWINGTON 1	NH	OIL
I71	PUBLIC SERVICE ELEC & GAS	MERCER	NJ	COAL/GAS
I72	ARIZONA PUBLIC SERVICE CO	FOUR CORNERS	NM	COAL
I73	PUBLIC SERVICE NEW MEXICO	SAN JUAN (NM)	NM	COAL
I74	NEVADA POWER CO	REID GARDNER	NV	COAL
I75	SIERRA PACIFIC POWER CO	NORTH VALMY	NV	COAL
I76	CENTRAL HUDSON GAS & ELEC	DANSKAMMER POINT	NY	COAL/GAS/OIL
I77	CENTRAL HUDSON GAS & ELEC	ROSETON	NY	OIL

Code	Operator	Unit	State	Type
I78	NEW YORK STATE ELEC & GAS	GOUDEY	NY	COAL
I79	NEW YORK STATE ELEC & GAS	GREENIDGE	NY	COAL
I80	NEW YORK STATE ELEC & GAS	HICKLING	NY	COAL
I81	NEW YORK STATE ELEC & GAS	MILLIKEN	NY	COAL
I82	NEW YORK STATE ELEC & GAS	SOMERSET 1	NY	COAL
I83	NIAGARA MOHAWK POWER CORP	ALBANY	NY	GAS/OIL
I84	NIAGARA MOHAWK POWER CORP	CR HUNTLEY	NY	COAL
I85	NIAGARA MOHAWK POWER CORP	DUNKIRK	NY	COAL
I86	ROCHESTER GAS & ELEC CORP	BEEBEE 12	NY	COAL
I87	ROCHESTER GAS & ELEC CORP	RUSSELL	NY	COAL
I88	CARDINAL OPERATING CO	CARDINAL	OH	COAL
I89	DAYTON POWER & LIGHT CO	JM STUART	OH	COAL
I90	DAYTON POWER & LIGHT CO	KILLEN 2	OH	COAL
I91	OHIO EDISON CO	NILES	OH	COAL
I92	OHIO EDISON CO	WH SAMMIS	OH	COAL
I93	OHIO POWER CO	MUSKINGUM RIVER	OH	COAL
I94	OHIO VALLEY ELECTRIC CORP	KYGER CREEK	OH	COAL
I95	METROPOLITAN EDISON CO	TITUS	PA	COAL
I96	PENNSYLVANIA ELECTRIC CO	CONEMAUGH	PA	COAL
I97	PENNSYLVANIA ELECTRIC CO	HOMER CITY	PA	COAL
I98	PENNSYLVANIA ELECTRIC CO	KEYSTONE	PA	COAL
I99	PENNSYLVANIA ELECTRIC CO	SEWARD	PA	COAL
I100	PENNSYLVANIA ELECTRIC CO	SHAWVILLE	PA	COAL
I101	PENNSYLVANIA ELECTRIC CO	WARREN	PA	COAL
I102	PENNSYLVANIA ELECTRIC CO	WILLIAMSBURG 5	PA	COAL
I103	PENNSYLVANIA POWER & LT	BRUNNER ISLAND	PA	COAL
I104	PENNSYLVANIA POWER & LT	HOLTWOOD 17	PA	COAL
I105	PENNSYLVANIA POWER & LT	MONTOUR	PA	COAL
I106	PENNSYLVANIA POWER & LT	SUNBURY	PA	COAL
I107	UGI CORP	HUNLOCK 3	PA	COAL
I108	WEST PENN POWER CO	ARMSTRONG	PA	COAL
I109	WEST PENN POWER CO	HATFIELDS FERRY	PA	COAL
I110	SOUTH CAROLINA ELEC & GAS	URQUHART	SC	COAL/GAS
I111	SOUTH CAROLINA PUB SERV	CROSS 2	SC	COAL
I112	BLACK HILLS POWER & LIGHT	BEN FRENCH 1	SD	COAL
I113	CENTRAL POWER & LIGHT CO	COLETO CREEK 1	TX	COAL
I114	HOUSTON LIGHTING & POWER	LIMESTONE	TX	COAL/GAS
I115	SOUTHWESTERN PUB SERV CO	HARRINGTON	TX	COAL
I116	SOUTHWESTERN PUB SERV CO	TOLK	TX	COAL
I117	TEXAS UTILITIES ELEC CO	BIG BROWN	TX	COAL/GAS
I118	TEXAS UTILITIES ELEC CO	MARTIN LAKE	TX	COAL
I119	TEXAS UTILITIES ELEC CO	MONTICELLO (TX)	TX	COAL
I120	WEST TEXAS UTILITIES CO	OAK CREEK (TX) 1	TX	GAS/OIL
I121	WEST TEXAS UTILITIES CO	OKLAUNION 1	TX	COAL
I122	PACIFIC POWER & LIGHT CO	CARBON	UT	COAL
I123	PACIFIC POWER & LIGHT CO	HUNTER	UT	COAL
I124	PACIFIC POWER & LIGHT CO	HUNTINGTON	UT	COAL
I125	APPALACHIAN POWER CO	CLINCH RIVER	VA	COAL
I126	VIRGINIA ELEC & POWER CO	CHESAPEAKE	VA	COAL
I127	VIRGINIA ELEC & POWER CO	CHESTERFIELD	VA	COAL
I128	PACIFIC POWER & LIGHT CO	CENTRALIA	WA	COAL
I129	WISCONSIN ELEC POWER CO	PLEASANT PRAIRIE	WI	COAL
I130	WISCONSIN PUBLIC SERVICE	WESTON	WI	COAL/GAS
I131	APPALACHIAN POWER CO	MOUNTAINEER 1	WV	COAL
I132	MONONGAHELA POWER CO	ALBRIGHT	WV	COAL
I133	MONONGAHELA POWER CO	HARRISON	WV	COAL

Code	Operator	Unit	State	Type
I134	MONONGAHELA POWER CO	PLEASANTS	WV	COAL
I135	MONONGAHELA POWER CO	RIVESVILLE	WV	COAL
I136	MONONGAHELA POWER CO	WILLOW ISLAND	WV	COAL
I137	OHIO POWER CO	KAMMER	WV	COAL
I138	VIRGINIA ELEC & POWER CO	MOUNT STORM	WV	COAL
I139	BLACK HILLS POWER & LIGHT	OSAGE	WY	COAL
I140	PACIFIC POWER & LIGHT CO	DAVE JOHNSTON	WY	COAL
I141	PACIFIC POWER & LIGHT CO	JIM BRIDGER	WY	COAL
I142	PACIFIC POWER & LIGHT CO	NAUGHTON	WY	COAL
I143	PACIFIC POWER & LIGHT CO	WYODAK 1	WY	COAL
M1	QEC	Callide B	Australia	Coal
M2	QEC	Tarong	Australia	Coal
M3	SECV	Loy Yang A	Australia	Coal
M4	SECV	Yallourn W	Australia	Coal
M5	SALT RIVER PROJECT	NAVAJO	AZ	COAL
M6	Ontario Hydro	Thunder Bay	Canada	Coal
M7	SaskPower	Boundary Dam	Canada	Lignite
M8	SaskPower	Poplar River	Canada	Lignite
M9	PLATTE RIVER POWER AUTH	RAWHIDE 1	CO	COAL
M10	ESB	Moneypoint	Eire	Coal
M11	JACKSONVILLE ELEC AUTH	ST JOHNS RIVER	FL	COAL
M12	ORLANDO UTILITIES COMM	CH STANTON 1	FL	COAL
M13	PPC of Greece	Amintaio	Greece	Lignite
M14	PPC of Greece	Kardia	Greece	Lignite
M15	PPC of Greece	St.Dimitr.	Greece	Lignite
M16	RICHMOND POWER & LIGHT	WHITEWATER VALLEY	IN	COAL
M17	KANSAS CITY BD PUB UTIL	NEARMAN CREEK 1	KS	COAL
M18	TENNESSEE VALLEY AUTH	PARADISE	KY	COAL
M19	LANSING BOARD WTR & LT	ERICKSON 1	MI	COAL
M20	SIKESTON BD OF MUN UTIL	SIKESTON 1	MO	COAL
M21	AMERICAN MUNI POWER OHIO	RH GORSUCH	OH	COAL
M22	GRAND RIVER DAM AUTHORITY	GRDA	OK	COAL
M23	Eskom	Arnot	S.Africa	Coal
M24	Eskom	Duvha	S.Africa	Coal
M25	Eskom	Kriel	S.Africa	Coal
M26	Eskom	Matla	S.Africa	Coal
M27	EGAT	Bang Pakong 1-2	Thailand	Oil/gas
M28	EGAT	Bang Pakong CCGT	Thailand	Gas
M29	EGAT	Khanom 1-2	Thailand	Oil
M30	EGAT	Mae Moh 1-9	Thailand	Lignite
M31	EGAT	North Bangkok 1-3	Thailand	Oil
M32	EGAT	South Bangkok 1-5	Thailand	Oil/gas
M33	TENNESSEE VALLEY AUTH	BULL RUN 1	TN	COAL
M34	TENNESSEE VALLEY AUTH	CUMBERLAND	TN	COAL
M35	TENNESSEE VALLEY AUTH	JOHN SEVIER	TN	COAL
M36	TENNESSEE VALLEY AUTH	KINGSTON	TN	COAL
M37	LUBBOCK POWER & LIGHT	HOLLY AVENUE	TX	GAS
M38	SAN ANTONIO PUB SERV BD	JT DEELY	TX	COAL
M39	TEXAS MUN PWR AGENCY	GIBBONS CREEK 1	TX	COAL
M40	CEGB	Aberthaw B	UK	Coal
M41	CEGB	Blyth A	UK	Coal
M42	CEGB	Cottam	UK	Coal
M43	CEGB	Drax	UK	Coal
M44	CEGB	Eggborough	UK	Coal
M45	CEGB	Ferrybridge C	UK	Coal
M46	CEGB	Fiddlers Ferry	UK	Coal

Code	Operator	Unit	State	Type
M47	CEGB	High Marnham	UK	Coal
M48	CEGB	Ratcliffe	UK	Coal
M49	CEGB	Rugeley B	UK	Coal
M50	CEGB	Staythorpe	UK	Coal
M51	CEGB	Thorpe Marsh	UK	Coal
M52	CEGB	West Burton	UK	Coal
M53	Scot Power	Methil	UK	Coal Slurry
M54	INTERMOUNTAIN PWR AGENCY	INTERMOUNTAIN	UT	COAL
M55	Taipower	Hsiehho	Taiwan	Coal/Oil
M56	Taipower	Hsinta	Taiwan	Coal/Oil
M57	Taipower	Linkou	Taiwan	Coal/Oil
M58	Taipower	Nanpu	Taiwan	Coal/Oil
M59	Taipower	Shen-Ao	Taiwan	Coal/Oil

Appendix 2.3: Chapter 7 Sample Plants (2 letter State codes refer to US state except UK)

Code	Operator	Unit	State
I1	ALABAMA POWER CO	BARRY	AL
I2	ALABAMA POWER CO	MILLER	AL
I3	ARKANSAS POWER & LIGHT CO	WHITE BLUFF	AR
I4	ARIZONA PUBLIC SERVICE CO	CHOLLA	AZ
I5	CENTURY POWER CORP	SPRINGERVILLE 1	AZ
I6	PACIFIC GAS & ELEC CO	POTRERO 3	CA
I10	PUBLIC SERVICE COLORADO	VALMONT 5	CO
I11	CONNECTICUT LIGHT & POWER	NORWALK HARBOR	CT
I12	UNITED ILLUMINATING CO	BRIDGEPORT HARBOR	CT
I13	UNITED ILLUMINATING CO	NEW HAVEN HARBOR 1	CT
I14	FLORIDA POWER CORP	CRYSTAL RIVER 4&5	FL
I15	GULF POWER CO	SCHOLZ	FL
I16	GEORGIA POWER CO	BOWEN	GA
I17	GEORGIA POWER CO	HARLLEE BRANCH	GA
I18	GEORGIA POWER CO	WANSLEY	GA
I19	SAVANNAH ELEC & POWER CO	MCINTOSH (GA) 1	GA
I24	HAWAII ELEC LIGHT CO	WH HILL	HI
I25	MAUI ELECTRIC CO	KAHULUI	HI
I27	ELECTRIC ENERGY INC	JOPPA	IL
I28	ALCOA GENERATING CORP	WARRICK	IN
I29	INDIANA-KENTUCKY ELEC COR	CLIFTY CREEK	IN
I30	Chugoku	Shinonoda	Japan
I31	Hokkaido	Ebetsu	Japan
I32	Hokkaido	Naie	Japan
I33	Hokkaido	TomatoAtsuma	Japan
I34	Shikoku	Saijo	Japan
I37	BIG RIVERS ELECTRIC CORP	DB WILSON 1	KY
I38	BIG RIVERS ELECTRIC CORP	GREEN	KY
I39	KENTUCKY POWER CO	BIG SANDY	KY
I40	CENTRAL LOUISIANA ELEC CO	DOLET HILLS 1	LA
I41	BOSTON EDISON CO	NEW BOSTON	MA
I42	CANAL ELECTRIC CO	CANAL	MA
I43	HOLYOKE WATER POWER CO	MOUNT TOM 1	MA

Code	Operator	Unit	State
I44	MONTAUP ELECTRIC CO	SOMERSET (MA)	MA
I45	NEW ENGLAND POWER CO	BRAYTON POINT	MA
I46	NEW ENGLAND POWER CO	SALEM HARBOR	MA
I47	BALTIMORE GAS & ELEC CO	BRANDON SHORES 1	MD
I48	POTOMAC ELECTRIC POWER CO	DICKERSON	MD
I49	POTOMAC ELECTRIC POWER CO	MORGANTOWN	MD
I50	CONSUMERS POWER CO	JC WEADOCK	MI
I51	CONSUMERS POWER CO	JH CAMPBELL	MI
I52	CONSUMERS POWER CO	JR WHITING	MI
I53	DETROIT EDISON CO	BELLE RIVER	MI
I54	DETROIT EDISON CO	MONROE (MI)	MI
I55	MINNESOTA POWER & LIGHT	CLAY BOSWELL	MN
I56	NORTHERN STATES POWER CO	AS KING 1	MN
I57	NORTHERN STATES POWER CO	SHERBURNE COUNTY	MN
I58	EMPIRE DISTRICT ELEC CO	ASBURY 1	MO
I59	KANSAS CITY POWER & LIGHT	IATAN 1	MO
I60	MONTANA POWER CO	COLSTRIP	MT
I61	MONTANA POWER CO	JE CORETTE 1	MT
I62	MONTANA-DAKOTA UTILITIES	LEWIS & CLARK 1	MT
I63	CAROLINA POWER & LIGHT CO	ASHEVILLE	NC
I64	CAROLINA POWER & LIGHT CO	MAYO 1	NC
I65	CAROLINA POWER & LIGHT CO	ROXBORO	NC
I66	DUKE POWER CO	BELEWS CREEK	NC
I68	MONTANA-DAKOTA UTILITIES	HESKETT	ND
I69	PUBLIC SER NEW HAMPSHIRE	MERRIMACK	NH
I70	PUBLIC SER NEW HAMPSHIRE	NEWINGTON 1	NH
I71	PUBLIC SERVICE ELEC & GAS	MERCER	NJ
I72	ARIZONA PUBLIC SERVICE CO	FOUR CORNERS	NM
I73	PUBLIC SERVICE NEW MEXICO	SAN JUAN (NM)	NM
I75	SIERRA PACIFIC POWER CO	NORTH VALMY	NV
I76	CENTRAL HUDSON GAS & ELEC	DANSKAMMER POINT	NY
I77	CENTRAL HUDSON GAS & ELEC	ROSETON	NY
I78	NEW YORK STATE ELEC & GAS	GOUDEY	NY
I79	NEW YORK STATE ELEC & GAS	GREENIDGE	NY
I80	NEW YORK STATE ELEC & GAS	HICKLING	NY
I81	NEW YORK STATE ELEC & GAS	MILLIKEN	NY
I82	NEW YORK STATE ELEC & GAS	SOMERSET 1	NY
I83	NIAGARA MOHAWK POWER CORP	ALBANY	NY
I84	NIAGARA MOHAWK POWER CORP	CR HUNTLEY	NY
I85	NIAGARA MOHAWK POWER CORP	DUNKIRK	NY
I86	ROCHESTER GAS & ELEC CORP	BEEBEE 12	NY
I87	ROCHESTER GAS & ELEC CORP	RUSSELL	NY
I88	CARDINAL OPERATING CO	CARDINAL	OH
I89	DAYTON POWER & LIGHT CO	JM STUART	OH
I90	DAYTON POWER & LIGHT CO	KILLEN 2	OH
I91	OHIO EDISON CO	NILES	OH
I92	OHIO EDISON CO	WH SAMMIS	OH
I93	OHIO POWER CO	MUSKINGUM RIVER	OH
I94	OHIO VALLEY ELECTRIC CORP	KYGER CREEK	OH
I95	METROPOLITAN EDISON CO	TITUS	PA
I96	PENNSYLVANIA ELECTRIC CO	CONEMAUGH	PA
I97	PENNSYLVANIA ELECTRIC CO	HOMER CITY	PA
I98	PENNSYLVANIA ELECTRIC CO	KEYSTONE	PA
I99	PENNSYLVANIA ELECTRIC CO	SEWARD	PA
I100	PENNSYLVANIA ELECTRIC CO	SHAWVILLE	PA
I101	PENNSYLVANIA ELECTRIC CO	WARREN	PA

Code	Operator	Unit	State
I102	PENNSYLVANIA ELECTRIC CO	WILLIAMSBURG 5	PA
I103	PENNSYLVANIA POWER & LT	BRUNNER ISLAND	PA
I104	PENNSYLVANIA POWER & LT	HOLTWOOD 17	PA
I105	PENNSYLVANIA POWER & LT	MONTOUR	PA
I106	PENNSYLVANIA POWER & LT	SUNBURY	PA
I107	UGI CORP	HUNLOCK 3	PA
I108	WEST PENN POWER CO	ARMSTRONG	PA
I109	WEST PENN POWER CO	HATFIELDS FERRY	PA
I110	SOUTH CAROLINA ELEC & GAS	URQUHART	SC
I111	SOUTH CAROLINA PUB SERV	CROSS 2	SC
I112	BLACK HILLS POWER & LIGHT	BEN FRENCH 1	SD
I113	CENTRAL POWER & LIGHT CO	COLETO CREEK 1	TX
I114	HOUSTON LIGHTING & POWER	LIMESTONE	TX
I115	SOUTHWESTERN PUB SERV CO	HARRINGTON	TX
I116	SOUTHWESTERN PUB SERV CO	TOLK	TX
I117	TEXAS UTILITIES ELEC CO	BIG BROWN	TX
I118	TEXAS UTILITIES ELEC CO	MARTIN LAKE	TX
I119	TEXAS UTILITIES ELEC CO	MONTICELLO (TX)	TX
I120	WEST TEXAS UTILITIES CO	OAK CREEK (TX) 1	TX
I121	WEST TEXAS UTILITIES CO	OKLAUNION 1	TX
I122	PACIFIC POWER & LIGHT CO	CARBON	UT
I123	PACIFIC POWER & LIGHT CO	HUNTER	UT
I124	PACIFIC POWER & LIGHT CO	HUNTINGTON	UT
I125	APPALACHIAN POWER CO	CLINCH RIVER	VA
I126	VIRGINIA ELEC & POWER CO	CHESAPEAKE	VA
I127	VIRGINIA ELEC & POWER CO	CHESTERFIELD	VA
I128	PACIFIC POWER & LIGHT CO	CENTRALIA	WA
I129	WISCONSIN ELEC POWER CO	PLEASANT PRAIRIE	WI
I130	WISCONSIN PUBLIC SERVICE	WESTON	WI
I131	APPALACHIAN POWER CO	MOUNTAINEER 1	WV
I132	MONONGAHELA POWER CO	ALBRIGHT	WV
I133	MONONGAHELA POWER CO	HARRISON	WV
I134	MONONGAHELA POWER CO	PLEASANTS	WV
I135	MONONGAHELA POWER CO	RIVESVILLE	WV
I136	MONONGAHELA POWER CO	WILLOW ISLAND	WV
I137	OHIO POWER CO	KAMMER	WV
I138	VIRGINIA ELEC & POWER CO	MOUNT STORM	WV
I139	BLACK HILLS POWER & LIGHT	OSAGE	WY
I140	PACIFIC POWER & LIGHT CO	DAVE JOHNSTON	WY
I141	PACIFIC POWER & LIGHT CO	JIM BRIDGER	WY
I142	PACIFIC POWER & LIGHT CO	NAUGHTON	WY
M1	QEC	Callide B	Australia
M2	QEC	Tarong	Australia
M3	SECV	Loy Yang A	Australia
M4	SECV	Yallourn W	Australia
M5	SALT RIVER PROJECT	NAVAJO	AZ
M7	SaskPower	Boundary Dam	Canada
M8	SaskPower	Poplar River	Canada
M9	PLATTE RIVER POWER AUTH	RAWHIDE 1	CO
M10	ESB	Moneypoint	Eire
M11	JACKSONVILLE ELEC AUTH	ST JOHNS RIVER	FL
M12	ORLANDO UTILITIES COMM	CH STANTON 1	FL
M13	PPC of Greece	Amintaio	Greece
M14	PPC of Greece	Kardia	Greece
M15	PPC of Greece	St.Dimitr.	Greece
M16	RICHMOND POWER & LIGHT	WHITEWATER VALLEY	IN

Code Operator		Unit	State
M17	KANSAS CITY BD PUB UTIL	NEARMAN CREEK 1	KS
M18	TENNESSEE VALLEY AUTH	PARADISE	KY
M19	LANSING BOARD WTR & LT	ERICKSON 1	MI
M20	SIKESTON BD OF MUN UTIL	SIKESTON 1	MO
M21	AMERICAN MUNI POWER OHIO	RH GORSUCH	OH
M22	GRAND RIVER DAM AUTHORITY	GRDA	OK
M24	Eskom	Duvha	S.Africa
M27	EGAT	Bang Pakong 1-2	Thailand
M28	EGAT	Bang Pakong CCGT	Thailand
M29	EGAT	Khanom 1-2	Thailand
M30	EGAT	Mae Moh 1-9	Thailand
M33	TENNESSEE VALLEY AUTH	BULL RUN 1	TN
M34	TENNESSEE VALLEY AUTH	CUMBERLAND	TN
M35	TENNESSEE VALLEY AUTH	JOHN SEVIER	TN
M36	TENNESSEE VALLEY AUTH	KINGSTON	TN
M37	LUBBOCK POWER & LIGHT	HOLLY AVENUE	TX
M38	SAN ANTONIO PUB SERV BD	JT DEELY	TX
M39	TEXAS MUN PWR AGENCY	GIBBONS CREEK 1	TX
M54	INTERMOUNTAIN PWR AGENCY	INTERMOUNTAIN	UT

Appendix 2.4: Chapter 8 Transmission and Distribution Sample Data (2 letter State codes refer to US state except UK)

Appendix 2.4.1 Sample Transmission Networks

(A) Small Transmission Companies

Code	Utility	State
1I	SAVANNAH ELECTRIC AND POWER CO.	GA
2I	INTERSTATE POWER CO.	IA
3I	IOWA ELECTRIC LIGHT AND POWER	IA
4I	IOWA POWER	IA
5I	IOWA ILLINOIS GAS AND ELECTRIC	IA
6I	CENTRAL ILLINOIS LIGHT CO.	IL
7I	ILLINOIS POWER CO.	IL
8I	SOUTHERN INDIANA GAS AND ELECTRIC	IN
9I	CENTRAL LOUISIANA ELECTRIC CO.	LA
10I	MAINE PUBLIC SERVICE	ME
11I	MICHIGAN POWER	MI
12I	UPPER PENINSULA	MI
13I	MINNESOTA POWER AND LIGHT	MN
14I	EMPIRE DISTRICT	MO
15I	ST JOSEPH LIGHT AND POWER	MO
16I	SIERRA PACIFIC POWER CO.	NV
17I	UGI CORP	PA
18I	NARRAGANSETT	RI
19I	NEWPORT	RI
20I	BLACK HILLS POWER AND LIGHT	SD
21I	NORTH WEST PUBLIC SERVICE	SD
22I	WEST TEXAS UTILITIES CO.	TX

Code	Utility	State
23I	MADISON GAS AND ELECTRIC	WI
24M	IMPERIAL IRRIGATION DISTRICT	CA
25M	PLATTE RIVER POWER AUTHORITY	CO.
26M	JACKSONVILLE ELECTRIC AUTHORITY	FL
27M	LAKELAND LIGHT AND WATER DEPARTMENT	FL
28M	ORLANDO UTILITIES	FL
29M	TALLAHASSEE ELECTRIC DEPT	FL
30M	MUNICIPAL ELECTRIC AUTHORITY OF GEORGIA	GA
31M	SPRINGFIELD	IL
32M	LINCOLN ELECTRIC SYSTEM	NE
33M	OMAHA PUBLIC POWER DISTRICT	NE
34M	EUGENE WATER AND ELECTRIC BOARD	OR
35M	SAN ANTONIO PUBLIC SERVICE	TX
36M	PUD NO1 OF DOUGLAS COUNTY	WA
37M	PUD NO2 OF GRANT COUNTY	WA

(B) Medium Transmission Companies

Code	Utility	State
38I	ARKANSAS LIGHT AND POWER	AR
39I	ARIZONA PUBLIC SERVICE CO.	AZ
40I	TUCSON ELECTRIC POWER CO.	AZ
41I	PUBLIC SERVICE CO. OF COLORADO	CO.
42I	UNITED ILLUMINATING CO.	CT
43I	POTOMAC ELECTRIC POWER	DC
44I	DELMARVA POWER AND LIGHT CO.	DE
45I	FLORIDA POWER CO.	FL
46I	GULF POWER	FL
47I	HAWAII ELECTRIC	HI
48I	IDAHO POWER CO.	ID
49I	CENTRAL ILLINOIS PUBLIC SERVICE	IL
50I	INDIANA POWER AND LIGHT	IN
51I	NORTH INDIANA PUBLIC SERVICE	IN
52I	PSI EN INC	IN
53I	KANSAS GAS AND ELECTRIC.	KS
54I	KANSAS POWER AND LIGHT	KS
55I	KENTUCKY UTILITIES CO.	KY
56I	KENTUCKY POWER	KY
57I	LOUISVILLE GAS AND ELECTRIC	KY
58I	SOUTH WESTERN ELECTRIC POWER	LA
59I	BALTIMORE GAS AND ELECTRIC	MD
60I	POTOMAC EDISON	MD
61I	CENTRAL MAINE	ME
62I	KANSAS CITY POWER AND LIGHT	MO
63I	MISSISSIPI POWER	MS
64I	MDU RESOURCES INC.	ND
65I	ATLANTIC CITY ELECTRIC	NJ
66I	PUB SERV CO. OF NEW MEXICO	NM
67I	NEVADA POWER CO.	NV
68I	CENTRAL HUDSON	NY
69I	ORANGE & ROCKLAND	NY
70I	ROCHESTER	NY
71I	CINCINATTI GAS AND ELECTRIC	OH
72I	OKLAH. GAS AND ELECTRIC	OK
73I	PUB SERV CO. OF OKLAHOMA	OK

Code	*Utility*	*State*
74I	DUQUESNE LIGHT	PA
75I	METROPOLITAN EDISON	PA
76I	PENNSYLVANIA ELECTRIC CO.	PA
77I	PENNSYLVANIA POWER AND LIGHT	PA
78I	PENNSYLVANIA POWER	PA
79I	SOUTH CAROLINA GAS AND ELECTRIC	SC
80I	EL PASO ELECTRIC	TX
81I	HOUSTON LIGHT AND POWER	TX
82I	SOUTH WESTERN ELECTRIC POWER	TX
83I	CENTRAL VERMONT	VT
84I	GREEN MOUNTAIN POWER CORP.	VT
85I	WASHINGTON WATER	WA
86I	WISCONSIN POWER AND LIGHT	WI
87I	WISCONSIN PUBLIC SERVICE	WI
88I	WISCONSIN ELECTRIC	WI
89I	MONONGAHELA POWER	WV
90M	SALT RIVER PROJECT	AZ
91M	SACRAMENTO MUNICIPAL UTILITY DISTRICT	CA
92M	NEBRASKA PUBLIC POWER DISTRICT	NE
93M	SOUTH CAROLINA PUBLIC SERVICE	SC
94M	LOWER COLORADO RIVER AUTHORITY	TX

(C) Large Transmission Companies

95I	ALABAMA POWER CO.	AL
96I	PACIFIC GAS AND ELECTRIC	CA
97I	SAN DIEGO	CA
98I	SOUTHERN CALIFORNIA EDISON	CA
99I	FLORIDA POWER AND LIGHT	FL
100I	GEORGIA POWER CO.	GA
101I	COMMONWEALTH EDISON CO.	IL
102I	INDIANA AND MICHIGAN	IN
103I	BOSTON EDISON	MA
104I	NEW ENGLAND POWER	MA
105I	DETROIT EDISON CO.	MI
106I	MONTANA POW CO.	MT
107I	DUKE POWER	NC
108I	PUB SERV CO. OF NEW HAMPSHIRE	NH
109I	CONSOLIDATED EDISON OF NEW YORK	NY
110I	LONG ISLAND LIGHTING CO.	NY
111I	NEW YORK STATE ELECTRIC AND GAS CORP.	NY
112I	CLEVELAND	OH
113I	COLUMBUS SOUTHERN POWER	OH
114I	OHIO EDISON CO.	OH
115I	OHIO POWER CO.	OH
116I	PACIFICORP	OR
117I	PORTLAND GAS AND ELECTRIC	OR
118I	PHILADELPHIA ELECTRIC CO.	PA
119I	CENTRAL POWER AND LIGHT	TX
120I	GULF STATES	TX
121I	TEXAS UTILITIES	TX
122I	APPALACHIAN	VA
123I	VIRGINIA ELECTRIC	VA
124I	PUGET SOUND POWER AND LIGHT	WA

Code	Utility	State
125I	NORTHERN STATES	WI
126M	LOS ANGELES DEPARTMENT OF WATER AND POWER	CA
127M	POWER AUTHORITY OF NEW YORK	NY
128M	BONNEVILLE POWER ADMINISTRATION	OR
129M	TENNESSEE VALLEY AUTHORITY	TN

Appendix 2.4.2 Sample Distribution Systems

(A) Small Distribution Companies

Code	Utility	State
1I	IOWA SOUTHERN UTILITIES	IA
2I	SOUTHERN INDIANA GAS AND ELECTRIC	IN
3I	CAMBRIDGE ELECTRIC	MA
4I	FITCHBURG GAS AND ELECTRIC	MA
5I	BANGOR HYDRO	ME
6I	MAINE PUBLIC SERVICE	ME
7I	MICHIGAN POWER	MI
8I	UPPER PENINSULA	MI
9I	OTTER TAIL POWER	MN
10I	EMPIRE DISTRICT	MO
11I	ST JOSEPH LIGHT AND POWER	MO
12I	MDU RESOURCES INC.	ND
13I	PENNSYLVANIA POWER	PA
14I	BLACKSTONE VALLEY	RI
15I	NEWPORT	RI
16I	BLACK HILLS	SD
17I	NORTH WEST PUBLIC SERVICE	SD
18I	GREEN MOUNTAIN POWER CORP.	VT
19I	MADISON GAS AND ELECTRIC	WI
20M	IMPERIAL IRRIGATION DISTRICT	CA
21M	LAKELAND LIGHT AND WATER	FL
22M	ORLANDO UTILITIES	FL
23M	TALLAHASSEE ELECTRIC DEPARTMENT	FL
24M	SPRINGFIELD	IL
25M	LINCOLN ELECTRIC SYSTEM	NE
26M	NEBRASKA PUBLIC POWER DISTRICT	NE
27M	EUGENE WATER AND ELECTRIC BOARD	OR
28M	SOUTH CAROLINA PUBLIC SERVICE	SC
29M	PUD NO1 DOUGLAS COUNTY	WA
30M	PUD NO2 GRANT COUNTY	WA

(B) Medium Distribution Companies

Code	Utility	State
31I	TUCSON ELECTRIC POWER CO.	AZ
32I	UNITED ILLUMINATING CO.	CT
33I	DELMARVA POWER AND LIGHT CO.	DE
34I	GULF POWER	FL
35I	TAMPA ELECTRIC	FL
36I	SAVANNAH ELECTRIC AND POWER	GA
37I	HAWAII ELECTRIC	HI

Code	Utility	State
38I	IOWA POWER	IA
39I	IOWA-ILLINOIS GAS AND ELECTRIC	IA
40I	IDAHO POWER CO.	ID
41I	CENTRAL ILLINOIS LIGHT	IL
42I	CENTRAL ILLINOIS PUBLIC LIGHT	IL
43I	ILLINOIS POWER CO.	IL
44I	NORTHERN INDIANA PUBLIC SERVICE	IN
45I	KANSAS GAS AND ELECTRIC	KS
46I	KENTUCKY UTILITIES CO.	KY
47I	KENTUCKY POWER	KY
48I	LOUISVILLE	KY
49I	CENTRAL LOUISIANA	LA
50I	SOUTHWESTERN ELECTRIC POWER	LA
51I	EASTERN EDISON	MA
52I	WESTERN MASSACHUSETTS	MA
53I	POTOMAC EDISON	MD
54I	MINNESOTA POWER AND LIGHT	MN
55I	UTILCORP UNITED	MO
56I	MISSISSIPI POWER AND LIGHT	MS
57I	MISSISSIPI POWER	MS
58I	MONTANA POWER CO.	MT
59I	PUBLIC SERVICE CO. OF NEW HAMPSHIRE	NH
60I	ATLANTIC CITY ELECTRIC	NJ
61I	CENTRAL HUDSON	NM
62I	PUBLIC SERVICE CO. OF NEW MEXICO	NM
63I	NEVADA POWER CO.	NV
64I	SIERRA PACIFIC	NV
65I	ORANGE & ROCKLAND	NY
66I	ROCHESTER	NY
67I	TOLEDO EDISON	OH
68I	PUBLIC SERVICE CO. OF OKLAHOMA	OK
69I	NARRAGANSETT	RI
70I	EL PASO ELECTRIC	TX
71I	WEST TEXAS UTILITIES CO.	TX
72I	CENTRAL VERMONT	VT
73I	WASHINGTON WATER	WA
74I	WISCONSIN POWER AND LIGHT	WI
75I	WISCONSIN PUBLIC SERVICE	WI
76M	SALT RIVER PROJECT	AZ
77M	SACRAMENTO MUNICIPAL UTILITY DISTRICT	CA
78M	JACKSONVILLE ELECTRIC AUTHORITY	FL
79M	OMAHA PUBLIC POWER DISTRICT	NE
80M	SAN ANTONIO PUBLIC SERVICE	TX

(C) Large Distribution Companies

Code	Utility	State
81I	ALABAMA POWER CO.	AL
82I	ARKANSAS LIGHT AND POWER	AR
83I	ARIZONA PUBLIC SERVICE CO.	AZ
84I	PACIFIC GAS AND ELECTRIC	CA
85I	SAN DIEGO	CA
86I	SOUTHERN CALIFORNIA EDISON	CA
87I	PUBLIC SERVICE CO. OF COLORADO	CO.
88I	CONNECTICUT LIGHT AND POWER	CT
89I	POTOMAC ELECTRIC POWER	DC

Code	Utility	State
90I	FLORIDA POWER AND LIGHT	FL
91I	FLORIDA POWER CO.	FL
92I	GEORGIA POWER CO.	GA
93I	COMMONWEALTH EDISON CO.	IL
94I	INDIANA POWER AND LIGHT	IN
95I	INDIANA AND MICHIGAN	IN
96I	PSI EN INC.	IN
97I	KANSAS POWER AND LIGHT	KS
98I	BOSTON EDISON	MA
99I	MASSACHUSETTS ELECTRIC CO.	MA
100I	BALTIMORE GAS AND ELECTRIC	MD
101I	CONSUMERS POWER	MI
102I	DETROIT EDISON CO.	MI
103I	NORTHERN STATES POWER CO.	MN
104I	KANSAS CITY POWER AND LIGHT	MO
105I	UNION ELECTRIC	MO
106I	CAROLINA POWER AND LIGHT	NC
107I	DUKE POWER	NC
108I	JERSEY CENTRAL POWER AND LIGHT	NJ
109I	PUBLIC SERVICE ELECTRIC AND GAS	NJ
110I	CONSOLIDATED EDISON OF NEW YORK	NY
111I	LONG ISLAND LIGHTING COMPANY	NY
112I	NIAGARA MOHAWK	NY
113I	NEW YORK STATE ELECTRIC AND GAS CORP.	NY
114I	CINCINATTI GAS AND ELECTRIC CO.	OH
115I	CLEVELAND	OH
116I	COLUMBUS SOUTHERN POWER	OH
117I	OHIO EDISON CO.	OH
118I	OHIO POWER CO.	OH
119I	OKLAHOMA GAS AND ELECTRIC	OK
120I	PACIFICORP	OR
121I	PORTLAND GAS AND ELECTRIC	OR
122I	DUQUESNE LIGHT	PA
123I	METROPOLITAN EDISON	PA
124I	PENNSYLVANIA ELECTRIC CO.	PA
125I	PENNSYLVANIA POWER AND LIGHT	PA
126I	PHILADELPHIA	PA
127I	WEST PENNSYLVANIA POWER CO.	PA
128I	SOUTH CAROLINA ELECTRIC AND GAS	SC
129I	CENTRAL POWER AND LIGHT	TX
130I	GULF STATES	TX
131I	APPALACHIAN	VA
132I	VIRGINIA ELECTRIC	VA
133I	PUGET SOUND POWER AND LIGHT	WA
134I	WISCONSIN ELECTRIC	WI
135I	MONONGAHEIA	WV
136M	LOS ANGELES DEPARTMENT OF WATER AND POWER	CA
137M	Eastern	UK
138M	EM (East Midlands)	UK
139M	LE (London Electricity)	UK
140M	MANWEB	UK
141M	MEB	UK
142M	Northern	UK
143M	Seeboard	UK
144M	SWEB	UK
145M	Yorkshire	UK

APPENDIX 3

STATISTICAL TESTS FOR DIFFERENCES BETWEEN SAMPLES

In this appendix we provide some notes on the 5 statistical tests that we use in chapters 5 to 8 to test our null hypothesis that there is no significant difference in the productive efficiency of publicly owned and privately owned electricity plants and firms. These statistical tests form the battery of tests with which we analyse the significance of differences in unit specific efficiency scores between the two ownership forms. We note the main characteristics of each of the tests below. In each case the statistic is distributed with an F or χ^2 distribution. If the estimated statistic lies outside the one-tail 95% confidence interval, then the null hypothesis is rejected in favour of the alternative hypothesis that one or other of the ownership forms has significantly higher productive efficiency. We acknowledge the helpful exposition in Brynes (1985), while Lehmann (1975) is a general reference on the non-parametric rank order tests (2) to (5). In chapters 5 to 8 we calculated these test statistics using the NPAR1WAY procedure in the computer package, SAS. The formulae for their calculation can be found in SAS Institute Inc. (1990) and in Brynes (1985).

All but the first statistic are based on the rankings of the efficiency scores rather than on their absolute values. These tests are said to be non-parametric or distribution free in that they make no assumptions about the precise form of the sample populations.

(1) Analysis of Variance

This parametric statistic is used to assess whether the difference in means between the two samples is significant. It assumes that the underlying distribution is normal and tests whether the means of the two groups are equal. This statistic follows an F distribution.

(2) Median Scores Test

This non-parametric test determines whether the two groups have been drawn from the same population or from populations with equal medians. It compares the samples on the basis of central tendency as measured by the median. This statistic follows a χ^2 distribution.

(3) Kruskal-Wallis (Wilcoxon) Test

This statistic is a non-parametric test of the hypothesis that the two samples were drawn from the same distribution. This statistic follows a χ^2 distribution.

(4) Van der Waerden (or expected normal scores) Test

This test uses the expected values of the order statistics for a normal distribution to test for a shift location between the two samples. This test is distribution-free and is highly efficient. We assume that this test follows a χ^2 distribution.

(5) Savage Scores Test

This statistic compares the samples using the expected values of the order statistics of an exponential distribution. It is a locally powerful test for comparing exponential distributions. We assume that this test follows a χ^2 distribution.

BIBLIOGRAPHY

Afriat, S.N.(1972). Efficiency estimation of production functions. *International Economic Review* 13(3): 568–598.

Aigner, D.J. and S.F.Chu (1968). On estimating the industry production function. *American Economic Review* 58(4): 826–839.

Aigner, D.J., C.A.K.Lovell and P.J.Schmidt (1977). Formulation and estimation of stochastic frontier production function models. *Journal of Econometrics* 6(1): 21–37.

Alchian, A.A.(1965). Some Economics of Property Rights. *Il politico* 30 (December): 816–829, reprinted in: A.A.Alchian (1977). Economic forces at work. Indianapolis: Liberty Press.

Alchian, A and H.Demsetz (1972). Production, Information Costs and Economic Organisation. *American Economic Review* 62: 777–795.

Ali, A.I. (1990). Data Envelopment Analysis: Computational Issues. *Computers, the Environment and Urban Systems* 14: 157–165.

Ali, A.I., C.S.Lerme and R.A.Nakosteen (1992). *Assessment of Intergovernmental Revenue Transfers.* Mimeo.

Al-Obaidan, A. and G.W.Scully (1991). Efficiency differences between private and state-owned enterprises in the international petroleum industry. *Applied Economics* 23: 237–246.

Aly, H.Y. and R.Grabowski, C.Pasurka and N.Rangan (1990). Technical, Scale, and Allocative Efficiencies in US Banking: An Empirical Investigation. *Review of Economics and Statistics* 72: 211–218.

Anglo-American Council on Productivity (1950). *Electricity Supply.* London: Anglo-American Council on Productivity.

A.P.P.A. (1991). *APPA Performance Indicators Survey 1990.* Washington: American Public Power Association.

Atkinson, S.E. and R.Halvorsen (1980). A Test of Relative and Absolute Price Efficiency in Regulated Utilities. *Review of Economics and Statistics* 62(1): 81–88.

Atkinson, S E. and R.Halvorsen (1984). Parametric Efficiency Tests, Economies of Scale, and Input Demand in the U.S. Electric Power Generation. *International Economic Review* 25 (October): 647–341.

Atkinson, S E. and R.Halvorsen (1986). The Relative Efficiency of Public and Private Firms in a Regulated Environment: The Case of U.S. Electric Utilities. *Journal of Public Economics* 29 (April): 281–294.

Averch, H. and L.L.Johnson (1962). Behaviour of the Firm under Regulatory Constraint. *American Economic Review* 52: 1052–1069.

Bailey, E.E.and R.D. Coleman (1971). The Effect of Lagged Regulation in the Averch-Johnson Model. *Bell Journal of Economics* 2: 278–292.

Banker, R.D., A.Charnes and W.W.Cooper (1984). Models for Estimation of Technical and Scale Inefficiencies in Data Envelopment Analysis. *Management Science* 30: 1078–1092.

Banker, R.D., A.Charnes and W.W.Cooper and A.Maindiratta (1988). A Comparison of DEA and Translog Estimates of Production Frontiers using Simulated Observations from a Known Technology. In A.Dogramaci and R.Fare *Applications of Modern Production Theory: efficiency and productivity.* Boston: KluwerNijhoff.

Banker, R., R.F.Conrad and R.P.Strauss (1986) A Comparat'ive Application of Data Envelopment Analysis and Translog Methods: An Illustrative Study of Hospital Production. *Management Science* 32(1): 30–44.

Banker, R.D., S.M.Datar and C.F.Kemerer (1991). A Model to Evaluate Variables Impacting the Productivity of Software Maintenance Projects. *Management Science* 37(1): 1–18.

Banker, R.D. and A.Maindiratta (1992). Maximum Likelihood Estimation of Monotone and Concave Production Frontiers. *Journal of Productivity Analysis* 3:

Banker, R.D. and R.C.Morey (1986). Efficiency Analysis for Exogeneously Fixed Inputs and Outputs. *Operations Research* 34(4): 513–521.

Baron, D.P. and D.Besanko (1984). Regulation, Asymmetric Information, and Auditing. *Rand Journal of Economics* 15: 447–470.

Baron, D.P. and D.Besanko (1987). Commitment and Fairness in a Dynamic Regulatory Relationship. *Review of Economic Studies* 54: 413–436.

Baron, D.P. and R.B.Myerson (1982). Regulating a Monopolist with Unknown Costs. *Econometrica* 50: 911–930.

Bartel, R. and F.Schneider (1991). The 'mess' of public industrial production in Austria: A typical case of public sector inefficiency? *Public Choice* 68: 17–40.

Battese, G.E. and T.J.Coelli (1988). Prediction of Firm-Level Technical Efficiencies with a Generalized Frontier Production Function and Panel Data. *Journal of Econometrics* 38: 387–399.

Bauer, P.W. (1985). *An analysis of multiproduct technology and efficiency using the joint cost function and panel data: An application to the US airline industry.* North Carolina, Chapel Hill: Unpublished doctoral dissertation.

Bauer, P.W. (1990). Recent Developments in the Econometric Estimation of Frontiers. *Journal of Econometrics* 46 (October-November): 39–56.

Bawa,V.S. and D.S.Sibley (1980). Dynamic Behaviour of a Firm Subject to a Stochastic Regulatory Review. *International Economic Review* 21: 627–642.

Berg, S.A., F.R.Forsund and E.S.Jansen (1991). Technical Efficiency of Norwegian Banks: The Non-Parametric Approach to Efficiency Measurement. *Journal of Productive Analysis* 2: 127–142.

Besanko, D. and D.F.Spulber (1991). Sequential Equilibrium Investment by Regulated Firms. *Rand Journal of Economics* 23(2): 153–170.

BIE (1991). *International Performance Indicators - Electricity.* Canberra: Bureau of Industry and Energy.

Boardman, A.E. and A.R.Vining (1989). Ownership and Performance in Competitive Environments: A Comparison of the Performance of Private, Mixed, and State-owned Enterprises. *Journal of Law and Economics* 32 (April): 1–33.

Boardman, A.E. and A.R.Vining (1992). Ownership versus competition: Efficiency in public enterprise. *Public Choice* 73: 205–239.

Bös, D. (1986). *Public Enterprise Economics: Theory and Application.* New York: North-Holland.

Bös, D. (1991). *Privatisation: a theoretical treatment.* Oxford: Clarendon Press.

Brynes, P. (1985). *Ownership and Efficiency in the Water Supply Industry: An application of the Nonparametric Approach to Efficiency Measurement.* Ph.D. Thesis, Carbondale Illinois: Southern Illinois University.

Brynes, P., R.Fare and S.Grosskopf (1984). Measuring Productive Efficiency: An Application to Illinois Strip Mines. *Management Science* 30(6): 671–681.

Brynes, P., R.Fare, S.Grosskopf and C.A.K.Lovell (1988). The Effect of Unions on Productivity: US Surface Mining of Coal. *Management Science* 34(9): 1037–1053.

Byrnes, P., S.Grosskopf and K.Hayes (1986). Ownership and Efficiency : Further Evidence. *Review of Economics and Statistics* 68:337–341.

Bunn, D. and K.Vlahos (1989). Evaluation of the Long-term Effects on UK Electricity Prices following Privatisation. *Fiscal Studies* 10(4): 104–116.

Button, K.J. and T.G.Weyman-Jones (1992). *X-inefficiency in the UK, Upper and Lower Bounds*. Loughborough University, Economic Research Paper No. 92/8.

Caillaud, B., R.Guesnerie, P.Rey and J.Tirole (1988). Government intervention in production and incentives theory: a review of recent contributions. *Rand Journal of Economics* 19 (Spring): 1–26.

Carter, S.B. (1991). Comments on Emmons, Whaples, and Wilson. *Journal of Economic History* 51(2): 466–469.

Caves, D.W., L.R.Christensen and W.E.Diewert (1982). The economic theory of index numbers and the measurement of input, output, and productivity. *Econometrica* 50: 1393–1414.

Central Electricity Generating Board (1986). *Annual Report and Accounts 1985–6*. London: Central Electricity Generating Board.

Charnes, A. and W.W.Cooper (1985). Preface to Topics in Data Envelopment Analysis. *Annals of Operations Research* 2: 59–94.

Charnes, A., W.W.Cooper and E.Rhodes (1978). Measuring the Efficiency of Decision Making Units. *European Journal of Operational Research* 2(6): 429–444.

Charnes, A.,W.W.Cooper and E.Rhodes (1981). Evaluating Program and Managerial Efficiency: An Application of Data Envelopment Analysis to Program Follow Through. *Management Science* 27(6): 668–697.

Charnes, A., W.W.Cooper, L.Seiford and J.Stutz (1982). A Multiplicative Model for Efficiency and Piecewise Cobb-Douglas Envelopments. *Operations Research Letters* 2(3): 101–103.

Charnes, A., W.W.Cooper, T.Sueyoshi (1988). A goal programming/constrained regression review of the Bell System breakup. *Management Science* 34: 1–26.

Chen, T-j. and Tang, D-p (1987). Comparing Technical Efficiency between Import Substitution orientated and Export orientated foreign firms in a developing economy. *Journal of Development Economics* 26: 277–289.

Christensen, L.R., D.W. Jorgenson and L.J.Lau (1971). Conjugate Duality and the Transcendental Logarithmic Function. *Econometrica* 39(4): 255–256.

Christensen, L.R. and D.W.Jorgenson (1969). The Measurement of U.S. Capital Input, 1929–1967. *The Review of Income and Wealth* 15 (December): 293–320.

Christensen, L.R., D.W.Jorgenson and L.J.Lau (1973). Transcendental Logarithmic Production Frontiers. *Review of Economics and Statistics* 55(1): 28–45.

Christensen L.R.and W.H.Greene (1976). Economies of Scale in U.S. Electric Power Generation. *Journal of Political Economy* 84: 655–676.

Coase, R.H.(1960). The Problem of Social Cost. *Journal of Law and Economics* 3:1–44.

Corti,G. (1976). Electricity Industry and Problems of Size. *National Westminister Bank Quarterly Review* (August): 8–15.

Cote, D.O. (1989). Firm Efficiency and Ownership Structure - The case of U.S. Electric Utilities Using Panel Data. *Annals of Public and Cooperative Economy* 60: 432–450.

Couch, J.F., K.E.Atkinson and W.F.Shughart II (1992). Ethics laws and the outside earnings of politicians: The case of Alabama's "legislator-educators". *Public Choice* 73: 135–145.

Cowling, K., P.Stoneman, J.Cubbin, J.Cable, G. Hall, S.Domberger, P.Dutton (1980). *Mergers and Economic Performance*. Cambridge: Cambridge University Press.

Cowling, T.G. and V.K.Smith (1978). The Estimation of a Production Technology: A Survey of Econometric Analyses of Steam Electric Generation. *Land Economics* 54(2): 156–186.

Crain,W.M. and A.Zardkoohi (1980). X-Inefficiency and Nonpecuniary Rewards in a Rent Seeking Society: A Neglected Issue in the Property Rights Theory of the Firm. *American Economic Review* 70: 784–792.

Crew, M.A. and P.R.Kleindorfer (1979). *Public Utility Economics.* London: Macmillan.

CSO (1987a). *Economic Trends Annual Supplement 1986.* London: HMSO.

CSO (1987b). *UK National Accounts 1986.* London: HMSO.

Danilin, S., I.Materov, S.Rosefielde and C.A.K.Lovell (1985). Measuring Enterprise Efficiency in the Soviet Union: A Stochastic Frontier Analysis. *Economica* 52(206): 225–234.

Dantzig, G.B. (1963). *Linear Programming and Extensions.* Princeton, NJ.: Princeton University Press.

DeAlessi, L. (1974a). An Economic Analysis of Government Ownership and Regulation: Theory and the Evidence from the Electric Power Industry. *Public Choice* 19(Fall): 1–42.

DeAlessi, L. (1974b). Managerial Tenure Under Private and Government Ownership in the Electric Power Industry. *Journal of Political Economy* 82: 645–653.

DeAlessi, L. (1977). Ownership and Peak-Load Pricing in the Electric Power Industry. *Quarterly Review of Economics and Business* 17 (Winter): 7–26.

Debreu, G. (1951). The Coefficient of Resource Utilisation. *Econometrica* 19(3): 225–234

Demsetz, H. (1967). Toward a Theory of Property Rights. *American Economic Review Proceedings* 57 (May): 347–359.

Demsetz, H. (1968). Why Regulate Utilities? *Journal of Law and Economics* 11: 55–65.

DiLorenzo, T.J. and R.Robinson (1982). Managerial objectives subject to political market constraints: Electric utilities in the U.S. *Quarterly Review of Economics and Business* 22 (Summer): 113–125.

Doble, M. and T.G.Weyman-Jones (1991). *Measuring Productive Efficiency in the Area Electricity Boards of England and Wales using Data Envelopment Analysis: A Dynamic Approach.* Leicester: Public Sector Economics Research Centre.

Eckel, C. and A.Vining (1985). Elements of a Theory of Mixed Enterprise. *Scottish Journal of Political Economy* 32 (February): 82–93.

Eckert, R.D. (1973). On the Incentives of Regulators: The Case of Taxicabs. *Public Choice* 14 (Spring): 83–100.

Edison Electric Institute (1985). *Analysis of the Differences among Alternative Forms of Utility Ownership in the U.S.A.* Washington, D.C.: Edison Electric Institute.

Electric World (1992). *Directory of Electric Utilities 1992.* New York: DRI McGraw-Hill.

Electricity Council (1986). *Annual Report and Accounts 1985–6.* London: Electricity Council.

Emmons, W.M. (1991). Private and Public Responses to Market Failure in the U.S. Electric Power Industry, 1882–1942. *Journal of Economic History* 51(2): 452–454.

E.N.E.L. (1987) *Annual Report and Accounts 1986.* Rome: ENEL.

Eskom (Various). *Eskom Annual Report* . Johannesburg: Eskom.

Farber, S.C. (1989). The Dependence of Parametric Efficiency Tests on Measures of the Price of Capital and Capital Stock For Electric Utilities. *Journal of Industrial Economics* 38: 199–213.

Fare, R., S.Grosskopf and E.C.Kokkelenberg (1989a). Measuring Plant Capacity, Utilisation and Technical Change: A Nonparametric Approach. *International Economic Review* 30 (August): 655–666.

Fare, R., S.Grosskopf, S-K.Li (1992). Linear Programming Models for Firm and Industry Performance. *Scandinavian Journal of Economics* 94(4): 599–608.

Fare, R., S.Grosskopf and J.Logan (1983). The Relative Efficiency of Illinois Electric Utilities. *Resources and Energy* 5: 349–367.

Fare, R., S.Grosskopf and J.Logan (1985a). The Relative Performance of Publicly Owned and Privately Owned Electric Utilities. *Journal of Public Economics* 26: 89–106.

Fare, R., S.Grosskopf, J.Logan and C.A.K.Lovell (1985b). Measuring Efficiency in Production: with an Application to Electric Utilities. In A.Dogramaci and M.R.Adam (eds), *Managerial Issues in Productivity Analysis*. Boston: KluwerNijhoff.

Fare, R., S.Grosskopf and C.A.K.Lovell (1985c). *The Measurement of the Efficiency of Production*. Boston, M.A.: Kluwer-Nijhoff.

Fare, R., S.Grosskopf and C.A.K.Lovell (1994). *Production Frontiers*. Cambridge: Cambridge University Press.

Fare, R., S.Grosskopf and C.Pasurka.(1989b). The effect of environment al regulations on the efficiency of electric utilities: 1969 versus 1975. *Applied Economics* 21: 225–235.

Fare, R. and C.A.K.Lovell (1978). Measuring the Technical Efficiency of Production. *Journal of Economic Theory* 19 (October): 150–162.

Fare, R. and L.Svensson (1980). Congestion of Production Factors. *Econometrica* 48(7): 1745–1753.

Fare, R. and W.Hunsacker (1986). Notions of Efficiency and Their Reference Sets. *Management Science* 32(2): 237–243.

Farrell, M.J. (1957). The Measurement of Productive Efficiency. *Journal of the Royal Statistical Society*, Series A, 120: 253–281.

Farrell, M.J. and M.Fieldhouse (1962). Estimating efficient production under increasing returns to scale. *Journal of the Royal Statistical Society*, Series A, 125: 252–267.

Ferrier, G.D. and C.A.K.Lovell (1990). Measuring Cost Efficiency in Banking: Econometric and Linear Programming Evidence. *Journal of Econometrics* 46: 229–245.

Foreman-Peck, J. and M.Waterson (1985). The Comparative Efficiency of Public and Private Enterprise in Britain: Electricity Generation Between the World Wars. *Economic Journal* 95: 83–95.

Forsund, F.R. and L.Hjalmarsson (1979a). Generalised Farrell Measures of Efficiency: An Application to Milk Processing in Swedish Diary Plants. *Economic Journal* 89(June): 294–315.

Forsund, F.R. and L.Hjalmarsson (1979b). Frontier Production Functions and Technical Progress: A Study of General Milk Processing in Swedish Dairy Plants. *Econometrica* 47(4): 893–900.

Forsund, F.R. and E.S.Jansen (1977). On Estimating Average and Best Practice Homothetic Production Functions via Cost Functions. *International Economic Review* 18(2): 463–476.

Forsund, F., C.A.K. Lovell and P.Schmidt (1980). A survey of frontier production functions and of their relationship to efficiency measurement. *Journal of Econometrics* 13: 5–25.

Fukuyama, M. (1993). Technical and scale efficiency of Japanese commercial banks: a non-parametric approach. *Applied Economics* 25: 1101–1112.

Funkhauser, R. and P.W.MacAvoy (1979). A sample of observations on comparative prices in public and private enterprises. *Journal of Public Economics* 11: 353–368.

Gong, B-H. and R.C.Sickles (1989). Finite Sample Evidence on the Performance of Stochastic Frontier Models Using Panel Data. *Journal of Productivity Analysis* 1: 229–261.

Gong, B-H. and R.C.Sickles (1992). Finite sample evidence on the performance of stochastic frontiers and data envelopment analysis using panel data. *Journal of Econometrics* 51: 259–284.

Grabowski, R. and C.Paskura (1988). The Relative Technical Efficiency of Northern and Southern US Farms in 1860. *Southern Economic Journal* 54 (3): 598–614.

Green, A., C.Harris and D.Mayes (1991). Estimation of technical inefficiency in manufacturing industry. *Applied Economics* 23: 1637–1647.

Green, R.J. and D.M.Newbery (1991). Competition in the British Electricity Spot Market. *Journal of Political Economy* 100(5): 929–953.

Greene, W.H. (1980a). Maximum Likelihood Estimation of Econometric Frontier Functions. *Journal of Econometrics* 13: 27–56.

Greene, W.H. (1980b). On the estimation of a flexible frontier production model. *Journal of Econometrics* 13: 101–115.

Greene, W.H. (1990). A Gamma-Distributed Stochastic Frontier Model. *Journal of Econometrics* 46(4): 141–163.

Greenwald, B.C. (1984). Rate Base Selection and the Structure of Regulation. *Rand Journal of Economics* 15: 85–95.

Griliches, Z. and V.Ringstad (1971). *Economies of Scale and the Form of the Production Frontier*. Amsterdam: North Holland.

Grosskopf, S. (1986). The Role of the Reference Technology in Measuring Productive Efficiency. *Economic Journal* 96(June): 499–513.

Guilkey, D.K., C.A.K.Lovell and R.C.Sickles (1983). A comparison of the performance of three flexible functional forms. *International Economic Review* 24 (3) October: 591–616.

Hammond, C.J. (1992). Privatisation and the Efficiency of Decentralised Electricity Generation: Some Evidence from Inter-War Britain. *Economic Journal* 102 (May): 538–553.

Hartley, N. and P.Culham (1988). Telecommunications Prices under Monopoly and Competition *Oxford Review of Economic Policy* 4 no.2: 1–19.

Hausman, W.J. and J.L.Neufeld (1991). Property Rights versus Public Spirit: Ownership and Efficiency of US Electric Utilities Prior to Rate-of-return Regulation. *Review of Economics and Statistics* 73(2): 414–423.

Hay, D.A. and D.J.Morris (1979) *Industrial Economics*. Oxford: Oxford University Press.

Helm, D. (1988). The Privatisation of Electricity. In B. Robinson (ed) *Privatising Electricity: Impact on the UK Energy Market*. London: Institute for Fiscal Studies.

Helm, D. and F.McGowan (1988). Electricity supply in Europe: Lessons for the U.K. In Helm, D.R., J.A.Kay and D.P.Thompson (eds), *The Market for Energy*. Oxford: Oxford University Press.

Hjalmarsson, L. and A.Veiderpass (1992a). Efficiency and Ownership in Swedish Electricity Retail Distribution. *Journal of Productivity Analysis* 3: 7–23.

Hjalmarsson, L. and A. Veiderpass (1992b). Productivity in Swedish Electicity Retail Distribution. *Scandinavian Journal of Economics* (Supplement) 94: S193–S205.

House of Commons Select Committee on the Environment (1989a). *Energy Policy Implications of the Greenhouse Effect Vol 1*. London: HMSO.

House of Commons Select Committee on the Environment (1989b). *Energy Policy Implications of the Greenhouse Effect Vol 3*. London: HMSO.

Huettner, D.A. and J.H.Landon (1977). Electric Utilities: Scale Economies and Diseconomies. *Southern Economic Journal* 44: 883–912.

IEA (1985). *Electricity in IEA Countries.* Paris: OECD.

IEA (1990). *Energy Prices and Taxes Second Quarter 1990.* Paris: OECD.

IEA (1993a). *Energy Policies of IEA Countries 1992.* Paris: OECD.

IEA (1993b). *Energy Prices and Taxes Fourth Quarter 1992.* Paris: OECD.

IEA (1994a). *Electricity in European Economies in Transition.* Paris: OECD.

IEA (1994b). *Electricity Supply Industry: Structure, Ownership, and Regulation in OECD Countries.* Paris: OECD.

I.M.F. (1990). *International Financial Statistics* various. Washington, D.C.: IMF.

Jackson, R. (1969). Regulation and Electric Utility Rate Levels. *Land Economics* (April): 372–76.

James Capel (1990). *The New Electricity Companies of England and Wales.* London: James Capel and Co.

Jenkins, G.P. (1985). Public utility finance and economic waste. *Canadian Journal of Economics* 18: 484–498.

Jenkins, G.P. (1987). Public utility finance and pricing: a reply. *Canadian Journal of Economics* 20: 172–176.

Jenkinson, T. and C.Mayer (1988). The Privatisation Process in France and The UK. *European Economic Review* 32: 482–490.

Jondrow, J., C.A.K.Lovell, I.S. Materov and P.Schmidt (1982). On the estimation of technical inefficiency in the stochastic frontier production function model. *Journal of Econometrics* 19: 233–238.

Jones, L.P., P.Tandon and I.Vogelsang (1990). *Selling Public Enterprise. A Cost-Benefit Methodology.* Cambridge, Mass.: MIT Press.

Joskow, P.L. (1989). Regulatory Failure, Regulatory Reform, and Structural Change in the Electric Power Industry. *Brookings Papers on Economic Activity* Microeconomics: 125–199.

Joskow, P.L. and N.Rose (1989). The Effects of Economic Regulation. In R.Schmalensee and R.Willig (eds) *Handbook of Industrial Organisation Vol.2* Amsterdam: North Holland.

Junker, J.A. (1975). Economic performance of public and private utilities: the case of U.S. electric utilities. *Journal of Economics and Business* 28: 60–67.

Kalirajan, K.P. (1990). On Measuring Economic Efficiency. *Journal of Applied Econometrics* 5: 75–85.

Kalirajan, K.P. (1991). An analysis of production efficiency differentials in the Philippines. *Applied Economics* 23: 631–638.

Kalirajan, K.P. and C.Yong (1993). Can Chinese state enterprises perform like market entities: productive efficiency in the Chinese iron and steel industry. *Applied Economics* 25: 1071–80.

Kamakura, W.A. (1988). A Note on 'The Use of Categorical Variables in Data Envelopment Analysis'. *Managment Science* 34(10): 1273–1276.

Kaserman, D.L. and J.W.Mayo (1991). The Measurement of Vertical Economies and the Efficient Structure of the Electric Utility Industry. *Journal of Industrial Economics* 39(5): 483–502.

Kay, J.A. and D.J.Thompson (1986). Privatisation: a Policy in Search of a Rationale. *Economic Journal* 96: 18–32.

Kennedy, W.P. (1976). Institutional Response to Economic Growth: Capital Markets in Britain to 1914. In L. Hannah (ed) *Management Strategy and Business Development.* London: Macmillan.

Kerkvleit, J. (1991). Efficiency and Vertical Integration: The Case of Mine-Mouth Electric Generating Plants. *Journal of Industrial Economics* 39(5): 467–482.

Koopmans, T.C. (1951). An Analysis of Production as an Efficient Combination of Activities. In T.C.Koopmans (ed), *Activity Analysis of Production and Allocation*. Cowles Commission for Research in Economics, Monograph No.13 New York: Wiley.

Kopp, R.J. and W.E.Diewert (1982). The decomposition of frontier cost function deviations into measures of technical and allocative efficiency. *Journal of Econometrics* 19: 319–331.

Kopp, R.J. and V.K.Smith (1980). Frontier Production Function Estimates for Steam Electric Generation: A Comparative Analysis. *Southern Economic Journal* 46(4): 1049–1059.

Kotowitz, Y. and F.Mathewson (1982). The Economics of the Union-controlled Firm. *Economica* 49: 421–433.

Kumbhakar, S.C. (1988). On the Estimation of technical and allocative inefficiency using stochastic frontier functions: the Case of US Class 1 Railroads. *International Economic Review* 29(4): 727–743.

Kumbhakar, S.C. (1989). Estimation of Technical Efficiency Using Flexible Functional Form and Panel Data. *Journal of Business and Economic Statistics* 7 (2): 253–258.

Kumbhakar, S.C. (1991). The Measurement and Decomposition of Cost-inefficiency: The Translog cost system. *Oxford Economic Papers* 43: 667–683.

Kumbhakar, S.C., S.Ghosh and J.T.McGuckin (1991). A Generalised Production Frontier Approach for Estimating the Determinants of Inefficiency in US Dairy Farms. *Journal of Business and Economic Statistics* 9(3):

Lau, L.J. and P.A.Yotopolous (1971). A test for relative efficiency and application to Indian agriculture. *American Economic Review* 61(1): 94–109.

Lehmann, E.L. (1975). *Nonparametrics: Statistical Methods based on Ranks*. San Francisco: Holden Day.

Leibenstein, H. (1966). Allocative Efficiency vs. X-Efficiency. *American Economic Review* 56 (April): 392–413.

Leibenstein, H. and S.Maital (1992). Empirical Estimation and partitioning of X-inefficiency: A Data-Envelopment Approach. *American Economic Review Papers and Proceedings* 82 (May): 428–433.

Littlechild, S. (1983). *Regulation of British Telecommunications Profitability*. London: HMSO.

Lindsay, C.M. (1976). A Theory of Government Enterprise. Journal of Political Economy 84(5): 1061–1077.

Lovell, C.A.K. and P.Schmidt (1988). A Comparison of Alternative Approaches to the Measurement of Productive Efficiency.In A.Dogramaci and R.Fare *Applications of Modern Production Theory: efficiency and productivity*. Boston: KluwerNijhoff.

Lucas, N.J.D. (1985). *Western European Energy Policy* . Oxford: Clarendon Press.

Lyon, T.P. (1991). Regulation with 20–20 hindsight: "Heads I win, tails you lose"? *Rand Journal of Economics* 22(4): 581–595.

Macmillan, W.D. (1986). The Estimation and Application of Multi-Regional Economic Planning Models using Data Envelopment Analysis. *Papers of the Regional Science Association* 60: 41–57.

Macmillan,W.D. (1987). The measurement of efficiency in multiunit public services. *Environment and Planning* A 19 p.1511–1524.

Maddala, G.S. (1983). *Limited Dependent Variables and Qualitative Variables in Econometrics*. Cambridge: Cambridge University Press.

Maloney, M.T., R.E.McCormick and R.D.Tollinson (1984). Economic Regulation,

Competitive Governments, and Specialised Resources. *Journal of Law and Economics* 27: 329–338.

Mann, P.C. (1970). Publicly Owned Electric Utility Profits and Resource Allocation. *Land Economics* 46 (November): 478–484.

Meeusen, W. and J. van den Broeck (1977) Efficiency estimation from a Cobb-Douglas production functions with composed error. *International Economic Review* 8: 435–444.

Melfi, C.A. (1984). *Estimation and decomposition of productive efficiency in a panel data model: An application to electric utilities*. North Carolina, Chapel Hill: Unpublished doctoral dissertation.

Melling, C.T. (1965). Performance and Accountability of a Nationalised Industry. *Scientific Business* p.8–9.

Meyer, R.A. (1975). Public Owned vs. Privately Owned Utilities: A Policy Choice. *Review of Economics and Statistics* 57 (November): 391–399.

Moore, J. (1986). The Success of Privatisation. In Kay, J.A., C.Meyer and D.Thompson (eds) (1986) *Privatisation and Regulation: The U.K. Experience*. Oxford: Oxford University Press.

Moore, T.G. (1970). The Effectiveness of Regulation of Electric Utility Prices. *Southern Economic Journal* 36 (April): 365–375.

National Power (1990). *Annual Report and Accounts 1989–90*. London: National Power.

Nerlove, M. (1968). Returns to Scale in Electricity Supply. In A. Zellner (ed). *Readings in Economics Statistics and Econometrics*. Boston: Little, Brown and Co. pp.409–439.

Neuberg, L.G. (1977). Two Issues in the Municipal Ownership of Electric Power Distribution Systems. *Bell Journal of Economics* 8 (Spring): 303–323.

New Zealand Ministry of Energy (1989). *Performance Measures and Economies of Scale in the New Zealand Electricity Distribution System*. Wellington: Ministry of Energy.

Niskanen, W.A. (1968). The Peculiar Economics of Bureaucracy. *American Economic Review, Papers and Proceedings* 58 (May): 298–305.

Niskanen, W.A. (1971). *Bureaucracy and Representative Government*. Chicago: Aldine-Atherton.

Niskanen, W.A. (1975). Bureaucrats and Politicans. *Journal of Law and Economics* 18: 617–643.

Norman, M. and B.Stoker (1991). *Data Envelopment Analysis: The Assessment of Performance*. Chichester: John Wiley and Sons.

Nowell, C. and J.F.Shogren (1991). The Timing of a Rate Request by a Regulated Firm. *Southern Economic Journal* 57(4): 1054–1060.

O.E.C.D. (Various). *Main Economic Indicators*. Paris: OECD.

Olson, M. (1965). *The logic of collective action: public goods and theory of groups*. Cambridge, Mass.: Harvard University Press.

Parker, D. and K.Hartley (1991). Organisational status and performance: the effects on employment. *Applied Economics* 23: 403–416.

Peltzman, S. (1971). Pricing in Public and Private Enterprises and Electric Utilities in the United States. *Journal of Law and Economics* 14: 109–147.

Peltzman, S. (1976). Towards a More General Theory of Regulation. *Journal of Law and Economics* 14: 109–147.

Perelman, S. and P.Pestieau (1988). Technical Performance in Public Enterprises: A Comparative study of Railways and Postal Services. *European Economic Review* 32: 432–441.

Pescatrice, D.R., and J.M.Trapani (1980). The Performance and Objectives of Public and Private Utilities Operating in the United States. *Journal of Public Economics* 13 (April): 259–276.

Picot, A. and T.Kaulman (1989). Comparative Performance of Government-owned and Privately-owned Industrial Corporations - Empirical Results from Six Countries. *Journal of Institutional and Theoretical Economics* 145(2): 298–316.

Pigou, A.C. (1932). *The Economics of Welfare.* 4th Edition. Reprinted 1950. London: Macmillan.

Pint, E.M. (1991). Nationalisation vs. regulation of monopolies - The effects of ownership on efficiency. *Journal of Public Economics* 44: 131–164.

Pint, E.M. (1992). Price-cap vs. rate of return regulation in a stochastic-cost model. *Rand Journal of Economics* 23(4): 564–578.

Pitt, M. and L-F.Lee (1981). The Measurement and Sources of Technical Inefficiency in the Indonesian Weaving Industry. *Journal of Development Economics* 9: 43–64.

Pollitt, M.G. (1991). *The Relative Performance of Publicly Owned and Privately Owned Electric Utilities: Some International Evidence* M.Phil Thesis, University of Oxford.

Pollitt, M.G. (1992). *Ownership, Scale and Efficiency in the Electricity Generation Industry: A cross-country study.* Paper presented to Industry Group Seminar, University of Oxford, 6th February, 1992.

Pollitt, M.G. (1993). *Efficiency and Ownership in Nuclear Power Production - An international application of Data Envelopment Analysis.* Mimeo.

Power in Asia (Various). London: Financial Times Business Information.

Power in Europe (Various). London: Financial Times Business Information.

Prager, R.A. (1989). The Effects of Regulatory Policies on the Cost of Debt for Electric Utilities: An Empirical Investigation. *Journal of Business* 62 (1): 33–53.

Price, C. and T.G.Weyman-Jones (1993). *Malmquist indices of Productivity Change in the UK Gas Industry before and after Privatisation.* Loughborough University, Economics Research Paper No 93/12.

Primeaux, W.J. and R.A.Nelson (1980). An Examination of Price Discrimination and Internal Subsidisation by Electric Utilities. *Southern Economic Journal* 47 (July): 84–99.

Primeaux, W.J. and R.A.Nelson (1988). The Effects of Competition on Transmission and Distribution Costs in the Municipal Electric Industry. Land Economics 64(4): 338–346.

Pryke, R. (1982). *The Nationalised Industries: Policies and Performance Since 1968.* Oxford: Oxford University Press.

Ramamurti, R. (1989). Book Review of Vickers, J.S. and Yarrow, G.K. (1988). Privatisation: An Economic Analysis Cambridge, Massachusetts: MIT Press in *Journal of Economic Literature* 27 (December): 1713–1714.

Rangan, N., R.Grabowski, H.Y.Aly and C.Paskura (1988). The Technical Efficiency of US Banks. *Economics Letters* 28: 169–175.

Rees, R. (1984a). *Public Enterprise Economics.* London: Weidenfeld and Nicholson.

Rees, R. (1984b). A Positive Theory of the Public Enterprise. In Marchand, M., P.Pestieau and H.Tulkens (eds), *The Performance of Public Enterprises. Amsterdam:* North-Holland.

Republic of China (Various). *Statistical Yearbook of Republic of China.* Executive Yuan: Directorate General of Budget, Accounting and Statistics.

Richmond, J. (1974). Estimating the efficiency of production. *International Economic Review:* 15 (2) June: 515–521.

Roberts, M.J. (1986). Economies of Density and Size in the Production and Delivery of Electric Power. *Land Economics* 62: 378–387.

Robinson, W.(1988). The Economics of Coal. In Helm, D.R., J.A.Kay and D.P.Thompson (eds), *The Market for Energy.* Oxford: Oxford University Press.

Roe, M.J. (1990). Political and legal restraints on ownership and control of public companies. *Journal of Financial Economics* 27: 7–41.

Rousseau, J.J. and J.H.Semple (1993). Notes: Categorical Outputs in Data Envelopment Analysis. *Management Science* 39(3): 284–386.

SAS Institute Inc. (1990). *SAS/STAT User's Guide, Version 6, Fourth Edition, Vol 2*. Cary, NC: SAS Institute Inc.

Schmidt, P. (1984). *An error structure for systems of translog cost and share equations.* Econometrics workshop paper 8309 (Department of Economics, Michigan State University, MI).

Schmidt, P. and Lovell, C.A.K. (1979). Estimating technical and allocative inefficiency relative to stochastic production and cost frontiers. *Journal of Econometrics* 9: 343–366.

Seiford, L.M. (1990). *A Bibliography of Data Envelopment Analysis (1978–1990)*. University of Massachusetts, Amherst.

Seiford, L.M. and R.A.Thrall (1990). Recent Developments in DEA - The Mathematical Programming Approach to Frontier Analysis. *Journal of Econometrics* 46: 7–38.

Seitz, W.D. (1971). Productive Efficiency in the Steam-Electric Generating Industry. *Journal of Political Economy* 79(4): 878–886.

Sexton, T.R. (1986). The Methodology of Data Envelopment Analysis. In: R.H.Silkman (ed) *Measuring Efficiency: An Assessment of Data Envelopment Analysis*. San Francisco: Josey Bass.

Sexton, T.R., R.H.Silkman and A.J.Hogan (1986). Data Envelopment Analysis: Critique and Extensions. In: R.H.Silkman (ed) *Measuring Efficiency: An Assessment of Data Envelopment Analysis*. San Francisco: Josey Bass.

Shapiro, C. and R.D.Willig (1990). Economic Rationales for the Scope of Privatisation. In: E.N.Suleman and T.Waterbury (eds) *The Political Economy of Public Sector Reform and Privatisation* Boulder: Westview Press.

Shephard, R.W. (1970). Theory of Cost and Production Functions. Princeton, N.J.: Princeton University Press

Shepherd, W.G. (1966). Utility Growth and Profits under Regulation. In Shepherd, W.G. and T.G.Gies (eds) *Utility Regulation: New Directions in Theory and Practice*. New York: Random House.

Shleifer, A. (1985). A Theory of Yardstick Competition. *Rand Journal of Economics* 16: 319–327.

South African Central Statistical Service (Various). *Bulletin of Statistics*. South Africa: Central Statistical Service.

Spann, R.M. (1974). Rate of Return Regulation and Efficiency in Production: An Empirical Test of the Averch-Johnson Thesis. *Bell Journal of Economics and Management Science* 5 (Spring): 38–52.

Spiro, P.S. (1987). Public utility finance and the cost of capital: comments on Jenkins. *Canadian Journal of Economics* 20: 164–171.

Stelzer, I. (1988). Britain's Newest Import: America's Regulatory Experience. *Oxford Review of Economic Policy* 4 no.2: 68–79.

Stelzer, I. (1989). Privatisation and Regulation: Oft-Necessary Compliments. in: Veljanovski, C. (ed) *Privatisation and Competition*: London: IEA pp.70–77.

Stevenson, R.E. (1980). Likelihood functions for generalized stochastic frontier estimation. *Journal of Econometrics* 13: 57–66.

Stewart, J.F. (1979). Plant size, plant factor, and the shape of the average cost function in electric power generation: a nonhomogeneous capital approach. *Bell Journal of Economics* 10: 549–565.

Stigler, G. (1971). The Theory of Economic Regulation. *Bell Journal of Economics* 2: 3–21.

Stigler, G. (1973). Economic Competition and Political Competition. *Public Choice* (Fall): 91–106.

Stigler, G. and C.Friedland (1962). What Can Regulators Regulate? The Case of Electricity. *Journal of Law and Economics* 5 (October): 1–16.

Sueyoshi, T. (1992). Measuring Technical, Allocative and Overall Efficiencies Using a DEA Algorithm. *Journal of the Operational Research Society* 43(2): 141–155.

Taylor, A.J. (1990). The CEGB and the Restructuring of British Coal *Royal Bank of Scotland Review* 165 (March): 36–45.

Thailand National Statistical Office (Various). *Statistical Yearbook.* Bangkok: National Statistical Office.

Thanassoulis, E., R.G.Dyson and M.J.Foster (1987). Relative Efficiency Assessments Using Data Envelopment Analysis: An Application to Data on Rates Departments. *Journal of the Operational Research Society* 38(5): 397–411.

Tieber,H. (1985). Public and Enterprise and Employment Policy. *Annals of Public and Cooperative Economy* 56 (1–2): 63–70.

Tirole, J. (1988). *The Theory of Industrial Organisation.* Cambridge, Massachusetts: MIT Press.

U.D.I. (1992). *Pocket Guide to US Electric Utilities.* Washington, D.C.: Utility Data Institute Inc.

U.N. (Various). *UN Statistical Yearbook for Asia and the Pacific.* Bangkok: UN Economic and Social Commission.

U.S. Energy Information Agency (1988). *Historic Plant Cost and Annual Production Expenses for Selected Electric Plants 1986.* Washington D.C.: U.S. Government Printing Office.

U.S. Energy Information Agency (1988). *Financial Statistics of Selected Electric Utilities 1986.* Washington D.C.: U.S. Government Printing Office.

U.S. Energy Information Agency (1992). *Historic Plant Cost and Annual Production Expenses for Selected Electric Plants 1989.* Washington D.C.: U.S. Government Printing Office.

U.S. Energy Information Agency (1992). *Financial Statistics of Selected Electric Utilities 1989.* Washington D.C.: U.S. Government Printing Office.

Varian, H. (1990). Goodness-of-fit in Optimising Models. *Journal of Econometrics* 46: 125–140.

Veljanovski, C. (1990). *The Economics and Law: An Introductory Text.* IEA: Institute of Economic Affairs.

Vickers, J.S. and G.K.Yarrow (1985). *Privatisation and the Natural Monopolies.* London: Public Policy Centre.

Vickers, J.S. and G.K.Yarrow (1988a). *Privatisation: An Economic Analysis.* Cambridge, Massachusetts: MIT Press.

Vickers, J.S. and G.K.Yarrow (1988b). Regulation of Privatised Firms in Britain. *European Economic Review* 32: 465–472.

Vickers, J.S. and G.K.Yarrow (1991a). Economic Perspectives on Privatisation. *Journal of Economic Perspectives* 5(2): 111–132.

Vickers, J.S. and G.K.Yarrow (1991b). The British electricity experiment. *Economic Policy* 12: 187–232.

Wagstaff, A. (1989). Estimating efficiency in the hospital sector: a comparison of three statistical cost frontier models. *Applied Economics* 21: 659–672.

Wallace, R.L. and P.L.Junk (1970). Economic Inefficiency of Small Municipal Electric Generating Systems. *Land Economics* 46 (February): 98–104.

Weinstein, M.A. (1964). The sum of the values from a normal and a truncated normal distribution. *Technometrics* 6: 104–5, 469–70.

Wenders, J.T. (1986). Economic Efficiency and Income Distribution in the Electric Utility Industry. *Southern Economic Journal* 52 (4): 1056–67.

Weyman-Jones, T.G. (1992). *Problems of Yardstick Regulation in Electricity Distribution.* Mimeo. Now published in M.Bishop, J.Kay and C.Mayer (1995). *The Regulatory Challenge.* Oxford: Oxford University Press.

Whitman, Requardt and Associates (1992). *Handy-Whitman Bulletin No.135.* Baltimore, Maryland.

World Bank (1993). *The World Bank's Role in the Electric Power Sector.* Washington D.C.: The World Bank.

Wyckoff, P.G. (1990). The simple analytics of slack-maximising bureaucracy. *Public Choice* 67: 35–47.

Yarrow, G.K. (1986). Privatisation in Theory and Practice. *Economic Policy* 2: 324–377.

Yarrow, G.K. (1988). The price of nuclear power. *Economic Policy* 6: 81–132.

Yarrow, G.K. (1989a). Does ownership matter? in: Veljanovski, C. (ed) *Privatisation and Competition*: London: IEA pp.52–69.

Yarrow, G.K. (1989b). Privatisation and Economic Performance in Britain. *Carnegie-Rochester Conference Series on Public Policy* 31: 309–344.

Yarrow, G.K. (1992). *British Electricity Prices since Privatisation.* Oxford: Regulatory Policy Institute.

Zieschang, K.D. (1983). A note on the decomposition of cost efficiency into technical and allocative components. *Journal of Econometrics* 23: 401–405.